"I found this book very entertaining and at the same time very informative. This is a must read for all security professionals in the hospitality industry."

Chris D. Brockway, MPA, CPP

"It is said that in the consulting business, 98% of the consultants can tell you hundreds of 'stories' about what 2% of the consultants have done or know. Darrell Clifton is a 2% consultant in the highly specialized field of hotel security. He has more than two decades of direct, practical experience. I want his book in my professional library."

John J. Strauchs, Co-author of *The Hallcrest Report II*
Private Security Trends 1970–2000

"Hotel and lodging security are some of the most difficult security disciplines within the hospitality environment. Darrell Clifton, CPP, has skillfully written a manual for anyone looking to gain valuable insight on how to tackle this job correctly and thoroughly. From a hotel tower resort to a boutique bed & breakfast, this book has it all. This is a must read!"

Mitchell R. Fenton, CPP, Chairman of the Hospitality,
Entertainment, and Tourism Council for ASIS International

"Darrell has produced a magnificent compendium covering all aspects of hospitality, entertainment, and tourism security. A must read for those entering the hospitality security industry after college or from law enforcement. The book serves as an excellent reference resource for the seasoned hospitality security professional."

H. Skip Brandt, CPP, CLSD, Executive Director,
International Lodging Safety & Security Association

"Darrell's vast knowledge and experience show through in his book. Hospitality Security is a challenge given its many moving parts; however, Darrell has created a road map for success that can be used at all levels of management and/or discipline. The book should be read by every operational manager to ensure their property is protected from the many forms of risk."

James C. Reynolds, CPP, CLSD, Hilton Worldwide

"Darrell is one of the most experienced hotel/resort industry security professionals that I know. This book is a must read for those starting in this ever-challenging, soft target security market."

Joe McDonald, CPP, PSP, CMAS, Chief Security Officer

HOSPITALITY SECURITY

Managing Security in Today's Hotel, Lodging, Entertainment, and Tourism Environment

Darrell Clifton, CPP

CRC Press
Taylor & Francis Group
Boca Raton London New York

CRC Press is an imprint of the
Taylor & Francis Group, an **Informa** business

CRC Press
Taylor & Francis Group
6000 Broken Sound Parkway NW, Suite 300
Boca Raton, FL 33487-2742

© 2012 by Taylor & Francis Group, LLC
CRC Press is an imprint of Taylor & Francis Group, an Informa business

No claim to original U.S. Government works

Printed in the United States of America on acid-free paper
Version Date: 20120420

International Standard Book Number: 978-1-4398-7436-3 (Hardback)

Library of Congress Cataloging-in-Publication Data

Clifton, Darrell.
   Hospitality security : managing security in today's hotel, lodging, entertainment, and tourism environment / author, Darrell Clifton.
      p. cm.
   Includes bibliographical references and index.
   ISBN 978-1-4398-7436-3 (hardback)
   1. Hotels--Security measures. 2. Restaurants--Security measures. 3. Hospitality industry--Management.
I. Title.

TX911.3.S4C55 2012
647.94068--dc23   2011047848

Visit the Taylor & Francis Web site at
http://www.taylorandfrancis.com

and the CRC Press Web site at
http://www.crcpress.com

DEDICATION

For

My mom and dad who taught me the difference between knowledge and wisdom,

Kenny who inspires me with his pride and appreciation of my accomplishments,

Kevin who motivates me with his kindness and love of everyone,

And the true love of my life

CONTENTS

SECTION 2   Policies

SECTION 3 Physical Security

SECTION 4 *The Security Executive*

FOREWORD

This outstanding overview of security operations in hospitality environments takes the reader through practical and easy to understand methods and best practices for establishing or improving a professional, proactive proprietary security force. The book stresses the importance of prevention and investigation into the root causes of incidents as a tool for avoiding future undesirable events.

The lodging component of a hospitality environment creates challenges to the security professional by its complex set of assets and amenities especially when combined with gaming environments. Darrell Clifton takes the reader through a logical and methodical process to first evaluate what risks are inherent to hospitality environments, how to asses those risks through threat and vulnerability assessments and methods to mitigate, eliminate or transfer them.

His approach for protection of people over assets is dead on and a concept that sometimes gets lost in the process of everyday business. Clifton emphasizes this important concept to include the training of security personnel in guest protection management. His three step approach for protecting guests, employees and property takes the reader through valuable insights into the business of renting rooms to transient lodgers and their wandering through a hospitality facility.

This is especially important in that each registered guest brings with them their own unique set of circumstances, family values, problems and social issues. The security function must operate to protect their individual rights, their right to privacy, and their desire to enjoy the facilities they are patronizing and contributing to the revenue stream. This must be balanced with the obligation, or duty, to provide reasonable care from foreseeable harm by the hotel to avoid incidents and litigation. Clifton clearly establishes and identifies practical, reasonable and cost effective ways to accomplish this balancing of guest enjoyment with guest protection.

I have had the pleasure of attending seminar sessions conducted by the author and have always taken away valuable insights from his experiences and successes in a difficult and challenging environment. He has a true grasp on policy and procedure from the development stage all the way through the implementation of the important self imposed standards that should be in place in any hospitality environment. If there is no policy or procedure in place, employees will react in a manner based on what they believe is the right thing to do and not always what is the desired response by management. Using the policy and procedures as the foundation for the training program and placing strong emphasis on training is a theme in his operations and in this book.

Section three of the book gets into the nuts and bolts of security operations to include actual strategies and methods to patrol casinos, arcades, parking lots, retail and food and beverage outlets. Patrol rarely gets the appropriate attention it should in training of security personnel. Patrol is often considered common sense and is probably one of the most important functions that security must perform. Clifton clearly identifies the documentation, training and methods to conduct effective patrol of a venue in easy to understand language.

He includes the technical side of securing a hospitality environment which is truly what is referred to as a "soft target" with many entrances and therefore opportunities for non guests or undesirables to access. CCTV system use by security personnel, alarm systems and communications to just name a few. The nightmare of dealing with "lost and found" is even covered which is rarely seen in any publication or article.

Clifton shares his knowledge and experience as a truly professional security executive with the reader to provide insights into his successful management style. Although hospitality environments tend to operate in an autocratic manner he has a true grasp on how to motivate, manage and obtain positive results from personnel which are always the hardest part of managing a security department.

Clifton takes his years as a proven industry professional and converts it in writing that should become a part of any hospitality security director's professional library. I consider him to be one of the best current gaming security directors in the business with a reputation of integrity, strong ethics, proactive approaches and creative management skills. This book will demonstrate to the reader what a true professional security director is and ways to become one.

Alan W. Zajic, CPP, CSP

PREFACE

Do not seek to follow in the footsteps of the wise. Seek what they sought.

Matsuo Basho, poet

Hotel Security Director. How many of you grew up dreaming of becoming a Hotel Security Director? I don't see many hands going up. The reality is that not very many of us aspired to this position or ever imagined ourselves in this career. We seem to evolve from two different worlds. See if one of these backgrounds describes you. The first comes from retired military or law enforcement. This professional has succeeded in his or her first chosen field of endeavor and now, for whatever reason, is taking on a logical next step. The second background type is the corporate climber. These career security professionals have started at some entry-level position in a hospitality company and proved their loyalty and knowledge to someone.

In both cases, the new Hotel Security Director comes to the position somewhat unprepared. Don't get me wrong. I do not question the knowledge, experience, or dedication of any security manager. I simply offer that, unlike the lawyer, doctor, cop, or soldier, there are few job-based learning or academic programs that actually train us how to do this job.

So, in the absence of a degree in Hotel Security Management, where does one acquire the knowledge necessary to excel in this career? There are many resources for management—even security management—but not much for Hotel Security Management. Those of us who have worked in the hospitality industry for any length of time know that there are just as many differences from other industries as there are similarities.

I suppose you could trace the history of hotels back to biblical times. As long as people have traveled, they have needed places to stay. The hotel industry has evolved right alongside the travel industry and tourism. Hotel Security, however, only dates back a few decades. In the early and mid-twentieth century, hotel detectives were hired to investigate the same crimes we still see today and to protect the occasional visiting dignitary.

In the late 1950s and early 1960s, one major thing happened to the travel industry—jet airliners. People traveling more often, farther from home, and for longer periods needed more hotels. The hotel security detective started to evolve around the same time. After casinos gained some notoriety in Las Vegas, they started to build huge hotels to attract affluent guests and entertainment. At first, these properties hired small security forces to protect their fortunes. The focus then was on protecting the money, catching cheaters, and keeping the undesirables out.

As corporations took over management of these resorts, they developed the megaresort. Security departments grew and it did not take long to learn that protection was needed not just for the money, but to protect the guests from scammers, con artists, and other guests. A 5,000-room hotel/casino has many more issues of internal theft, property loss, and accidents than it ever does with theft and robbery of casino funds.

By the 1980s, lawyers were finding the hotel/casino accident business to be quite lucrative. Courts in Nevada were assigning some premise liability to those property owners.

Hotels all over the world, many of them with franchises in Las Vegas, realized that they needed a security force to protect themselves from the guests as well as the criminals. Today, we find most hotels of medium size have full-time security and, more importantly, a Security Director to prevent problems as well as resolve them.

I offer that brief perspective to impress upon you the importance of prevention. Many Security Directors in hotels think of themselves as police chiefs of their own small town with a private police force. While a large hotel functions just like a city, we have a different duty of preventing problems. While a police chief or sheriff is tasked with upholding laws, our responsibility is "protection of assets." While catching bad guys, solving crimes, putting out fires, and breaking up fights are some of the things we do, they do not necessarily protect or prevent anything.

Whether you are the only manager of a small motel or a Chief Security Officer of a large hospitality chain, this book is for you. The security function does not change based on the size of the facility. Your success as a Security Director will depend on your ability to prevent bad things, not respond to them. This confounds many security professionals because it is hard to prove success based on things that did not happen. However, the rest of us—and your bosses—know that a Security Department that sees less crime and maintains a safe and comfortable environment for its guests is the most successful of all.

Having managed one and visited most of the largest and busiest Security departments in the world, I always think I have seen it all—and, of course, I haven't. But I have taken each of those unique incidents and worked them backward to find how they could be prevented. I believe every incident is preventable and it is our job to decide if the prevention is practical and affordable. I encourage you to share your stories and the steps you took to prevent incidents from recurring. The safety of our guests and employees in the hospitality business is success for all of us.

In the chapters that follow, I have endeavored to include at least an introduction of everything you need to know to operate a Security Department in a hotel, nightclub, amusement park, or any other hospitality venue. It is experience-based, proven methods for preventing and resolving the challenges faced by today's hospitality practitioner. Whether you are new to this position, aspiring to meet this challenge, or are a veteran of our exclusive club, you will find some valuable information contained herein. You will either learn best practices or validate those that you already employ. One of our favorite axioms, "If it isn't written, it didn't happen," can certainly be applied to this book. Successful security methods cannot be shared and hold their value without being documented.

Reading this book cover to cover is certainly the best way to get its full value, as there are industry standards and best practices throughout. However, some may find it more useful as a reference guide to be consulted for specific methods and procedures. As for standards, you will learn early in the next two chapters that our industry has few. We have developed, over the last several hundred years, some preferred methods that we call "Best Practices." Standards, Best Practices, and personal preferences are referenced and identified as such. Keep in mind that many of these security methods are subjective and vary with not only opinion, but also the type of establishment, its location, and its management. If they are successful, then they are not wrong, so consider ideas that oppose your own as alternatives.

INTRODUCTION

The hospitality industry is a complex group of different types of businesses. Their commonality is that they provide a service to visitors. Lodging is a big piece of the hospitality pie and includes hotels, motels, bed & breakfasts, and even college dorms or government housing (as far as security is concerned, anyway). Another aspect of our industry is amusement parks. Theme parks, water parks, aquarium or marine life venues, golf courses, ski resorts, and many others fall into this category. Casinos are a huge player in the hospitality industry. Not only do they have their own hotels—and even theme parks—they also have their own way of doing business unique to the industry. Bars and nightclubs are other unique facets of Hospitality that have their own special considerations. Convention facilities round out this industry and include meeting space properties, arenas, stadiums, and outdoor event venues.

As for security in the hospitality industry, we are in the dubious position of having to keep our assets as secure as possible, while keeping our property as open and welcoming as we can. This conundrum compounds the complexity of our job functions, and is why we refer to our properties as "soft" targets. While it is hard enough to protect a nuclear power plant from intruders, terrorists, thieves, and spies, it is even more difficult to keep those same persons out of a hotel that is open to the public. Many of the traditional methods of security, such as locks, alarms, and cameras, are still used at our facilities, but we also have to employ more creative methods, such as patrol, behavioral recognition, and passive deterrence (signs, reminders, and awareness).

Moreover, the risk assessment is slightly more complicated because instead of hardening a target against intrusive threats, we have to take guest safety and crimes against persons into account. In fact, they take a priority over our intrinsic assets because they have a higher value—life over money.

This book will take you through the process of protecting those hospitality assets—guests, employees, and property. I have segmented this process into three sections. First is Planning. We will learn how to create a Risk Assessment where our threats and vulnerabilities are calculated with probabilities to determine risk. Once we know our risks, we can develop a Security Plan, where we decide how to apply various layers to mitigate the risks. Budgeting is included in this section because we need money to implement our plan and the amount we get will directly reflect where we go next.

The second section is entitled Policies. This is where we get into the establishment of an actual Security Department. We will start with documentation of our policies into a Security manual, training manual, emergency procedures manual, and incident action plan. We then add some dimension to the department by adding staff. That chapter will review scheduling, wages, deployment, and even contract security. After we hire them, we have to train them, so that is introduced in Chapter 6. I included some specialized training, such as use of force and bike patrol. Safety is first, so before we put those security officers to work, we will look at safety and awareness programs that every facility should have.

Section 3 is Physical Security and this is where all of our planning is turned into action. We start with a detailed look at patrol procedures in all areas of the hotel including restaurants and nightclubs. The next chapter is the technical stuff. We look at alarm and camera systems, various software programs, video, and lost and found. Chapter 10 is about emergency procedures and response, examining response planning and the specific recommended response to certain emergencies. Investigations are reviewed in great detail. I think you will enjoy learning about this more glamorous part of our job. We talk about follow-up, interviews, crime analysis, internal crime, and even a few specific investigation types.

The book ends with Section 4 and one final chapter on Executive Skills. I consider this chapter more subjective and my goal is to have you learn from the successful leadership styles that I have seen and practiced. This is not designed to offend any particular style or person, but simply breaks through some of the stereotypes and traditions of those who have assumed the position of Security Director. I sincerely hope you will learn some things that will make you a successful leader. I welcome, encourage, and look forward to your feedback.

ABOUT THE AUTHOR

Darrell Clifton, CPP, is the director of Security at Circus Circus Hotel Casino in Reno, Nevada, having worked his way through every position in that department from front-line security officer. Clifton was very fortunate to have cross-trained in every operational department within the hotel and casino, which he feels has rounded his perspective on the relationship between Security and the success of the entire company. During his 25 years in Security Management, he has specialized in the process of prevention. This experience has led to the creating, writing, and implementation of new policies and programs on such topics as Workplace Violence Prevention, Hotel Security, Casino Security and Surveillance, Crime Prevention, Emergency Preparedness and Business Continuity, Drug Recognition, and many others.

Clifton chairs several community and national organizations including the Downtown Police Tax District, Alcohol Advisory Board, Washoe County Business Preparedness Committee, and the Northern Nevada Chapter of American Society for Industrial Security (ASIS). He also sits on the board of directors for Secret Witness, AlertID, and is the vice chairman of the Hospitality, Entertainment and Tourism Council. He is a frequent contributor to *Security Magazine*, *Casino Journal*, and as a speaker at ASIS, Reed Exhibitions, University of Nevada–Reno, and Gamepath.

Clifton is also a FEMA-certified Continuity of Operations Manager and participates in several state task forces to plan, write, and implement Continuity of Operations (COOP), Continuity of Government (COG), and other emergency plans. He was named by *Security Magazine* as one of the most influential people in the security industry.

Section 1

Planning

1

Risk Assessment

Despite the scoring, the results are absolutely in accord with our risk assessment.

—Marc Short
U.S. Homeland Security spokesman, defending a grant program

Whether your property is in design phase, recently completed, or an established destination facility, a Risk Assessment needs to be completed. A properly researched and considered Risk Assessment will not only help management plan protective measures, but also it will provide a legal defense for those measures.

Many hotels have been in operation for years and have never completed a formal Risk Assessment. Informal Risk Assessments are performed constantly by security professionals, engineers, and risk managers. Formal or informal, the process is largely the same. Your first decision is whether you should do this process yourself or hire a professional.

EXTERNAL RISK ASSESSMENT

An outside consultant can add some integrity to your Risk Assessment. The professional has the experience and the resources to do a thorough job and the résumé to add credibility to the finished product. The only reason not to have this contracted out is the cost. However, as we learn later in this book, costs can be justified by savings in other areas.

INTERNAL RISK ASSESSMENT

Besides saving money on hiring this process out, the education you will gain and the knowledge of your own property will be priceless for you.

A Risk Assessment is quite simply a calculation of severity and probability. Don't let the math scare you. Security professionals perform these assessments on a regular basis—and they do so in their head. Each time a security officer approaches someone in the hotel, a mental Risk Assessment is being performed. The immediate results of that mental calculation are used to determine the officer's stance, demeanor, reaction, and level of readiness. For example, a petite, elderly, intoxicated woman trying to get her room key to work generally would not pose the same threat or prompt the same response as a tall, muscular, younger man. That is a simple Risk Assessment. In his head, he calculated the probability of that person being a threat (attacking him) and he counted the severity of that threat (big guy versus little old lady) and made an instant decision to prepare himself.

The Risk Assessment process takes this simple calculation, expands it for a variety of threats, and formalizes it so that a security plan can be developed and documented for use later in justification. So, why do we need to go through all of this if we can do it in our heads? To protect our assets in court. I will explain toward the end of this chapter, but first, the assessment. This process can be divided into five steps. First, we will divide the property into sections. Then we will list all the possible threats and hazards for each area. Next, we will compile some historical data to determine probability. After that, severity will be figured into the process. Finally, we will work with the resulting values to determine risk.

Step 1—Divide the Property

Step 1 is to categorize the property into areas. Each area is like its own business with its own particular threats and risks, so it will be simpler to work with them separately. Do this by physical location, department, or revenue center—whatever makes sense to you. We will do a separate Risk Assessment for each of these areas, such as front desk, nightclub, guest rooms, and retail store. Some threats and hazards are to the entire property—such as floods and hurricanes—although the likelihood and severity will depend on your location. These are addressed in Chapter 10. We will use "Guest Rooms" as an example of one of our sections for the remaining steps (see Table 1.1).

Step 2—List Threats

Step 2 is to list the threats for each area. Consider every threat, no matter how remote its possibility. For our purposes, threats are crimes, natural hazards, and accidents. In

Table 1.1 Risk Assessment Example (Guest Rooms)

Threat/Hazard	Severity	Probability	Risk
	10 = Most Serious 1 = Least Serious	10 = Most Likely 1 = Least Likely	Severity × Probability

Table 1.2 Listing Possible Threats

Threat/Hazard	Severity	Probability	Risk
	10 = Most Serious **1 = Least Serious**	**10 = Most Likely** **1 = Least Likely**	**Severity ×** **Probability**
Robbery			
Domestic violence			
Property theft			
Assault on employee			
Noise complaint			
Fire			

Table 1.2, some examples of threats are robbery, domestic violence, property theft, assault on employee, noise complaint, and fire.

Step 3—Severity

Severity is completely subjective. We are going to fabricate these numbers based on our own common sense or opinions. Different persons may evaluate severity a bit differently, but even that will not matter for this exercise. Even though opinions vary, most people will rate incidents relatively the same. Death is more serious to everyone than vandalism, so the values are not as important as their ranking with the other threats.

For the purpose of this Risk Assessment, Severity is a rating of 1 to 10 on how bad the event would damage the assets or persons. Death would be a 10 and excessive noise in a hotel room is likely a 2. In Table 1.3, I have assigned values to each of the threats

Table 1.3 Determining the Severity of Threats

Threat/Hazard	Severity	Probability	Risk
	10 = Most Serious **1 = Least Serious**	**10 = Most Likely** **1 = Least Likely**	**Severity ×** **Probability**
Robbery	8		
Domestic violence	2		
Property theft	5		
Assault on employee	8		
Noise complaint	2		
Fire	9		

5

based on my opinion of a sample hotel. I made "Fire" the most serious with a rating of 9 because it can do the most damage and disrupt business most severely. I rated "Domestic Violence" and "Noise Complaint" as least severe with 2 each. Both of these types of incidents cause a minor disruption to a few other guests and it is unlikely the hotel would suffer any loss from either. Your ratings may be different and that is fine as long as you can justify them.

Step 4—Probability

In order to determine probability, we need to do some research. Although our severity numbers in the table were subjective, the probability numbers better have some backing or you will look ignorant in a deposition. Backing comes in the form of historical crime data.

GATHERING LOCAL CRIME DATA

Before risk can be assessed, some data need to be gathered. First is historical "neighborhood" criminal activity. Criminal activity would include just about every type of activity that could happen at the hotel. Few crimes that occur at businesses, residences, or on the street are not a potential threat to a hotel, so just about every type of crime is pertinent.

There are several possible sources for local crime data, the most likely of which is the local police department. Many police departments provide regional crime data and calls for service through public source Web sites. Others provide it by less technically advanced means like paper reports available from the police station or city hall. Most large cities like Los Angeles, Las Vegas, and Chicago have easy-to-navigate Web sites that provide crime data that can be filtered and sorted. Many smaller cities provide this service as well. The easy way to find out is to do a Web search for your city name and "crime data."

There are other privately owned, but free, Web sites that provide this service for most cities using public information. Try searching "crime data by city" or "crime data by zip code." Of course, a few crime analysis companies provide this data for a fee. The price may include the Risk Analysis that is being explained here and other valuable information from other sources combined into one professional presentation. Consider these services to save time.

If the local law enforcement agency does not provide this data in an electronic form, it may be necessary to query them personally. This is public information, but there may be a fee associated with compiling the information or copying files.

Other sources for historical crime data are the Business Improvement District, Business Owners' Association, or Chamber of Commerce. The hotel may already belong to such a group, which generally has this information compiled or can easily access it through its law enforcement liaisons.

Many security departments will task someone with keeping this neighborhood crime activity documented and categorized (see Chapter 11). There are other investigative reasons for doing this, but for the Risk Assessment, it fulfills the data-gathering requirement. This is an easy process to set up and the events can be taken from a police blotter in the newspaper, personal contacts at the police department, or regular phone calls to the report desk.

When gathering crime data, it is important to establish the radius or area from which the data are derived. This depends entirely on the location of the property. If the property is in a downtown urban setting, the entire downtown region should be used. If it is more of a suburban area with a couple of other hotels around, those few square acres might be enough. This may seem subjective and it is. Two requirements apply here. First is that the area surveyed is the same every time the data are collected. Second is that the area is large enough to find reported crimes and a good cross section of types of crimes.

It is also important to establish a time frame for the criminal activity. This may be limited by the source. Las Vegas, for example, only provides 60 days' worth of stats. It would be advisable to go back a year to cover all seasons and weather periods as well as tourist and economic cycles.

COMPILING LOCAL CRIME DATA

Once the information is gathered, there may be a murder, a couple of robberies, a few auto burglaries, and so forth. This is only the start. For the Risk Assessment, it will be necessary to know time of day, type of business, violent or property crime, etc. It also will be helpful to note the type of security in place at those places for comparison later. (See Table 1.4 for an example of local crime data.)

From our fictional crime data (Table 1.4), we can draw several conclusions with just a cursory look. There has not been a history of hotel homicides, which is why we did not include them in our Risk Assessment earlier in this chapter. Assaults also are not an issue, and judging by the stats, are probably mostly domestic. Robberies, however, are a problem. Of the robberies in this area, 20% were in hotels. Auto thefts were also a sizable percentage of the total, likely because of the nice selection in most hotel parking lots.

Table 1.4 An Example of a Crime Data Table

Local Crime Data—Downtown Any City				
Crime	Daytime	Nighttime	Hotel	Other Business	Residential
Homicide	1	2	0	0	3
Sexual assault	3	5	2	1	5
Robbery	10	15	5	15	5
Assault	25	26	4	11	36
Burglary	30	24	6	16	32
Theft	49	54	10	76	17
Auto theft	17	18	5	14	16

GATHERING PROPRIETARY INCIDENT DATA

Besides knowing what is going on around the property, it is necessary to know what is happening on the property as well. Proprietary data should be the easiest to get. Depending on what types of records are kept, the form they are in, and how long they are held, they can be the most useful. Ideally, the hotel has some reporting system in which data can be mined, sorted, and filtered into what is necessary.

If you are coming into a new property and do not have the historical records that you might expect, then you may need some help. Just as you did previously, consult the local police for their records. This will not have everything (only those incidents reported to the police), but it will provide something with which to work. You might even do this if you do have your own reports because some victims report crimes to the police and not to the hotel. Another dataset to ask for is "Calls for Service" by address. This will give you a great idea of incidents like domestic violence that do not always have an associated police report. The data, when compiled, will look like the police data already compiled (Table 1.4). Rather than create another table, just add the new data to the existing data.

GATHERING MARKET INCIDENT DATA

The third type of data needed is market data. This will be the same crime activity gathered previously, but it will be from like properties in the same market. A hotel located by itself may not have neighbors with which to compare, so it has to be assumed that similar hotels in the same region are going to have similar crime activity, threats, and risks. For this research, location of the other property or properties is less important than their type. If the property for which the Risk Assessment is being performed is a multistory, medium-priced resort, then it should not be compared to a budget motel. It is better to find a similar property in another city.

This information can be retrieved online or from the police as explained previously, but is best when taken from the source. Security directors who share the same market and have similar crime victims should already be communicating. They certainly should not have any problems sharing anonymous crime data. Unlike colleagues in the sales department, security operations should not compete. Competition when it comes to guest safety does not help anyone and ultimately results in a bad reputation for your region or tourist market. Relationships with peers are discussed in more detail in Chapter 12. Add this third data set to the existing data. The result should be a table showing what crimes are more likely to occur at our hotel based on neighborhood crime data, our own proprietary reports, and industry averages.

DETERMINING LIKELIHOOD

We will use all of the data compiled previously to determine trends and probability. The future cannot be predicted, but history provides a very good view of what is likely to happen. Applying this data in a simple list makes some things very clear. In the example

Table 1.5   Determining the Probability of Threats

Threat/Hazard	Severity	Probability	Risk
	10 = Most Serious 1 = Least Serious	10 = Most Likely 1 = Least Likely	Severity × Probability
Robbery	8	4	
Domestic violence	2	6	
Property theft	5	4	
Assault on employee	8	3	
Noise complaint	2	8	
Fire	9	1	

in Table 1.5, the Risk Assessment is performed on guest rooms. Not all of the crimes are relevant to guest rooms. Auto theft data, of course, will be used for our assessment of the parking areas, but robbery, assaults, and other thefts may be important to assess risk in guest rooms. These data are objective as they are derived from actual events and require little guesswork or assumptions. The Risk Assessment is almost complete.

In Step 4, probability—or likelihood—is determined. For each event, what is the likelihood (on a scale of 1 to 10) that it will happen? As before, the actual number does not matter as much as the order of events. The most likely should be high on the scale, and the least likely should be at the bottom (near 1). Confusion often arises in this step. Are we to determine the probability of the occurrence without security measures taken, or with mitigation? For example, the likelihood of theft with no lock on the door is higher than if there is a working lock. This will be discussed in more detail later, but for this assessment tool, it is better to determine the likelihood using existing or normal preventive measures. Therefore, when figuring the values in this column, assume that working locks are in place, proper lighting exists, and so on.

In Table 1.5, I assigned a rating of 1 to "Fire" because in my sample hotel there is a no-smoking policy, bed linens meet modern fire retardant standards, and we have never had a fire in our hotel. "Robbery" and "Property Theft" each earned a 4 because we have had both occur with almost equal regularity and other hotels in our area have had them as well. "Noise Complaint" was rated highest because we are a value-oriented hotel and we get noisy guests all the time. Once again, your values may be different based on your history, type of hotel, and your surroundings.

DETERMINING RISK

The final step of the Risk Assessment is the easiest, and for those visual learners, the most revealing. Multiply the severity value by the probability for each threat to determine risk. In some exercises, you may add these numbers instead of multiplying them. Using the

Table 1.6 Determining the Risk of Threats

Threat/Hazard	Severity	Probability	Risk
	10 = Most Serious 1 = Least Serious	10 = Most Likely 1 = Least Likely	Severity × Probability
Robbery	8	4	32
Domestic violence	2	6	12
Property theft	5	4	20
Assault on employee	8	3	24
Noise complaint	2	8	16
Fire	9	1	9

likelihood as our multiplier will give us a broader range of values when we are finished, making it easier to distinguish one risk from another.

In our example in Table 1.6, we had some expected results and maybe a surprise or two. Robbery was high, as expected. Domestic violence and Fire came out low as risks. We probably will not devote as many resources to prevent these in our Security Plan. (Remember, Fire is already addressed in building construction and existing detectors and alarms as per fire code.) "Assault on Employee" was higher than expected. This is a risk that is not always sufficiently addressed in Security Plans, but there are plenty of high-profile examples where housekeepers have been attacked, raped, and even killed by hotel guests. We will address this in our Security Plan in Chapter 2.

Insurance companies use this same formula to calculate your insurance premiums. They just use many more variables for severity and probability. Probability factors for car insurance, for example, are driving record, geographical location, age, gender, etc. Severity factors are cost of vehicle, income level, deductible, etc. These factors and others are entered into complicated algorithms to determine what type of risk you are. You can get just as complicated with your property Risk Assessment if you want to take the time. In fact, your business insurance company has likely done something similar to this already.

FORESEEABILITY

Foreseeability is the trump card to the Risk Assessment. Foreseeability means that if an event has occurred on the property before, then it is possible that it will happen again. As mentioned before, history is a good indicator of potential hazards, so if the environment allowed an incident to occur, and the security environment does not change to meet that threat, then it can happen again. This becomes a liability issue. If it does happen again, it will be considered as having been foreseeable by the courts. The event happened because of the inadequate security, nothing changed to prevent it from happening again, it did happen again, and now it is management's fault.

In 2008, an employee sued an Oklahoma hospital for inadequate security after she was abducted and sexually assaulted in the parking lot. The hospital did provide cameras and an employee monitored 30 camera feeds simultaneously. It was discovered later that the suspect's van was visible on camera circling the garage with duct tape obscuring the license plate. Within the previous year, there had been several incidents of assault, battery, abduction, and robbery.

The hospital management had plenty of notice due to prior acts that this particular event was foreseeable. In this case, it was deemed that the video system proved inadequate to keep the employee safe. The hospital attempted to have the case dismissed, claiming it was not responsible for the criminal actions of third parties. The Supreme Court of Oklahoma denied the hospital's motion and sent the case back for trial.

Suppose an incident occurs in the parking garage—like a strong-arm robbery. If basic security measures had been taken—such as proper lighting, security patrol, and emergency call boxes—then there may be a good defense for the hotel in the lawsuit that arises. In most cases, a good security manager will re-assess the area and determine what security measures could have prevented the incident entirely. Perhaps adding cameras, increasing patrols, and gating the entrance points would be considered appropriate. If a similar incident occurs again, there is likely a good defense that the management is doing everything reasonable to prevent such events and protect its guests.

Suppose after the first robbery, the company decides that its security measures are adequate and changes nothing. If a second robbery occurs, the company is going to be in a very difficult position to defend itself because the second incident was foreseeable.

MANAGING FORESEEABILITY

The word *foreseeability* is not found in many dictionaries. Legal and risk professionals created it and it means that one should have the "ability" to "foresee" events based on previous events that occurred. In other words, if a crime or incident happens, there is foreseeability that it will happen again.

In 2010, a man who was attacked in his motel room sued a popular U.S. motel chain. The perpetrators had knocked on the victim's door; he allowed them entry and was severely beaten. The suit claimed that the motel chain had a duty to ensure his safety and prevent criminal acts. The plaintiff also alleged that the motel lacked security cameras and patrols, among other things. The motel responded that the attack was "unforeseeable" because motel employees were not aware of the attackers' presence

11

on the property and that there were no known similar incidents at that motel or within the immediate vicinity. The court agreed with the motel, stating that even if the motel had the security measures in place, the crime would not have been prevented because the victim had opened his own door, resulting in the attack.

As we learn in this chapter, even though the motel won this case, they are now on notice. If a similar crime were to occur at that property again, they may be held liable because it is now foreseeable. Strike one.

Some legal professionals refer to foreseeability as the "one-strike rule." The company can defend against that first incident if it was unexpected and reasonable precautions had been taken (strike one). But, the second event is one that should have been expected—foreseen. Therefore, the liability falls more on the property that should have taken steps to prevent the event (strike two—you're out).

The remainder of this book is written with the expectation that security directors want to keep their employees and guests as safe as they can and that reasonable steps will be taken to prevent crime and accidents.

Most security directors are reading this and thinking that they have already done their Risk Assessment in their head. This is a great skill, but there are two important reasons for documenting the process. First, collecting written data and compiling it in written form is likely to catch some errors or some omissions that may occur during the thought process. Second, and most importantly, the documentation is vital for litigation. It is difficult to remember and to defend a mental determination, especially if it is years old. If another director or management team takes over, he or she will have no idea how the original assessment came to the conclusions that it did. The written assessment allows the company's legal counsel to show how and why certain security measures were taken if they are challenged. "If it isn't written, it didn't happen."

In November 2005, a man walked into a shopping mall with a rifle, pistol, and guitar case full of ammunition. He shot mall patrons at random, hitting eight of them before being arrested by police. The eighth man sued the mall for inadequate security, claiming the mall could have provided better security measures to prevent the shooting. The mall filed for summary judgment and was at first denied, but upon reconsideration, the court granted the dismissal. The court agreed with the mall that a random shooting in the mall was not foreseeable and the mall had no duty to protect against it. Now that the mall has "notice" of this type of incident, it will likely take some additional security measures (revise its security plan) because it will not be able to use the same defense if a shooting happens again.

In the next chapter, the Security Plan will be introduced and implemented. First, it is important to realize that the Risk Assessment is never completed. Each time a new aspect of the security plan is implemented, that part of the Risk Assessment will have to be re-assessed. Severity may not change, but probability definitely changes each time an area is fortified. Ideally, all of the values in the Risk Assessment are low and maintained low. Other factors may change the Risk Assessment. Seasonal factors, demographic changes in the area, special events, economy, regional crime, police patrol, and even the company marketing strategy may change probability and require a new assessment. These specifics will be discussed later throughout the book.

2

Security Plan

I have six locks on my door all in a row. When I go out, I lock every other one.
I figure no matter how long somebody stands there picking the locks, they are
always locking three.

Elayne Boosler, Comedian

In an ideal security world, we would take our Risk Assessment and come up with a perfect plan to mitigate every risk. In reality, the plan you create and implement will be influ-
enced by your style, education, and experience and that of your manager and maybe your
lawyer. That is why I do not presume to tell you how to run your department. Instead, I
offer some proven methods, best practices, and even some unusual ideas that I have seen
or tried myself. It will be up to you to apply the ones you think will work for you and
your property.

The security plan is a document that explains what security measures will be taken
to mitigate risks (prevent crime and accidents) on and around the property. This process
is a bit subjective for hotels and entertainment venues because there are generally no
standards or codes that address them. In an airport or nuclear facility, there are government regulations that standardize access control and other physical security aspects.
Hotels, amusement parks, nightclubs, and similar facilities are not so regulated. There
are certainly fire and building codes, OSHA guidelines, and other applicable regulations, but in general, cameras, lighting, security staffing, and other security measures are
not included. The hospitality industry has not yet standardized physical security either.
However, there are some best practices and corporate policies applied by larger hotel
chains. These will be used throughout this reference and should be used whenever possible in the security plan.

Remember, as with risk assessment, the main purpose of the security plan is to defend
the security posture of the property in court. Since there are no standards, a plaintiff lawyer is sure to compare the security at the defendant's property with one that has better
security. So, for the purposes of this plan, the best practice will be recommended every
time. Your goal is to provide the best defense (security plan) that you can within your
budget.

SECURITY IN COURT

When an unfortunate event happens on hotel property, the victim of the act often names the hotel in a lawsuit. The victim sues the hotel—not because the hotel caused the act, but because the hotel did not take adequate measures to prevent the crime or incident from occurring. It is for this reason that the risk assessment and the security plan are so important. The plaintiff's lawyer will try to find where the security was weak or below standards. Since there are no standards, the only way to prove substandard security is by comparing to other properties. The risk assessment will show where the other properties were examined and the security plan will show that the security was equal to or the same as other properties.

The first defense is a good offense. The risk assessment sheds light upon the potential for events, such as a robbery in a parking garage. The security plan will deal with those initial security defenses. If a robbery does occur, it does not mean that the security defenses were weak, but they were obviously weak enough to allow the event to happen. The Security Director then has two choices: (1) leave security as it is and hope for the best or (2) fortify security in the garage and prevent it from happening again.

Option 1: Leave security as is. This option is riskier, but less expensive. Many businesses manage risk in this manner, hoping, gambling, and calculating that another incident will not occur. This is usually a measured risk, weighing the option of spending money on security or spending money on litigation later. This option usually does not appeal to the Security Director, but it is a product of the business world. There is a strong likelihood that the property management makes these types of decisions for the Security Director (more on this topic in Chapter 12).

Option 2: Fortify security. This option may be considered safer, and even morally correct, but is obviously more expensive. There will be costs associated with purchasing and installing equipment and paying wages for increased labor. This option also may be viewed as better for the business's image: It takes safety seriously and does what it takes to provide it to its guests.

SECURITY PLAN

We cannot create a Security Plan until a Risk Assessment has been completed (Chapter 1). The plan includes security staffing amounts, cameras, lighting, access control, CPTED (crime prevention through environmental design), and many other physical aspects. It may also include policies and procedures. Many organizations create and follow very detailed and lengthy plans that explain and outline all of these pieces of their security posture. Other, maybe smaller, properties do not make a written plan. Most security directors are either operating under a plan written by a predecessor or do not have a written plan at all. They rely on their mental notes and personal philosophy to create policies and organize their protective measures.

Like the Risk Assessment, the Security Plan is not very valuable unless it is written. Those who do not have a written plan simply have not had to justify their security to their boss for the purposes of obtaining funds for staffing and hardware. They also have not been deposed on their justification for why they had a certain level of staffing, certain video or alarm systems, or policies that did not address certain aspects of security. The formal Security Plan is not that difficult to write and may save time and money later.

What does the plan look like? In the Risk Assessment example in Chapter 1, guest rooms were evaluated. Guest rooms will be one portion of the plan. The plan will take the risks identified in the assessment and outline how to mitigate them. For example, if robberies were a documented risk, security patrol, cameras, controlled access, and peepholes might be recommended in the Security Plan. By the time each area's security plans are compiled and added to other components like policies and procedures, it becomes apparent that the Security Plan is a comprehensive and lengthy document.

OUTLINING THE PLAN

Part of the Security Plan will be a Policy Manual. To make the plan-writing process easier, the plan presented here will be designed like the manual. This will save time and allow for some solid consistency between the Plan and its key component. The outline of the Security Plan will look something like this:

Department Mission
Organization
Policies and Procedures
Overall Property
Specific Areas

Each of these components of the Security Plan is explained in more detail.

Department Mission

The mission is the overall strategy of Security for the property or organization. This is vital to the plan so that the reader knows what the intent of the Security Department is. While most hotels might presume to have the same mission, they actually do vary. As we see in every type of business that we frequent, there are many missions with many different goals. In a multiuse facility, the focus may have to be explained. Is the mission guest safety, protection of company assets, or life safety, or all of the above? Other departments or contractors may be responsible for one or more of these components, so we will leave those missions to them.

Most hotels are basically the same. The mission might be "to protect the assets of the hotel and its guests and employees while maintaining a safe and comfortable environment for everyone." That is a good mission statement, but the plan will need some more detail. A high-end hotel or a brand-reliant property may incorporate "brand protection" or "luxury" into its mission statement. A budget property or family-oriented facility might not want to include these elements in their plan. Security is a general element of every mission

17

statement, but other elements specific to the type of property also can be included because they will affect decisions on security applications in the plan.

EXAMPLES OF MISSION STATEMENTS

"The Mission of Southwest Airlines is dedicated to the highest quality of Customer Service delivered with a sense of warmth, friendliness, individual pride, and Company Spirit."

"The Ritz-Carlton Hotel is a place where the genuine care and comfort of our guests is our highest mission. We pledge to provide the finest personal service and facilities for our guests who will always enjoy a warm, relaxed, yet refined ambience. The Ritz-Carlton experience enlivens the senses, instills well-being, and fulfills even the unexpressed wishes and needs of our guests."

Remember, we are working on a Security Department mission statement. It is not the mission statement for the entire organization. They are separate and different. It may make sense to follow the corporate mission statement in security, but the corporate statement does not address security decisions. Reading the mission statement of the Ritz-Carlton in the adjacent textbox, you would have to assume that the mission of their Security Department is consistent with the hotel's mission of "finest service" and "unexpressed wishes." It is likely that security's mission is something along the lines of discretion, comfort, and service that supports the objectives of the hotel. As for Southwest Airlines, their Security Department probably focuses on the keywords in the corporate statement like warmth, service, and friendliness.

Your Security mission statement should be consistent with your corporate mission, so consider looking at other departments to see what they have. You also may talk to those who wrote the corporate mission statement and get ideas from them. Finally, as I mention throughout this book, ask your own employees to help develop your mission. Your mission statement is not just something to hang on the wall; it will be used to make important decisions on the type of security used throughout the property. Refer to it each time you make a decision or create a policy. This will help you remain consistent.

Organization

Organization of the Security Department includes the chain of command—or hierarchy—from executive down to front line. The purpose of this section is to make clear who reports to whom and who has which responsibilities. Names are not important—just positions. Why is this important in the plan? One reason is that those who read this plan (lawyers, your boss, and your successors) need to know how decisions are made and at what level. Do frontline employees operate on their own, with minimal supervision, relying on management from other departments to make important decisions or is the organization large enough where there is a shift manager to whom officers report? This may be a vital component of the plan when, in court, your company is trying to defend a poorly made decision.

Starting at the top, who has the highest, or ultimate, responsibility for security matters? This depends on the corporate structure, the size of the organization, and the corporate philosophy. Many companies have an executive security position reporting to the CEO or property manager. This is most preferred and explained in more detail in Chapter 12. Some companies have the security leader (director, manager, etc.) reporting to Legal, Human Resources, or Facilities. There are good reasons for each reporting structure, but that reasoning is probably out of your control. So, for the purpose of the Security Plan, we are simply documenting it, whatever it is.

This organization chart is going to look somewhat like a pyramid and the previous paragraph describes the point at the top. Next is the second line of management. Large organizations use an operations manager in this senior middle position. It also may be divided between operations and investigations or administration. Instead of having two managers in this position, the Ops manager can take the Personnel/Operations side and the director can take the Administrative or Investigative side. The director is still the highest authority, but it saves a position. (It is advisable not to have two persons in charge of the entire operation.)

The above level can be skipped entirely if the organization is small-to-medium in size. The third (or second) tier is middle management. This position could be called supervisors or shift managers, depending on the number of frontline staff. The ideal proportion of supervisor to officer is 1:5. So, if there are 10 officers on a shift or team, there should be 2 supervisors. This is not to say that if the property has decided to use a "shift manager" format, that two managers are needed per shift. It means that each five persons need a supervisor, so this can be accomplished through different levels of supervision.

The next level might include supervisors (if managers are used above) or senior (lead) officers. If a property has 15 officers on a shift, there could be a manager and two or three supervisors, or a supervisor and three senior officers.

Keep in mind that a small property may not have many levels of supervision in Security. If there is one officer on duty at night, he or she may report to a hotel manager or similar position. However, your ideal ratio depends on the size of your property, the skill

V.A. Graicunas developed the term *Span of Control* in 1933 when he researched the effectiveness of varying management ratios. He determined that there were several factors, such as the physical location of the employees (whether they work together or separately), personalities, types of work performed, and the capabilities of the employees. That ratio was found to be acceptable at 4 employees to 1 supervisor all the way to 22:1 depending on those factors. Police departments operate at about 4:1 and fire departments operate at about 3:1.

In the 1980s, a new factor was found to influence the effectiveness of this ratio: technology. Computers and other automation systems took away some of the duties of supervisors and managers and many corporations "flattened" their chain of command. Middle management positions were eliminated as duties were given up to technology. We still look today to eliminate middle management as one way to save money, so if your ratio is higher than those described in this chapter, don't worry.

level of your employees, and other factors. This needs to be drawn out in the organizational chart as well.

The final level—the base of the pyramid—is the officer. This is the front line and the most important because they do the most work.

The organizational pyramid likely includes other units of responsibility besides Operations. Investigations, Training, Administration, and Safety are common units to include in your chain of command and organizational chart. Others included in some hotels are Lifeguards, Lost and Found, Shuttle Drivers, Parking Attendants, etc. Whatever legs of your pyramid you might have, each has to have an "upline" and a "downline" of who reports to whom from the director on down.

Job Description

Each of the positions described previously and each position held in your department requires a job description. The purpose of a job description is to outline the job functions of that position. This description may be needed in litigation, for progressive discipline, coaching, training, promotion processes, and light-duty determinations.

A job description is relatively simple to create and your Human Resources Department may have already done this for you. Following is an outline of a generic job description.

Position title
Department
Pay range
Reports to
Subordinate positions
Minimum qualifications
Physical requirements
Hours or schedule (if applicable)
Job functions
Revised date

It is important to be as specific as possible, but to leave that last and famous line "and other duties as assigned." That line avoids the insubordinate retort: "That's not in my job description." When all the job descriptions are complete, all of the duties under your authority should be documented. If anything is missing, that will explain where you lack accountability.

Policies and Procedures

This is not going to be the complete security policy manual (that will come later in Chapter 4). For the Security Plan, there will need to be some basic policies that dictate how security will function in each area so that it can be applied later in the plan. This may involve other stakeholders. The Risk Manager (legal counsel), the General Manager, and affected department heads may have a say in how security operates and performs certain functions.

In this section of the plan, it is decided how Security patrols, prevents crime, and reacts or responds to certain events. The Security Director needs to decide in advance of the Security Plan if security is contracted or staff positions, if they will be armed, if they will handle violent, medical, or life-saving situations, and if they will perform other skilled functions, such as profiling and gang intervention.

In November 2008, 2,000 shoppers lined up outside a major retail store seeking to take advantage of Black Friday specials. Just before the doors were about to open, the crowd broke the doors, and trampled an employee, killing her. Arguably, this incident was not foreseeable and was considered a horrible tragedy. In fact, the major retailer avoided criminal prosecution and any civil penalties by reaching a modest settlement that included changes to procedures that would prevent the situation from occurring in the future. In the years following that event, every store in the chain implemented procedures that prevented the stampede for bargains and the chain had no further incidents. In November 2010, another large retailer had an incident very similar to the one in 2008. In this scenario, the crowd rushed the doors—also seeking bargains—and trampled a fellow shopper. Nobody was killed. What if the injured shopper was killed? Was there foreseeability? Could it be argued that the retailer was negligent? Would you like to be the lawyer or the Security Director for that store?

Overall Property

The security posture of the property also needs to be decided in advance of the deployment of the plan. The director and executive team has to decide if the property will have uniformed security, and if they want to be visible and highly aggressive or discreet and reactive. Generally, the hospitality industry tries to be open and inviting, so bollards, guard posts, cameras, fences, and restrictive signage go against that philosophy. This is not to say that those measures will not be deployed, if necessary, but they need to be justified. CPTED is one way the property and its management can decide to mitigate risk while maintaining that hospitable feeling for its guests.

One of the first things learned in law enforcement or the military is the concept of layered security. If you think you are not familiar with it, don't be so sure. Anything that is protected is protected in layers. Your home, for instance, likely has several layers of security. Obviously, there is a door with a lock. There probably is also lighting, a peephole, neighbors watching, a standoff area (lawn), white picket fence, a barking dog, and maybe an alarm. These are all layers of security. Our hotel uses layers as well, and we will be documenting these layers in the Security Plan.

Layers of security in the hospitality environment are, primarily, physical, technological, and human. Layers can be considered as concentric rings around the asset, such as fences and walls around a prison. Layers do not have to be physically concentric. Just as in the previous example of your own home, the dog and the alarm are not actually concentric to the house. They are simply another level of security.

A layer is anything that detects, delays, deters, or denies entry to the asset. Examples of layers used in the Security Plan are thus explained.

Physical Layer
A common example of a physical barrier is a wall. Shrubs, trees, bollards, rivers (moats), rocks, and fences also can be physical layers. Potentates and presidents use people as physical layers. Traditionally walls and fences were less attractive, uninviting layers of denial. Advances in architecture and landscape have applied design to this science in the last few decades so the hospitality industry can protect its assets and maintain the beauty and convenience of the property. Each of these types of layers is discussed specifically throughout the book.

Technological Layer
Cameras, alarm sensors, radar, and lighting are examples of technological layers. Cameras provide detection—if they are being monitored—and provide deterrence if they are visible to would-be offenders. Alarm sensors, such as motion detectors, can be an active or a passive form of detection. Radar, not generally used in hospitality applications, is an active form of detection. Lighting is one of the most common layers of security. It is regularly misused or under-used as a decoration or a practical visual aid. When used correctly, lighting allows cameras to work better, deters crime by eliminating hiding places, provides an appearance of activity, and detects criminals in otherwise dark places. Technology also allows us to use tools, such as biometrics and video analytics, as another layer of security.

Human Layer
There are several ways to use staff as a protective layer. Fixed guard posts, walking, driving, and bicycle patrols are common and effective measures used outdoors. Behavioral recognition, undercover officers, and intelligence gathering are some of the more advanced methods of human intelligence used by all types of properties and assets. Personnel are the most effective type of security because they provide detection, deterrence, delay, and denial while providing subjective, intelligent decision making and the ability to interact with guests and provide guest services and other duties. Humans are also the most expensive layer so tend to be used as little as possible.

About 80 school children on a field trip to a water park in Concord, CA, in 1997, caused a major accident. Trying to break a record for the most kids on a slide, the kids overloaded the slide against the orders of the lone ride attendant. The slide, which was designed for single riders, was overcome by the weight and collapsed, killing one and injuring dozens.

Personal responsibility for reasonable behavior does not apply in the hospitality/ recreation industry—especially when children are involved. The property needs to take reasonable steps to prevent foreseeable incidents.

Several hotel cases in a few different states are currently shaping the concept of fore-seeability. They are considering the presence of other factors such as due care by the hotel, and prior, similar incidents. Even the word "similar" is not a term agreed upon by most litigants. These discussions are too complex and lengthy for this forum, so we will leave that to our legal experts.

The bottom line for any security director to remember is that if an incident occurs, it will be used against you later. How you document that incident and how you react – to the point of making substantial changes to your Security – will be scrutinized. Incident documentation is presented later in this book, but the Security Plan is where we document the changes after an incident.

Specific Areas

While there will be a general security posture for the property as explained previously, there may be some exceptions. Areas behind the scenes or "back-of-the-house" may have less attractive barriers to protect valuables than those in view of guests. A motel in a high-crime neighborhood may use a walk-up window at night for check-in. Many newer luxury hotels have eliminated the check-in counter altogether. Guests at these resorts approach a kiosk for check-in and are helped face-to-face by a customer service representative who can provide a more physically engaging experience. You can imagine that this technique does not work for all hotels in all markets.

Deployment

Deployment includes where officers are needed, how many, and what their purpose is. Some hotels use the "shotgun" approach to staffing and deployment: Hire as many officers as the budget will allow and spread them around the property to provide as much visibility and coverage as possible. This approach is obviously lacking in efficiency or logic. Even if money is no object, the idea of providing security based on geography, rather than risk, may leave the property wasteful in one area and negligent in another.

For example, the retail area of a hotel property would need more of a physical presence during business hours than it does during times when the shops are closed. That is because the risks associated with a retail area change as the chance of robberies, shoplifting, violent crimes, and even accidents are reduced when customers are not present.

Similarly, the retail area may require less of a physical security presence than a nightclub when both are open for business. A nightclub generally has higher risk factors, such as intoxicated people, fights, and larger crowds. (The documented Risk Assessment for each area would exemplify and justify these variances in security posture.)

Waste would occur where officers are placed in these lower risk areas, especially where locked doors and gates or cameras might suffice. Negligence might apply when something happens in the nightclub and an officer is assigned to patrol other areas instead of the nightclub.

Using risk factors to determine staff deployment in the Security Plan is much more efficient, and easier to justify to management and lawyers. Other factors besides risk need to be considered in placing bodies around the property. Image, guest service, and other duties of the officers are explained next.

In a hotel/casino, security officers do most of the moving of money. This is generally not because of the risk associated with theft, but because most casino regulations require a department independent of the casino to be the third party in a transaction to avoid collusion. This goes against the popular belief that the casino places all its security officers around the cage and the pits for protection. The casino actually has much more to lose from a guest being robbed in its parking garage than it does with a theft from a blackjack table.

Upscale hotels do not earn their reputations lightly. These hotels, known for their high ratings, high-profile guests, and high prices might want smartly dressed officers in the lobby and porte-cochère as a visual comfort to their guests even though there is not necessarily any higher risk in these areas. This type of property is not only reducing physical risk and protecting its assets. It is also protecting the reputation and image in which it has invested so much.

Conversely, a smaller hotel with few staff members might have no visible security because they are not concerned as much with their aesthetic image. The security budgets are understandably smaller and it might assign its security to drive the company airport shuttle. Security does this function because they have a driver's license, can handle most off-property guest situations, and probably because they are the only employees not assigned to other duties. This is not an ideal use of Security, but sometimes it is a reality in the hospitality business.

These variables will have to be calculated into the Security Plan depending on the situation of the property and after the other risk factors have been addressed. To mitigate the risk factors into the Security Plan, take each area that was evaluated and decide if it needs an officer to mitigate it. The Risk Assessment in the preceding section was made either by area or by type of incident. Either way, the Security Plan is better segmented by area of the property. As each area is reviewed, determine if it needs a fixed post, if it is part of some type of patrol route, or if other tactics can be used to mitigate the risk.

Work Force

There is no widely accepted formula to calculate work force in a hotel. Various groups and individuals have tried to assign ratios, such as one officer per number of square feet, or per quantity of hotel rooms, or per amount of floors. This might work in a warehouse, factory, or office building, but not in a hotel. The variable is "people." It completely depends on the quantity and demographic of the guests, the neighborhood, and the region. A hotel attached to a theme park or a casino has entirely different staffing needs than a business hotel in a downtown city or in a rural agricultural community. It may be easier to determine staffing if you had a magic formula, but it would be more difficult to justify it later. This is why we did the Risk Assessment. The reality of a Security Plan is that you can justify and document all day long, but if your company does not allow that level of staffing, you will have to make due.

If you are having trouble justifying your staffing level, or you want to justify more, here are three suggestions for your overall staffing.

1. Hire as many as your budget will allow. If you already have an established staffing level and budget, you are unlikely to justify more. If you are starting with a new operation, check the properties around you or in your brand line and take the highest number.
2. Use your Security Plan. Add up your total posts and patrol areas figured into your security plan and hire enough to fill those positions. Do not forget breaks and supervisors. Also, consider how many you need to handle a major emergency like an evacuation. A large hotel needs several officers to clear all the rooms. Select the higher of this number and the number of posts.
3. Find an established precedent. Any hotel that has been sued for having inadequate security has had to justify their staffing numbers. This is not only a very accurate estimate, but is already proved in court to be adequate. If you have been through this, consider it the silver lining of all those deposition hours. If you have not been through it, find a similar property that has and compare those numbers.

It will be extremely difficult to decrease security staffing once you set your number. This is perceived as taking away protection from guests. This leaves your guests more vulnerable and you more liable. If you have to reduce staffing, take the staff away from noncritical areas such as supervision, administrative duties, or merchandise protection.

In 2005, a man walked into a shopping mall wearing a trench coat with a rifle and pistol underneath. He called 911 and told the operator he was about to commence shooting. He shot seven people and took four as hostages before being taken into police custody. One of the victim's families sued the mall for inadequate security. The plaintiff argued that the mall did not take even the most basic steps to protect its patrons—armed security or off-duty police, tracking of past crimes, public address system, and coordination with police to prevent attacks. The mall owners argued that the incident was not foreseeable and, therefore, not preventable. The court sided with the plaintiff that the incident was foreseeable and the mall should have implemented procedures such as those argued above.

Combining Layers

Other ways to secure an area or reduce risk involve the use of hardware or some type of equipment, such as cameras or locks. In some ways, hardware—or technology—offers a better and cheaper option for a layer of security. Locks, doors, and fences are generally infallible and cannot be distracted or overwhelmed. They also do not offer any subjectivity, which makes humans the better choice in some instances. However, humans cost more and have to have days off, lunch breaks, and insurance benefits.

Fixed posts, regular patrol, and security systems are most often combined to provide the most secure environment. It is the security director's responsibility to determine the best combination and application to reduce risk in each area. The director's experience, education, and training come into play here, but here are some basics that anyone can follow in securing an area in the most efficient and effective way possible.

Begin with the easiest and cheapest method of security possible. Then add layers until the risk has been mitigated. As you evaluate each risk, decide which security measure will most effectively and inexpensively prevent it. That may include a combination of measures or multiple layers such as a lock and an alarm, or prickly shrubs and a camera. This requires knowledge of those measures and layers and the experience of knowing what works and what does not. Do not hesitate to consult with an expert if you are not sure about whether it will work. You will find some good suggestions of what works throughout this book.

Using the standard hotel room as an example, the first layer of security is the lock on the door. In the old days, this was the Security Plan and you would be finished. As we figured out that keys could be lost, stolen, or duplicated, another layer was added. The key lock was replaced with a magnetic key lock and most of those issues were alleviated. Dead bolts and secondary door locks were added so guests would feel safe from the intruding housekeeper or technologically advanced burglar. For most hotels, the Security Plan is finished with the door locks. If the Risk Assessment includes the chance of robbery or room invasion, the next cheapest security method is the peephole. There is still the risk of door pushers, stalking crimes, and other violent acts, so it may be necessary to add cameras in the hallways or elevators. The final layer to add is physical patrol. Adding layers to physical patrol is achieved by increasing the frequency all the way up to a standing post.

Summary

The Security Plan is a justification for your policies, deployment, staffing, and all the neat gadgets you have acquired. You may never need to justify these to anyone, but you need to be prepared to explain why you spent this much money protecting this and that much money protecting that. The Security Plan keeps this process objective. For example, 20 years ago cameras were installed in elevators. That was seven directors ago and now your new hotel manager wants to know why we are spying on people in elevators. A Security Plan would explain to you and your new boss that a sexual assault in an elevator cost the hotel $750,000 to settle.

You also may find yourself on the witness stand trying to explain why the previous security director did not put a lock on the fitness center when it was built last year and a hotel guest was robbed. This is why you want to update your Risk Assessment and your Security Plan often and especially when you take over the responsibility for each. Each time you make a change to your plan—adding cameras, reducing workers, remodeling the nightclub—consider how it will affect your liability. Ask yourself if you will be able to justify this change to your boss, to a jury, or to your successor if something goes wrong.

The format of the plan is not as important as the content. If you are not sure of your format, use the previously mentioned outline or the one for the Security manual in this book. As long as you can read it and use it to provide your justification, you will be fine.

You need to keep current on new technology, current events, industry standards, and market practices. This knowledge is needed to keep your Security Plan current. (See Chapter 12 on career improvement.) At the very least, subscribe to magazines and newsletters that provide this information to you. Track cases and case law on matters of security and hospitality. Attend as many local and national seminars and organizations as you can. As I mention many times in this book, you need to be the subject matter expert on hospitality security to adequately protect your business.

SPECIALIZED PATROL

There is an entire chapter (Chapter 8) devoted to patrol techniques and types, but the programs that follow are important enough to change your entire Security Plan, so they are included here.

Armed Security

Most advocates for armed security will tell you that an unarmed security guard is about as effective as a doorstop against an armed assailant. Opponents of "guards with guns" will argue that the cost and liability of carrying guns is just too great. Although I am one of the advocates, I agree that guns have their limitations. I think I can present this program to you in a way in which you might agree.

Management Buy-In

The decision to arm security officers is usually way above the director's pay grade. If you want to issue guns, you will need buy-in from the executives (the general manager [GM] or owner) and their legal counsel. As soon as you mention it, images of Barney Fife—the incompetent TV deputy played by Don Knotts on *The Andy Griffith Show* who was not trusted with bullets for his duty weapon—and little old ladies with bullet holes lying in your hotel lobby will come to mind. This is not a good starting place, so instead of starting at the bottom, let's come in from the top.

Your Risk Assessment should have identified the need for armed security. You may be located in an urban area that experiences armed robberies, gang shootings, homicides, and other violent crimes. You may have even had some incidents on your property with guns, knives, or other dangerous weapons. Your hotel may have been identified as a piece of critical infrastructure and is therefore a target for terrorism. Finally, the prevalence of active shooter incidents from disgruntled workers or domestic violence in the workplace has likely come very close to your property.

These incidents, including any others, such as police chases through your property, law enforcement warrant service, or felony traffic stops in and around your hotel should be documented. Just as you did for the Risk Assessment, keep a running tally of these occurrences and be prepared to use them to justify guns both before and after the program is in place. Next, compile some lawsuit data.

Many security law publications do this for you. Alternatively, you can do a Web search for accidental shootings by security officers, negligent training security, security shot bystander, security shot suspect, etc. Find every lawsuit you can for the past 10 years that shows guns, good or bad, in the hands of Security. One more thing to research: employees (guards) who have sued their employer for not providing the proper equipment to save their own life. I can think of a couple of world famous headlines where Security was sued for not taking action because they lacked the proper tools. Then there is the guest who could probably prove that a gunman in your hotel was foreseeable and that your security was inadequate because you had no armed personnel to mitigate the threat.

All of this data and anecdotes make a great presentation, but the GM still has that vision of Barney Fife. You need to dispel this image by presenting a quality training and firearms program. It cannot hurt to show some examples of successful (no bad shots fired) armed security programs in your area or at least in hotels similar to yours. Your objective, like any other proposal, will be to show how the positives outweigh the negatives. So, before you make that presentation, let's work through the cons and turn them into pros.

Policy

Usually, when I am asked for advice on starting an armed security program, the questions are about training and bullet strength. Unfortunately, it is not that simple. Way before we get to that, we have to develop a firearms policy. Your policy will protect you, your employees, and your company from those bad things in your lawyer's head. The policy covers the rules involved with purchasing, storing, maintaining, loading, carrying, pointing, shooting, and reporting (the use of) a firearm. You cannot establish your training program until you work out the parameters involved in those aspects of the program. This book is not going to cover everything you need to know, but here are some things to consider.

Hiring—As you hire new officers, you should assume that they will be armed at some point. This may change the questions you ask, the experience you seek, and the background check that you perform. It is more difficult to switch from unarmed to armed officers because you were not considering this when hiring your current staff.

Armed officers—There are many arguments on whether to arm officers indoors. Many properties choose to arm only those officers who patrol outdoors or supervisors and managers. A firearm in a crowded nightclub may actually do more harm than good—unless you are faced with somebody shooting at you. Arming officers who only work outside may be a good way to get management comfortable with the idea.

Open carry—The decision to carry weapons openly on a uniform or to conceal them under a blazer is entirely dependent on your Security Posture (discussed earlier in this chapter). One is a deterrent and reactive and the other is only reactive. There also will be considerations of permits and governmental regulations for carrying.

Use of force—You should already have a use of force policy that specifically justifies what level of force to use depending on the force presented by a suspect. This policy is used to justify your actions and protect you and your officers, but also to enforce the policy. Those officers who abuse their ability to carry a deadly weapon are dealt with swiftly and severely.

Use of force continuum—This is discussed in more detail in Chapter 6, but an important consideration is "use of force options." If you provide firearms and nothing else, you may be negligent in not providing some less-than-lethal force option as an intermediary to avoid unnecessary use of deadly force.

Pay differential—You may want to pay armed officers a bit more than their unarmed counterparts. This not only recognizes their additional training and experience level, but also shows them, and possibly a court, that you take this program seriously. Whereas some "guard" companies just throw a gun on their hip and go out, hoping for the best, your company provides quality training of quality officers who receive a reasonable pay.

Equipment—You have probably seen security companies that allow officers to bring their own weapons, holster, and leather gear, with any type of ammunition and style and caliber of gun. It creates a bad image to have a bunch of "cowboys" or "hired guns" protecting your assets. Take time to research and invest in quality equipment that is consistent, maintained by the company, issued in a proper fashion, and carried like a professional.

Training

Training is absolutely the most important part of this program. It is difficult to decide how to start. I have two suggestions. One is to certify an in-house instructor (or two) with the National Rifle Association (NRA) or other qualified firearms trainer. These schools, usually a week long, teach everything from tactics to policy to instructional methods. Do not just pick the employee who grew up with hunting rifles or used to be a police officer. A qualified trainer, combined with firearms aptitude and devotion to the company, is best.

The second suggestion is to connect with local law enforcement trainers. They are definitely qualified, but you may have to remind them that your rules of engagement are different from a police officer's rules. Where the police may draw their weapons on any felony suspect, our policy is likely something like "only in the defense of our life." (This is only an example—policies vary.)

Once you have the policies and the trainer in place, you will need a training program. Look to other companies and your local police departments for guidance on what your program will look like. Even though you may think you don't have the time and budget to copy a police program, you may be surprised how little time they spend on firearms training. Devoting the same time and money to your program as the local police or a local "competitor" looks very good for you. Remember that if you are sued for a shooting, the amount of training and the quality of your program will be scrutinized.

Make sure your training program includes the following components: relevant laws associated with firearms, use of force policy, operation and basic functions of all types of firearms, firearm malfunctions, loading and unloading, near and distant shooting, tactics, stance, intuitive decision-making skills, tactical loading, range safety, and much more.

Discipline/Enforcement

How you enforce the policies for firearms is very important to the integrity of the program. Allowing officers to use poor judgment in drawing their weapons will diminish the perception of your level of competency. Those who violate these policies need to be held strictly accountable. A review and reporting process for any firearms or use of force related incident is vital. Once you allow someone to blur the boundaries or make a mistake, your firearms program is threatened.

The reality is regardless of what preconceived notions your lawyer and GM may have, Security Departments that deploy armed officers do not engage in random, accidental, or reckless use of firearms. If they did, they would not stay armed and you would not even consider it. Accidental or unlawful shootings by trained security officers are so rare that there is no trend or pattern that could lead anyone to prove otherwise. It is much easier to show where armed officers have saved lives, prevented crime, and kept many properties safe.

Nonlethal Weapons

In 2003, security officers used pepper spray to subdue a fight at a Chicago nightclub. The aerosol spray spread throughout the club causing minor irritations and vomiting for some customers. A panic stampede resulted from most of the 1,500 guests not knowing what the odor was; many assumed it was a poison terror attack. The only exit used was the front doors, which opened inward, then led to a steep flight of stairs down. Twenty-one people died and the club owners received prison sentences for code violations.

Doors opening inward and stairs leading directly to a door are fire code violations and an unsafe practice. Pepper spray in its aerosol form is not advisable indoors and, in this case, turned a nonlethal weapon into a deadly one.

I mentioned nonlethal weapons in the "Armed Security" section and they are justified in Chapter 6. If you do decide to deploy an intermediate weapon to avoid deadly force, there are options.

Taser®
The Taser is a revolutionary device that emits projectiles that apply a high-voltage electric charge to a suspect. The charge contracts muscles and usually incapacitates an aggressor. This weapon is very controversial and is under enormous legal scrutiny. In my personal opinion, the problem with the Taser is not its function, but in its application. Many police departments have failed to properly place this device on their use of force continuum and even when they do so, they fail to enforce its correct usage. We have all seen this device used as a *first* resort or in an inappropriate situation. Most police departments have a limit on how much they have to pay in a lawsuit, but private corporations do not.

If you have a hard time selling firearms to your executive team, it will be impossible to sell the Taser. Just to be clear, I think this is a great device and very effective when used correctly, but until the tendency for every "victim" of its use to sue goes away, it will not be in your financial interest to use it.

Baton/Impact Weapons
Like the Taser, batons have taken a beating in the courts due to their misuse. Baton training was always of a defensive nature, but Rodney King-type situations have left the legal

perception that it is offensive. If you use a baton, and there is a death due to a blow to the head or vital organ, your defense will be expensive.

Other impact weapons include asps, saps, straight sticks, kubutons, and any other device used to strike or apply pressure to a combatant. When used correctly, these can be amazing instruments with very effective techniques. Unfortunately, a serious injury from a stick will just produce dollar signs for most plaintiff lawyers.

Pepper Spray/OC

Oleoresin capsicum (OC) is an oil-based organic substance derived from hot peppers. It is designed to burn and distract the combatant to the point that he or she cannot focus on the offense. Several years ago, it replaced tear gas and MACE as the preferred chemical irritant for most police and security departments. Most police officers will use the aerosol form of OC because it quickly affects the lungs and eyes of assailants, incapacitating them faster. Unfortunately, aerosol also affects others nearby including the officer. See the accompanying textbox on previous page.

Pepper Stream was developed to avoid the problems associated with aerosol, but it also splatters and does not affect the assailant as severely. Pepper Foam is relatively new. It hardly splatters and remains on the skin longer, but does not affect the lungs and eyes as much. However, in my experience, it is quite effective. The downfall of OC is that it does not affect everyone the same and some not at all. The positive is that there has never been a death directly associated with its use and the effects wear off.

Like everything else we talk about in this book, we have to look at weapons not just for their effectiveness, but also from a liability standpoint. The best device to protect our guests and ourselves may not be the best to protect our assets. Choose your not-so-lethal weapons wisely.

Dispatch

To some properties, Dispatch is a function of communication, to others it is a room where systems are monitored, and to the rest of us it may be a method of gathering and documenting activities. Call it a Dispatch Office, a Command or Control Center, an Operations Center, or whatever. The function should be all of the above.

Communication

Dispatch, in this sense, is just like a police department or a taxi service. Calls are received, prioritized, and dispatched to your officers. In smaller facilities, your hotel phone operators or front desk personnel may do this. A large property may have several persons devoted to the dispatch function. This becomes a highly specialized function, requiring advanced training and above-average intelligence. Many hotels and tourist venues provide training similar to 911 centers to do telephonic medical triage, phone etiquette, radio procedures and language, hostility de-escalation, and more. On top of all this, we often ask them to handle housekeeping or engineering calls as well as the functions listed next. Training and experience are highly encouraged for this position, as it is an expectation of service from your responding agencies as well as your guests.

System Monitoring
Because Dispatch is usually a constantly staffed, isolated room, it is the perfect place to monitor video systems, fire alarms, panic and intrusion alarms, access control systems, and even facility monitoring (HVAC, boilers, etc.). Some of these functions are explained in more detail in Chapter 9.

Documentation
What better position to log all of our activities than the dispatcher? While you are answering routine and emergency phone calls, dispatching a dozen officers, watching 20 television screens, and answering alarms, why not write all of this stuff down for us? There are computer-aided dispatch systems that make this job a bit easier, but it is still a huge task, although a vital one for your department.

VIP Protection

As a proprietary Security Department, protecting celebrities, politicians, and executives hardly falls into the mission of protecting the company's assets. However, we all know that these individuals show up, sometimes announced, sometimes not, sometimes prepared with Security, sometimes not. Whichever way they present themselves to you, their presence will definitely disrupt your business and create a threat in one way or another. So, on occasion it may become your duty to protect these people from themselves and from others.

In most cases, your department will be one layer of security (such as with the president). On the other hand, you may be the proprietary source of information to the personal team that needs to get around the property easily. With some would-be celebrities or newsmakers, they may not bring their own staff, which puts you on the spot. Finally, some security staff or bodyguards may be your biggest threat.

Planning for this event is straightforward—if you are the one doing it. If you were planning it, you would first conduct a Risk Assessment. List the possible threats and their likelihood. Then create a Security Plan. Document how each threat is mitigated. This is also called an Incident Action Plan. Then you have to arrange these plans, such as crowd control for celebrities, personal protection for a rich executive (and his or her family), and so forth. It is helpful to have a small group of officers or managers go through some sort of executive protection training to provide expertise in these situations. You also can contract this service to professionals.

As with the president or a very famous person, he or she will have his or her own security and only need you to assist with access and travel through the property. In this case, assign a liaison from your staff to theirs to help this process run smoothly. Remember for whom you work. Your mission is to protect your company. The best way to do that is to collaborate with these people, as a negative incident on your property is not good for business.

Special Events

Just about any event that is not normal for your property, or that disrupts your regular business, is a special event. These also require an Incident Action Plan (Chapter 4) and some special policies and procedures. Crowd control, access control, evacuation routes, and other procedures not normal to your operation need to be addressed in the plan.

How many officers you will require, what they do for certain emergencies, will you search attendees, and many other issues need to be addressed in the Plan.

MEDICAL PROGRAM
Defibrillators

It was said at the turn of this century that you were safer in a Las Vegas casino than anywhere else if you were going to have a heart attack. Automatic external defibrillators (AED) used to be reserved for larger properties with highly trained security departments. Any property that has them has probably seen them not only used, but also used successfully to save lives. Ironically, most properties use AEDs more than they use fire extinguishers. Like most technology, they are now cheaper, easier to use, and more prevalent. This does not negate the need for a robust policy and training program for their use.

Defibrillators are a portable, battery-operated diagnostic heart monitor that measures heart rhythm and automatically delivers a shock if it detects the need for one. The user needs only to turn it on and connect it properly. AEDs also include audio recording, voice prompts, and other features. Just because technology has made them easier to use does not mean that you can just buy a couple and stand by to save lives. Just as you would not buy guns and pass them around to your officers without training and a strict use policy, you cannot do this with AEDs. A program is absolutely required before, during, and after being equipped with these units.

Justification

If you do not have AEDs, get them tomorrow. There is no acceptable reason not to have them these days. Serious brain injury occurs after four minutes of a stopped heart. Moreover, even if you live across the street from a hospital, the only way to get a shock to the heart in four minutes is to have an AED within two minutes of every person in your facility. When you are sued for not having AEDs, and you will be, what excuse will you give for not having them? Cost? Convenience? Time? There is no excuse.

Medical Sponsor

Many large hotel chains contract with a heart physician to oversee their AED program. This doctor, who must practice and maintain his or her education in cardiac and emergency medicine, advises on policy and training and reviews each incident where the AED was connected to a person. For a stand-alone hotel, you may be able to do this on a per diem basis with a local physician. The local ambulance company, fire department, and even the health department in your area may provide this service as well.

Training

To protect your liability, training should be done with a certified AED/CPR (cardiopulmonary resuscitation) trainer from a reputable organization. There are nonprofit associations that provide this training and can train trainers to lessen costs. Most training sessions for first responders are approximately eight hours and include CPR, basic emergency aid, and AED use. If you have read any part of this book, you know I am going to recommend every security officer have this training. The last thing you want is to have your one or two trained officers busy when the call comes out for a cardiac arrest. Try explaining that to a jury.

If you have a small security department, you may want to train other employees on your property that are mobile and easily deployed in the event of a medical emergency. This would include any department with radios.

Policy

This policy saves lives, but can also cost lives if not implemented and followed properly. Training is most important. Next is a policy requiring when the AED unit is dispatched to a medical call. You need to decide if you will bring it to calls of a sleeper, no-answer-to-knock calls, check-the-welfare calls, etc. Since we are not doctors, or even paramedics (in most cases), who are we to decide if the AED is needed at each particular medical call? As soon as a person is suspected of being unresponsive, or worse, the AED should be automatically sent. This is usually by the second officer (if there are two or more) or by the first if there is only one. This allows the closest officer to get on scene, perform a quick assessment, and start CPR if necessary. It would be an unfortunate mistake if the security officer assumed someone was just sleeping, fainted, faking, or otherwise and it turned out to be a fatal incident. Better to bring it each time and not use it.

A hotel in Nevada wisely deployed defibrillators and trained each officer on their proper use. This program was quite successful and saved several lives. However, in one incident, caught entirely on video, a man was found unconscious in the lobby. The first officer responded in seconds, but did not bring the defibrillator (AED) as trained. The second and third officers also responded very quickly and did not bring the defibrillator. The supervisor arrived, also with no AED. The officers could detect no heartbeat but heard gurgling so they assumed the man was breathing. An ambulance was called and paramedics were on scene eight minutes after the man went down. They immediately deployed their defibrillator, which malfunctioned.

The supervisor called for the hotel's AED and the man was revived after being shocked by the AED. The man survived but his family sued, as he did not fully recover from the brain damage. In court, the family subpoenaed video and reports from seven other incidents where the first officer to the scene brought the AED. They also showed the hotel's training program, which mandated the AED be brought to every medical call. The hotel claimed that they thought the man was just drunk and unresponsive because they heard him gurgling. As you guessed, the hotel took a serious hit because the training was not consistently applied.

In this case, the hotel had AEDs, had a policy to bring them, and violated their own policy. It was easy for the plaintiff to prove that they contributed to the man's ill health.

You should also have very strict policies on inspection and testing of the units and their associated equipment, changing of the batteries, storage area access, security, etc.

Storage and Access

You have seen AEDs in shopping centers and airports mounted very conspicuously for everyone to see and use. Other places, such as casinos, keep them behind the scenes. The difference is usually the size of the security force. A smaller staff will rely on other employees or even guests to retrieve the AED and use it or to get it for the single security officer that may show up. Casinos and other large businesses use more expensive and advanced units and prefer to keep them safely stowed away, but in convenient locations. However you decide to do it, make sure they are accessible regardless of the crowd you have and that they are placed conveniently for an officer to grab quickly.

It is not necessary to have them spread throughout a hotel tower. If you are going to have the second responder obtain the AED, then he or she is most likely coming from someplace other than the tower. The lobby, bell desk, or adjacent area is a wiser choice.

If you have a smaller security staff, you may need to train employees from other departments on how to use the AED.

Follow-Up

After an AED incident, it is advisable to have a review by your medical sponsor. Using the recording and data stored in the unit, he or she can evaluate the performance of the officers and provide constructive feedback as to where they can improve and what they did well. Regular training drills and this type of feedback will make this process much less stressful and more successful. There is nothing more rewarding than saving someone's life in this manner.

Medical Calls

Accidents and illnesses are certainly the most common types of calls in a tourist-based business. The policy for medical calls is property-wide and requires training, or at least an awareness, of all employees. Every employee needs to know that Security is the first responder so all calls that are related to a medical problem are routed to security. Perhaps the hotel operator will call local paramedics if there is no full-time Security Department. On the other hand, the front desk personnel could do this.

The hotel operators will receive most calls from guests for medical assistance. They need to have the most basic training: location and type of problem. Security is on the way. Then they transfer the call to Security, staying on the line to ensure the call goes through. There are three stages in this process for when Security should call an ambulance (or whoever provides your emergency medical services [EMS]).

1. If the guest asks for an ambulance, do not question it. Call the ambulance. It is okay to obtain information, but do not delay or deny EMS.

2. After the dispatcher takes basic information, he or she will have to make a decision to call paramedics and send Security.
3. Send officers to the scene to make a decision.

Determining when to call paramedics is very easy. If they are conscious, ask them. Would you like an ambulance? No? How may we help you? If they are unconscious, call the paramedics—every time. Varying from this policy will open your company to great liability.

Medical Personnel

In the old days, fancy hotels had a "house doctor" on staff that would help sick guests. We have come a long way from that luxury, partly due to economics and malpractice insurance, and mainly due to advances in emergency medicine and "911." In fact, in the 1990s many large hotels hired and trained Emergency Medical Technicians (EMTs) or registered nurses to provide an increased level of service for guests. The theory was that this would be an added layer of safety for guests. What happened was EMTs and nurses were expected to diagnose medical problems and save a trip to the hospital. You can imagine an EMT telling a guest with a bad headache that they need to take aspirin and rest, and then the guest turns out to have a stroke or a tumor. That only needs to happen once for a hotel to think twice about those EMTs. In an effort to save the EMTs, we ended up sending them *and* the outside agency to every call. It was soon declared redundant and a waste of money, so most hotels discontinued their medical programs.

Almost every city in the world has some sort of emergency response network that sends specially trained personnel with special equipment to deal with almost every situation. What that means to a modern hotel facility is that we have become the intermediary between the guest and this public service. Our service, therefore, is one of stabilizing and relaying information to the authorities. The expectation of service has even risen above that which we would receive in our own homes if we had a heart attack.

Whether or not you agree with it, we have to meet these expectations by providing at least that level of service for which we can reasonably train security officers. AEDs, for example (discussed in the next section), allow a superficially trained person to shock a heart back to life. As these advances become more prevalent, such as an automatic baby deliverer or brain surgeon, perhaps we will be expected to provide those services as well. Until then, we will provide that which is expected and keep our eye on the next technology and adjust accordingly.

In 2010, we have evolved (backward) to providing basic first aid care. We can respond quickly, assess the situation, and relay that information to the responding agency. Our training is limited to CPR, AED, and stabilizing shock. Let me be clear on this: You still need to designate a 24-hour team (Security) to respond to medical calls. They still need to have at least basic first aid training and CPR. This training may have to be more advanced if you are located in a rural area where paramedic response is farther away.

As with every policy introduced in this book, place yourself on a witness stand trying to explain why you did not train your officers to do CPR. There is no right answer.

Medical Equipment

Equipment is needed corresponding to the level of training. If you are training in CPR and AED, you will need oxygen and associated canulas, breather masks, and regulators. First aid supplies may include bandages, eyewash, thermal blankets, etc. This equipment needs to be stored in a central location depending on the layout of the property. A suitable bag or case should be issued to transport the items to the scene. You should also consider one or more wheelchairs to move sick persons to a taxi, intoxicated individuals back to their rooms, etc.

Inspections and stocking of the above items is just as important as having them. When one item is used, it must be replaced. I suggest keeping a stock of all items in a closet somewhere and inspecting the medical bag every shift or daily to make sure items were replaced.

ANTITERRORISM

Hotels have been soft targets for terrorism for years before 9/11. 9/11 brought the idea home to us here in the United States that it could actually happen here. Hotels are considered "soft" because they are not hardened to intrusion. By their nature, they are open to the public and have very little access control. They are "targets" because they offer the opportunity to provide mass casualties, visually dramatic destruction, economic impact, and iconic news coverage.

The good news is that 9/11 raised awareness and concern (and spending) on counterterrorism. Unfortunately, we are taking too long (over 10 years now) to get to the level of protection we need to reach. The federal government—and by grants, local and state governments—is spending huge amounts of money on developing plans and buying equipment that is not following any specific strategy or purpose. For example, following 9/11, we knew that radio communications between agencies was nonexistent. In 10 years, very few agencies have resolved this issue. This is not meant to be critical of the government, because they have thwarted and prevented many major attacks on the United States and should be recognized for such. It is to say that as private entities, we have some, if not most, of the burden of making our properties hardened to this threat.

We are not the government, and do not get much of the funding described previously, so we have to do what is best for our guests and us. We have to balance our risks—all of them—with our budget and practicality. We have to be smarter rather than harder. Therefore, I will not be recommending any of those cool automatic bollards or x-ray cameras. I will review some effective and simple countermeasures we can use to prevent terrorism. The best way to do that is to understand first what terrorism is, and then how we can prevent it.

The FBI defines terrorism as "the unlawful use of force or violence against persons or property to intimidate or coerce a government, the civilian population, or any segment thereof in furtherance of political or social objectives." You can argue with that definition that gang activity is terrorism. For the sake of this section, we will focus on al-Qaeda and others who have designs to attack targets in the West and any that may suit their designs. For the sake of prevention and behavioral recognition, these terrorists do not choose their

37

target based on personal reasons or monetary gain. We know from previous incidents that they choose a target based on high media value (popular place), symbolism (e.g., World Trade Center), or high body count (which would include hotels).

Just like criminal networks, terrorists operate in organized or solo ways. The "lone wolf" is a radicalized individual who is moved to militancy because of extreme ideology or political views. Timothy McVeigh and Charles Manson were lone wolves. (Manson was a lone wolf who successfully created his own terror network.) Groups of terrorists are called "cells," which operate within either highly structured or loose organizations. There are active cells, fringe cells, and sleeper cells. Because Muslim terrorist groups think of their Jihad as a long-term war, there may be sleeper or fringe cells anywhere that can activate at any time. Authorities have been successful routing out some of these groups, but there is no way of knowing how many there are or where they are hiding, which is likely in plain sight.

According to the U.S. Department of Homeland Security (DHS), al-Qaeda leaders have called for Westerners to conduct simple, small-scale attacks against familiar targets that do not require extensive funding, support, or training. In recent years, we have seen numerous attempts foiled by the FBI and there is no reason to think that terrorists will not continue to learn and alter their strategy based on these arrests. Terrorist groups are very structured in their ability to compartmentalize plans and missions while using technology like the Internet to communicate and train.

Attacks in other countries and attempted attacks on U.S. soil usually include bombs (improvised explosive devices—IEDs), but some—like in Mumbai, India—combined bombs with small arms fire. Our government authorities and oversees hotel colleagues have learned a great deal from these attacks and we have the good fortune of being able to learn and plan based on this intelligence. Here are some recent incidents involving hotels.

> In January 2008, several men lobbed grenades at security guards at the access gates of a luxury hotel in Kabul, Afghanistan. Once they made entry to the fortified hotel, one man activated a suicide bomb. Six were killed, mostly security and staff. The terrorists were disguised as local police to get close to the gates and guards.
>
> A truck filled with explosives approached the front gate of a Western luxury hotel in Islamabad, Pakistan, in September 2008. The driver exchanged gunfire with gate guards and then detonated the explosives. The explosion and ensuing natural gas leak and fire destroyed most of the hotel, killing 60 people, and injuring 250. It was believed that the lone terrorist was targeting a group of U.S. marines who were staying in the hotel.
>
> In November 2008, 10 heavily armed men, operating simultaneously in teams of two, attacked several targets in Mumbai, India. They entered the rear of the hotel—with help from employees—while detonating IEDs at the entrances of the two hotels to prevent first responders from entering. IEDs also were detonated in taxis around the city to distract and deter police. The gunmen took hostages in the hotels and engaged first responders with guns and IEDs, which set the building on fire. The incident lasted 3 days and at least 173 died.

A car filled with gunmen exchanged small arms fire with gate guards at another luxury hotel in Peshawar, Pakistan, in June 2009. They forced their way through a gate and detonated a car bomb near the hotel, which killed 7 and wounded approximately 40.

In July 2009, bombs ripped through two iconic hotels in Jakarta, Indonesia. They were detonated five minutes apart, killing 7 and wounding approximately 50. After an unexploded bomb was found in a hotel room, it was determined that it was intended to activate first, causing guests to flee toward the lobby where that blast would have caused more fatalities. This is referred to as a "secondary explosion" and is intended to exploit panic resulting from a primary explosion.

Four Baghdad, Iraq, hotels were targeted in simultaneous attacks in June 2010. Each of the attacks involved explosives that killed 36 people and caused extensive damage to each hotel. Witnesses reported one of the vehicles containing a bomb was disguised to look like an emergency vehicle with flashing red lights.

In Mogadishu, four men disguised as government security forces shot their way through security in August 2010. Most members of the Somali parliament who were at the hotel for a conference were shot and killed.

On June 28, 2011, nine assailants armed with automatic weapons, rocket-propelled grenades, and explosives attacked the Intercontinental Hotel in Kabul, Afghanistan at 10:30 p.m. The attack began with a suicide bombing at a side entrance, which allowed other assailants to avoid heavier security at the main entrance. Once inside, the assailants killed as many guests and employees as possible. As NATO-led forces arrived, the attackers fled to the roof where some detonated their suicide vests and military personnel in helicopters killed others. The siege ended at 3 a.m., but one terrorist hid in the building until 8 a.m. when he detonated his vest, killing two police officers and a civilian. In all, 20 people were killed and approximately 18 were injured. The Taliban claimed responsibility for this attack and has vowed to carry out similar attacks in the West.

These attacks were carried out overseas and we have no reason to believe these types of attacks could occur on U.S. soil. Or do we? We had the same outlook before the World Trade Center Bombing (and soon after it). Let's take advantage of the information we have and take the simple steps to harden and prevent *before* something happens instead of afterward.

Note that the bombings and shootings mentioned previously all occurred in the past few years, post-9/11, and each of the properties had hardened themselves to prevent those types of incidents. That hardening had varying levels of success depending on the intelligence done by the terrorists, their financial and physical capabilities, and the personnel resources available to them. Some were military or government-backed and many used "inside" personnel. Most hotel security directors overseas will tell you that hiring is their biggest problem. Determining and relying on the loyalty of security officers hired locally when faced with a fellow citizen with a gun or bomb is a risky proposition.

In the United States, we are fortunate that we do not have this problem to the same extent, but we still need to make sure our background and hiring processes are consistently strong. Once hired, it is important to have an employee awareness program. Many corporations and hotels in our industry have adopted the federal government's "See Something, Say Something" program. This is a very simple program because it quite succinctly reminds the employee to report suspicious activity to a supervisor or security. DHS has videos available to show your employees in each department what they should be looking for. These are free or you can buy them from various companies. Following is a list of indicators that may indicate suspicious behavior. This list should be incorporated in training for security and other employees.

- Front desk
  - Using false ID or no ID at check-in
  - Requests for anonymity on registration
  - Paying for room with cash
  - Using someone else's credit card
  - Third-party registration
  - Extending stay one day at a time
  - Requests for specific room, floor, or view

- Housekeeping
  - Refusal of service for long periods
  - Little or no luggage in room
  - Renting room, but not using it
  - Leaving all belongings in room upon check-out
  - Multiple visitors or deliveries to room

- Security
  - Attempt to access employee areas
  - Unusual interest in hotel security, access, cameras, stairwells, etc.
  - Use of alternate entrance and exits to avoid being seen
  - Not following hotel policies
  - Unusual interest in staff shift change, operating procedures, etc.

Other target-hardening measures will depend on your risk assessment and your location. I would not expect a hotel in the Midwest to be as heavily hardened as a hotel in New York City. You will have to decide, based on cost and feasibility, which, if any, of these procedures and equipment you want to acquire.

Standoff

Standoff distances for hotels vary between extremes. At a minimum, there should be some sort of bollards blocking runaway vehicles from entering doors and windows. Valet concourses built before 9/11 were designed for door-to-door convenience, but new construction since then has blocked or removed the traffic lane that is closest to the building.

Generally, hotels will back off traffic as far from the building as possible without making it too inconvenient for guests. Bollards in a hotel setting need to be decorative, so a popular choice is a big flowerpot. These likely will only stop a slow-moving car. Rather than purchase the expensive, in-ground bollards, I suggest using a wedge-shaped pot or planter. When these are tipped over, they create a wedge that brings any size vehicle up off its front wheels.

Metal Detectors

Metal detectors are contrary to the hotel business and I would not use them unless there was a specific threat. Bag searches may be a more friendly option if you find searches necessary.

X-Ray Luggage

After 9/11, many hotels started using x-ray machines for luggage that went through the main entrance. These machines are very expensive to maintain, they break down a lot, and they are not foolproof as TSA (Transportation Security Administration) has reminded us.

Bomb Dogs

Several hotels throughout the United States have sniffer dogs. This is a large expense and is not practical for 24-hour operation. Hotels that have them use them for random patrol, for investigating suspicious packages, and for a visible presence.

Countersurveillance

Part of the countersurveillance process includes behavioral recognition (discussed in Chapter 8). The other component involves assigning an investigator to inspect the property on a regular basis to identify those who may be gathering information on the property. Their other function is to identify vulnerabilities from the terrorist's point of view. If you send someone out to try to "break" your defenses, he or she will find vulnerabilities for which modifications can be recommended.

Video Surveillance

Your digital video system should have analytics that can be used for counterterrorism. Your system should be able to "see" packages or bags left unattended, persons in unauthorized areas, license plate recognition, facial recognition, and many other bells and whistles.

Many other counterterrorism procedures and agencies can help with this process. DHS offers free site inspections and can make recommendations on your vulnerabilities and mitigation suggestions.

DOMESTIC TERRORISM

The previous section was mostly geared toward traditional Islamic terrorism. We must not forget that the United States and other Western countries have their own domestic terrorists. Their goals are generally the same: death and destruction to bring attention to their cause. There are known cases of environmentalist, animal rights, antiabortion, and White supremacist groups that have bombed buildings, assassinated executives, and set fire to structures to raise awareness for their "cause." For our purposes, most of the measures in the last section still apply, but generally, these groups have specific targets. Intelligence and research are the keys to prevent being a target of these groups. For a hospitality venue, we need to watch what groups rent our meeting space, what executives or dignitaries visit our guest rooms, and what vendors with which we do business.

Keep an eye on your Sales and Convention departments and make sure they inform you of every group coming on property. A simple Internet search can answer most of your questions, or at least cause you to make the appropriate alarm. You are not looking out for just the initiators of violence, but also the potential victims of it. For example, a hunting group may be targeted by an animal rights organization, or an obstetrician symposium may be attacked by an antiabortion group. Besides violence and property destruction, the last thing you want is a protest on your sidewalk by one of these groups.

DATA SECURITY

This book is primarily about physical security, but we cannot ignore the convergence with data security. Those of you who deal with this collaboration might not describe it as such. These days, trying to run physical security without IT (information technology) support is like trying to be captain of a ship without an engine room. Some companies have figured this out and they put that captain in charge of his or her own engine room. Others have IT and Physical Security report to the same person. Still others are trying to work together, but with entirely different operations and agendas.

I suspect most hotels operate like the latter because they have not quite accepted that IT flows through every department and all aspects of the operation. In Security, that flow is through alarms, access control, video, reports and admin functions, and even patrol systems. Physical Security is using more "bandwidth" and more "systems" than ever before. Convergence has been the term used in most security circles to describe the new relationship between these two entities. If you have ever had any drug recognition training, you know that convergence means two eyes working together to focus on one target. If that is true, then we don't have to look at IT as a threat or an intruder in our world, but one with whom we can collaborate to achieve a common goal. After all, one eye without the other cannot perceive depth.

Several years ago, I was embarking on a project to switch from analog to Internet Protocol (IP) cameras. My logical assumption was that I would be working with IT to transmit my data from the camera to the recording source, but also throughout the property to several end users. I called a meeting of Security, Engineering, and, of course, IT. As we gathered around waiting for the meeting to start, we all discussed with some excitement the new technology that was about to open many doors for us. The IT Director walked in quietly, went to the whiteboard, and wrote "NO" in large letters. We looked at each other and then him, and asked what he meant. He said, "No, you cannot use *my* network for video." A long argument ensued about whose network it was, whose side he was on, and so on. Then he walked out.

That IT guy does not work there anymore, but that decision came too late as I had to build an entire network for video from scratch. I would have saved money, time, and probably improved the company intranet if he had been more cooperative. I hope you can learn two things from this story: One is that you need buy-in when you tromp into someone's field as I did, and two, don't act as he did when you need to work together on a project. The fact is there are hardly any projects or any equipment you will acquire where you won't need the expertise of the IT department.

You need IT probably a bit more than they need you (which may lead to some of that animosity), so build that relationship with them before you really need it. IT doesn't really need me to get into their office, but I rely on IT to make sure my network is up, that I have Internet and email, that my password works, and that all my systems are operating properly. I hope that you have a good person who understands we are all here to protect the assets and the guest. This is one of the first relationships you need to build if you have not done so already.

Besides convergence, there is another side to data security that has nothing to do with physical security. While you may have bad guys that occasionally come into your property to do bad things, your data are under attack constantly. There are people in other countries who do nothing all day but exploit vulnerabilities in your network or data chain. If you have email, Internet, or any other link to the outside world—and you do—your data are at risk. Your data may be the most valuable asset your business has. Credit card info, personal identities, client lists, payroll, and employee lists are all on your servers and your servers all connect in some way to China, Nigeria, and who knows where else.

This is not a full-time job; worse, it is a job for an entire department of experts. For every inebriated guest or shoplifter you physically deal with, there are another thousand attacks on your network. I am not a professional in data security, so I say leave it to the experts and support them 100 percent. One of the biggest risks to data security comes through employees. Either inadvertently, or intentionally, employees are responsible for the vast majority of data leaks, breaches, thefts, and viruses. Your IT department should already have policies in place that address these vulnerabilities, but they are often enforced by Security—as are most thefts. Some policies regarding data security are as follows:

Confidentiality—Most employees do not leak information on purpose. It is often through a clever scam or accidentally opening a bad link. Still, everyone must sign and adhere to a confidentiality policy and be held accountable if they break it. Training sessions on scams and Internet dangers should supplement these policies whenever possible.

Unauthorized hardware—This is often an unintentional breach as well. Employees bring in their music device or that free flash drive they received from the trade show. That device was probably made in China and its origins or intent are dubious. Companies should exclude all external drives and USB plug-ins for this reason. Besides, that sales manager who found a better job down the street just might like to supplement his income with the convention client list from your hotel. There is technology now that detects these devices being inserted into a desktop computer.

Personal electronic devices—Besides the USB devices just mentioned, cell phones and other data devices are problematic for several reasons. Cell phone cameras, Wi-Fi,

Bluetooth, and hardwire connections are great ways to accomplish data theft. Some of the more advanced data companies can detect these devices being used, but no one has been able to detect a photo being taken of a computer screen. Cameras have some other ramifications. There have been sexual harassment and privacy cases against companies that allowed employees to have cameras on them at work.

Passwords—Password sharing is still the biggest problem for data security. Usually among co-workers, password sharing leads to some policy violations and access control issues, but when shared accidentally with outsiders, it can lead to real problems. A policy against password sharing should be enforced.

Internet/email filtering—Many companies have Web filters; presumably to keep workers from being distracted by nonwork-related Web sites. A more important reason is to avoid malicious sites. Just entering an unverified site can download a virus or cause other technical problems. Those filters usually are experienced-based, meaning that they are not put on the exclusion list until someone finds out about it. This means an email can have a link to a malicious site that has not been vetted and can inadvertently download something bad.

One thing you do not want at work is your employees abusing the Internet. Besides being a distraction of their real work, and the possibility of downloading viruses (mentioned previously), there are some other issues. Viewing and downloading pornography, for example, could result in sexual harassment issues. What if it is child pornography or exploitation? Keeping these filters current and strict keeps everyone out of trouble.

A few years ago, and probably still today, we were being bombarded with the Nigerian 419 scams. These people would send out millions of emails hoping to get just a few suckers and they did. One that affected businesses was the charming guy that convinced the lonely secretary to rescue him from his life of poverty with a promise of riches to be unlocked by the two of them later. This scam coaxed many an employee to use their business contacts and accounts to make airline reservations, long distance phone calls, and wire transfers, with the understanding that it would just be a "loan" to be paid back when their newfound wealth arrived.

DATA INVESTIGATIONS

Another point of convergence for IT and Security comes in the form of investigations. Data evidence is critical in many investigations now and both departments need to work together. For example, it is common to use archived emails as evidence in a sexual harassment case. There are many systems within a hotel that house or process information that you will need from time to time. You need to set up that relationship in advance so you can get to the data quickly and cleanly when needed. A good IT department can go one step farther and alert you when problems occur. Web filters can monitor attempts to enter pornography sites, emails with key words, unusual login times and frequency, access level violations, etc. These triggers can be set in advance with a consistent response from Security and Human Resources (HR).

3

Budgeting

Don't tell me where your priorities are. Show me where you spend your money and I'll tell you what they are.

James W. Frick, politician

The budget is really the biggest difference in Security policy from one property to another. We all want to protect our guests and we all want the best equipment and highest paid staff, so the only thing that usually separates us is the amount we spend. In this chapter, we will talk about how to prepare a budget and then look at some creative ways to save and get more money to do the job you would like to do.

BUDGETING BASICS

Even if someone else does your annual budget, you should participate in this process. Budgeting alarms some of us who are more physical managers rather than administrators. Like anything else, once you understand it, budgeting is not so bad. The budget is your "forecast" or plan on how much you will be spending on what.

The Process

Almost every department in every company in the world budgets the same way: Take the prior year's income and expenses, multiply by how much you think those will go up or down, and you are finished. Security has little revenue (income) to speak of, so half of the job is out the window, and all we need to calculate is expenses.

Prior Year

Prior Year (sometimes called current year) refers to the fiscal year that is just before the fiscal year for which you are budgeting. (A fiscal year is the 12 months used by the company for its budget—often the anniversary of the day the company opened.) If your fiscal year begins May 1, you may be planning your budget around February. That means February,

March, and April have not yet occurred, so you have no expenses to compare for those months. For those months, you would have to estimate how they are going to turn out based on how the other nine months did that year.

New Year

New Year is the year for which you are doing your budget. In the previous example, it is May through April.

Full-Time Equivalent (FTE)

Full-Time Equivalent (FTE) is a common and useful term in budgeting your staff. It is simply the number of employee positions you have based on the hours worked. You may have 60 part-time employees who work a number of hours to equal 40 FTEs. This number is the total hours worked in a month divided by the number of work hours in the month (approximately 168). Since some departments have part-time employees and give extra days off, sick days, early-outs, and other variables, FTE allows you to compare wages evenly from year to year.

Expenses

Expenses are divided into several categories. To complete the budget, take the prior year's expenses and add or subtract the amount you expect it to change. Following are common expenses and how to calculate them.

Wages
Wages, the largest part of most security budgets, is usually divided into hourly, salary, and overtime expenses. These amounts change year to year if your staffing numbers change or if your hourly wage changes. If you provide a cost-of-living increase of 3 percent each year, then you would add 3 percent to the hourly and salary amounts. If you downsize your department by six positions, you would subtract those six salaries from the budget. Overtime is usually not planned in a budget. The objective is to operate without overtime, so it is usually calculated into the hourly amount. In other words, use the sum of the prior year's hourly and overtime amounts to equal the hourly amount in the new year. Overtime would be forecast to be zero. Wages might be separated further into holiday, vacation, bonus, commission, and other amounts included on employee checks. They are budgeted in the same way.

Benefits
Benefits are a cost we often neglect. Your accounting department does not. These carry over to the next year consistently unless there is a significant change in benefit costs. Benefits include cost of health insurance, life insurance, retirement, etc.

Operating Expenses
Operating expenses in the Security Department include almost every other expense. (Revenue departments have cost of sales, food, goods sold, etc.) These may be separated

into such categories as equipment, office supplies, travel, and so on. You may have 20 or more line items that you may or may not use. These lines usually correspond with lines used by other departments. The concept for budgeting is the same as before. If you spent X on office supplies this year, then that is likely to be what you will spend next year. This holds true for each line unless you know of some significant change in spending habits. Significant changes include a change in vendors or some other addition or subtraction in the way you buy things.

Capital Expenses
This is a separate budget and is addressed later in this chapter.

THE PAPERWORK

Paperwork? I bet your hotel does not do this on paper. Imagine the full trashcans and worn out erasers. At a minimum, you probably use a program like Excel® or an accounting program designed just for budgeting. Don't be intimidated by their complexity. These programs do most of the work for you and you should only have to enter a few numbers as described previously. Some programs allow you to enter the number of employees you will have and the programs do the rest.

YOUR BUDGET

You are responsible for this budget, so take ownership of it and follow it. Doing these calculations and forecasts will help you stay on track. You will see where your department is spending money and possibly even find ways to save money. When the boss tells you to cut your budget by 5 percent, you will have an idea where to start looking and what impact it will have.

CAPITAL EXPENSES

Each year, the company takes a portion of its profits and invests it back into the property as improvements. This infusion of cash is called capital and may vary from year to year. This money is not spent on salaries or regular expenses because it is an investment intended to provide a return on investment (ROI). Remodeling rooms is a good example of a "CapEx" in a hotel. The hotel manager will generally have this money spent years in advance and is not looking for suggestions from Security. It is your job to make sure security improvements are considered in allocating capital. A new video system, an upgrade of guest-room door locks, or an employee access control system are popular examples of capital expenditures.

Requests for capital are usually made in writing and often decided in a special meeting. Creating this document is important and needs to be done right. Here are some suggestions and necessary elements of a request for capital.

Collaboration. Your request is more likely to be approved if it has the support of more than one department. Seek those persons or departments that share the need for the improvements and get their buy-in and assistance in justifying the expense. The hotel manager will share your need for a guest-room lock upgrade, the restaurant manager might support you on a new camera system for the nightclub, and the Human Resources Director wants an access control I.D. badge system for employees just as much as you do.

Research. You will be responsible for gathering all of the information necessary to make a decision. Don't say, "We need IP and HD video recording because everyone else has it" and expect a green light without making your case. You will need prices, references (who else uses it and what is their success), ROI (return on investment), and how it will improve or benefit the company or its guests.

Pricing. If possible, get more than one bid and be prepared to document why you selected the preferred bidder. Their work experience, their price, and prior relationship with the company might be reasons to select a certain vendor.

ROI. A capital improvement needs to show a potential to make money for the company, even if it is indirectly. For example, a new camera system does not generate profits, but you may be able to justify the cost by the amount saved on repairing the old system, lack of usable video the old way, and even potential losses recovered. Do not make this stuff up. Just like in eighth grade algebra, you need to show your work.

Benefit to business. Not every capital expense is backed with ROI. A new outdoor heater in valet does not increase profits, but it does increase comfort of the guests, which adds to their experience. It also brings the property up to what might be an industry standard for cold-weather hotels. If you cannot show an ROI or a benefit to business, don't even bother asking for the money.

Preparing the request. If you have ever written a business plan, you know how to write this request. You will include all the information that you gathered previously, putting it into an easy-to-read format, with photos of what it looks like, charts and graphs that support your findings, and an executive summary.

Executive summary. This is a short, maybe one page, summary of the entire request. Just the facts so the decision maker can decide if he or she wants to look into it deeper. Be prepared to answer questions even though they are answered in your written material.

The pitch. You may go through this entire process, and it may be approved on several different levels until it gets up to the grand executive president of all hotels. You may be called to the office to plead your case. The president will nod his or her head in agreement. The president will smile and take many notes. He or she may ask questions and enter numbers in a calculator. Then, after you are exhausted and exhilarated from your most brilliant performance ever, the president will say, "You're right. We need one of those gizmos. I agree 100 percent." Then, "But we can't buy one this year."

The moral. Don't expect to get to this level. There are many things they want to buy and many factors, besides security, that affect their decision. They may consider new televisions in the guest rooms or adding on a sports bar more urgent because it will increase profits. Without those profits, we may not make it through the year. However, they have validated your proposal and may put it on next year. Do not give up. Shelve it until next year and then try again.

SECURITY REVENUE

Security is just a big business expense to most general managers. They don't like paying for it, but they know it is necessary. There is no reason why Security cannot contribute to the bottom line. You may already be pulling some of your own weight without realizing it. Not all of these ideas will work in all organizations, but at least you may be acknowledged for your efforts.

Restitution

Your investigators can cover some of their expenses by recovering losses from employee thefts. In Chapter 11, we discuss the investigations process and loss recovery. Loss recovery should be tracked and reported to your boss and the controller each month or quarterly. This will show positive income being generated by the Security Department. Otherwise, it is deposited in some miscellaneous operating account and lost in the numbers.

Court restitution is a different matter entirely as it is actual revenue instead of savings. When you make an arrest for theft or vandalism, have a prepared document ready to include with the arrest report detailing the costs incurred by your department in making this arrest. The unrecoverable loss in a theft, the items broken, and the property damaged all have a value. Then there is the cost of the arrest itself. Two officers multiplied by two hours equal another amount. Then there are administrative costs associated with processing the arrest. Writing the report, copying it, and reading it all have value. Total this and you might have a couple of hundred dollars that you will submit to the court as restitution. The judge may or may not honor all or part of it and you may not ever get any of it, but whatever you get is more than you would have if you did nothing. You also may speak to your accounting department as to whether they can "write off" these amounts as unrecovered losses.

Parking

Many hotels use an outside service to manage or at least enforce parking. They call a certain tow company to haul away a car and that company makes hundreds of dollars each time. Why not do it yourself? So, you don't have any tow trucks or a tow yard. That is okay. How about disabling the vehicle with a "boot"? A boot costs a few hundred dollars and keeps a vehicle from being moved. Then, your department charges the drivers when they return to their vehicles. This may not be advisable for your guests' cars, but it is perfect for employees of the office building next door or the nightclub down the street. If you have plenty of parking, maybe you need to think about charging for it per hour or per month.

Special Events

Your Catering or Convention Departments may have certain events that require physical security. Look at how those departments address this with their clients. Either they allow them to hire their own contract security company or they assign you to provide this service. You need to assess the risk of having an outside company exposing you to liability on your property. Can you vouch for their training? What if they use excessive force on an intruder? What if one with a criminal record is caught in the storeroom with the boss' daughter? Consider limiting the security presence at these events to your own personnel, or at least to a company that you contract. Either of these options puts revenue into your department and gives you some control over the risk on your property.

Lost and Found

As we will discuss in Chapter 11, unclaimed merchandise can really pile up in a large hotel. There are numerous ways to earn money from these items. First, you can sell the items to the employees in a "rummage sale." Second, you can actually sell many of the items on eBay and get a higher price. Phone chargers, for example, are worth at least a couple of bucks on an auction site. Lastly, you can donate the items to charity and collect a write-off. Ask the controller if the write-off can be credited to Security because your department did all the work. This is, of course, after a certain period of time and after all efforts to find the original owner have been exhausted.

Back-Charging

You may feel like the revenue-generating departments take advantage of having their own private security force to do things that they cannot or do not have the work force to do. Talk to your boss about charging these departments for these tasks. This will accomplish two things. First, it will add revenue to your bottom line. Second, because it adds expense to the other departments, they just might reduce their calls for service. Your department wins either way.

Please remember that some of these ideas have to be proposed in the right context or you might be thrown out of the boss's office. Think about it before you just hand a list to someone. I have been successful with all of the ideas presented here, but I presented them one at a time and sought buy-in from other departments beforehand.

JUSTIFYING SECURITY IN A DOWN MARKET

We have probably all been in the meeting or received the memo to reduce our expenses by 5 percent. The hospitality industry seems to be the first to suffer when the economy is down and the last to recover when it rebounds. Unfortunately, a reduction in business volume or revenue does not necessarily mean a reduction in crime or the need for security. Also unfortunate is the fact that the boss may not see it the same way. He needs to see a cut across the bottom line and this means everyone—including you—must bite the bullet. It is your job to educate your boss on why you actually need more security during these slumps, not less. You may meet somewhere in the middle with no cuts and that is a good compromise.

Crime Rates

You need to arm yourself with some facts: In a down economy, criminals have to work harder. Their hard-earned stolen money does not go as far, so they have to increase their thefts. Financial desperation leads to new criminals. Those who may have just been scraping by may now be "forced" into stealing to make ends meet. Crimes of opportunity increase. Whereas before if someone left their keys in their car or their bag unattended, they were less likely to be a victim. Now, those opportunists are increasing in numbers and are more likely to take advantage of any opportunity given. We need to maintain a certain presence of uniforms and active security to prevent crime on and around our property.

Internal Crime

In a down economy, chances are that hours have been reduced, wages are frozen, and people are being laid off. Employees become desperate and some even justify their crimes this way. "The hotel still has business; the bosses are probably getting their bonuses, so it is only fair if I take a little off the top." They will become more creative, greedier, needier, and, if not stopped, will drive the business down even more. Cuts in security reduce the number of audits on these employees.

Guest Comfort Level

Everyone can feel the crime increase, especially when traveling. Guests want to get away from troubles like those described previously. When crime is up, Security needs to ramp up equally to provide the same level of protection that it did before. Guests are not necessarily looking for security, but feel it when it is not there.

Terrorism

Don't forget about this threat that has been looming over us for decades. It has not gone away and is not likely to go away. Whether or not you see an increase in terrorism around you, realize you are not immune and you cannot let your guard down. One incident, no matter how small, even if it fails, can ruin everything. You may never recover from this loss of business and guest confidence. Reducing the staff that keeps this threat away is a huge mistake.

MAKING THOSE CUTS

Before the boss starts cutting salaries and laying off security officers, let's throw in some bones to keep him happy without hurting our operation.

Creative Scheduling

I know you probably do this already, but take a hard look at your schedule. Do you need all those officers at all of those times? Maybe your patrol frequency ebbs and flows and you do not need three shifts with the same number of people. Look at staggering shifts so that different start times allow for staffing levels to rise and fall according to the need for security during those times. Look into four-day workweeks of 10-hour shifts. See if this works just for your high volume shifts to give you an overlap while the nightclub is open. Depending on the type of business you have, perhaps you are fully loaded on day and swing and run a skeleton at night. You know your business. Just take a close look. Taking an inconvenient cut is better than a slash from the top.

Briefing

If you pay your officers for a preshift briefing, consider using this time for the operational duties of the department. See if the briefing can be done through email, pass-down logs, or even on the radio. Put pertinent information on a bulletin board and require officers to read it before starting work. I like the camaraderie and consistent information flow of a preshift briefing, but I would rather lose that than officers from the hotel.

Several lawsuits have been filed over the years by security officers claiming they should be compensated for time spent preparing for shifts and attending preshift briefings. These lawsuits, some of them class actions, have been decided in favor of both sides. The consensus is that officers do not have to be compensated for time spent on minimal activities preparing for work, such as putting on uniforms, obtaining their firearms, etc. However, briefings have been perceived as a work-related meeting and therefore compensable.

Getting ready for work is not unique to security officers and not an activity that most courts consider part of payroll. It is generally not fair to require workers to attend a meeting and not pay them for it. Check with your HR Director or legal counsel to ensure that your policies do not violate labor laws.

Supervisors

Look at the duties of your supervisors. If they are spending their entire shift in the office, there is something wrong. They need to be "on the floor" supplementing the shift. They can cover breaks, vacations, and delegate some of their duties to others.

Spending

You should look at cutting your spending before someone else does. Look at that current year budget and see where all the money goes. Copier repairs? Really? Do we need all those copies? How about radio repairs? New radios now can be cheaper than the repair on the old ones. Prioritize your spending into needs and wants. Then make the cuts yourself. Even 5 percent will not hurt you, but it will please the boss.

Procedural Changes

If you are still doing things the way you always have, there is a chance you can save some time and money by re-examining your procedures. Labor is the largest part of your budget, so what are those officers doing all the time? For example, if you have two door hosts and two floor officers in a small nightclub, perhaps you can have one of each and a third that watches both. That is a 25-percent cut! You also can start the night with minimal staffing and ramp up to full strength at peak time.

Patrol Areas

If officers have time to stand around talking, they are either goofing off or their patrol area is too small. Try increasing the area they have to cover. They should be on the move all the time, giving you good coverage. The boss will think you are over-staffed if he or she sees officers standing around talking while he or she is asking for cuts. In other chapters, we discussed how to set up patrol areas and whether to use physical patrol, video, gates, etc. Take a closer look and see if you really need that physical patrol in that area or if a camera can cover it as well.

Arrests/Reports

Arrests should be the last option when dealing with any situation. An arrest not only opens you up to liability for false arrest, but there are also injury claims (from the suspect and the officer) and they take up a huge amount of time and resources. Make sure your supervisors know that an arrest is warranted only if nothing else works. Be unreasonably reasonable with irrational persons. Reports also take a lot of time. Determine why you are taking the report. Remember that you are not a police department and you have no obligation to take crime reports. Your reports are to protect you and they do nothing at all for the guest. Burglary from a vehicle in the parking lot: You probably deny those claims anyway, so why do the report? Damage in the hotel hallway: You have no suspect and you will not. The damage will be repaired whether or not you write a report. Think of all the incidents for which you write reports and ask yourself what they are for. Maybe a log entry will suffice to have a record that the incidents occurred.

There are many ways to save money in security staffing. It is much better if it comes from you rather than an arbitrary across-the-board cut. If you make these decisions now, you can cut staff through attrition (people leaving on their own) rather than having to lay off employees.

Section 2

Policies

4

Security Manuals

There were policies, there were standard operating procedures. But we found as we looked at our operations that there was this gap that should be filled by a directive.

Bryan Whitman, Pentagon spokesman

Many of us are results-oriented directors. We want to take care of business and rules and regulations seem to get in the way. That is not to say that we don't follow the rules, but we despise the fact that we have to create rules, document them, and enforce them—especially the ones that seem superfluous. In addition, we would rather be out there greeting our guests and working alongside our employees instead of writing a bunch of stuff no one will read. But deep down we know that it will be read, most likely when we are being sued or when our job is at stake. So, take some time and get this part done right. It will make it easier for you in the end.

HIERARCHY OF RULES

Let's come to an agreement on some basics first. I know that you likely know this stuff, but it confuses the average person or officer. These seem to be in order of their severity, but they are actually in order of how many they affect. This will be important later.

Crimes—Crimes are acts or omissions of laws forbidding or commanding them in which there is a penalty. Crimes include homicide, theft, disturbing the peace, etc. There are federal, state, local, and other crimes. Each of these jurisdictions may have laws that are more restrictive than the ones "above" them. Most municipalities enforce misdemeanors, and felonies belong to the state. There are many variations here; this is not a law class and it is just for illustration. Everyone has to abide by these laws.

Codes/Ordinances/Regulations—These are also rules (or crimes in some instances) that are applied to certain groups or businesses. Fire, health, and business codes are examples of these. They are generally enforced by a government body and apply only to businesses or certain types of buildings.

Industry Standards—These are not laws, but generally rules imposed by an industry on itself. They only apply to the industry and the penalty may be no greater than exclusion from the industry. A good example of this is motion picture ratings. Movie theaters impose age restrictions on movies as a condition of belonging to their association. It is not necessarily a crime for a juvenile to see an "R"-rated movie.

Now we are starting to get into the thick of rules where lines are often blurred.

Best Practices—These are not rules or regulations at all, but techniques or methods that have proved to best achieve the desired result. A best practice may come about in our industry from a trial where it was proved that a certain practice was the "best" way to do a certain thing. A good example of a best practice is the manual that we are going to create in this chapter. Nobody says you have to have one, you will not be arrested if you do not have one, and there is no fine to pay if you don't have a manual. It has simply been proved over thousands of court cases that a documented manual of policies is a good defense in court as well as a valuable training tool. I put this category here because these practices likely dictate—or should dictate—how your company and department operate.

The next three rungs of the hierarchy ladder are the company manual, the department manual, and the training and emergency manuals. These and the incident action plan are discussed next.

TYPES OF MANUALS

Four types of manuals apply to Security. The company manual, or corporate manual, contains the policies for the entire organization. The security manual is the comprehensive set of rules for the Security Department. The training manual is the guide used to train employees within the Security Department. The emergency manual applies to the entire organization, but is specific to emergency preparedness and business continuity.

Company Manual

The company manual is a set of rules for the entire company. This may be a corporate manual that applies to all properties in a chain or it may be a property manual that applies to all departments at that property. There also may be both: a corporate and a company manual. Of course, this manual sets the rules for every department to follow, and generally only those rules that apply to all departments. This document is usually created and maintained by Human Resources, company counsel, or a specific regulatory department.

In most organizations, the company manual is used as the guideline or framework for the department manual. Where the company policy might dictate general policies, the department manual will expand those policies into specific procedures. For example, most hotel companies have a general appearance and grooming policy. This policy may require business attire, neatly groomed hair, and a presentable appearance. Then each department will expand on that to address uniform standards, hair length, beards, moustaches, piercings, nails, etc.

The company manual, which was already written by someone else, will make a good outline for the security manual. Keep this in mind when the security manual outline is discussed later in this chapter.

Another company manual is the regulatory manual. In the casino industry, there are minimum internal controls that set guidelines for all aspects of gaming. The cruise line industry follows several similar documents relating to maritime and Homeland Security regulations. Then there are rules and contracts for unions, trade groups, conventions, health and fire codes, and many other rules and policies that may have an effect on hotel policies. These documents, like the company manual will provide a framework for many of the procedures for the Security Department.

Creating these company or regulatory manuals will not be discussed in this book because the Security Director is not likely to have to create one. However, as mentioned previously, these manuals provide the guidance for the production of the Security Manual.

Security Manual

The security manual is the book to which this chapter is devoted. It is simply the rules and policies for the entire Security Department. Some departments will separate it into two manuals: a policy manual and a procedures manual. Others may separate it into a policy manual and a training manual. The procedures and training manual are very similar and are introduced in the next section. For this section, however, the policies and procedures will be combined into one manual.

The need for a current and complete security manual is based on consistency. As explained in Chapter 1, the manual is an asset for defending the hotel in court. This value will only come when the manual is followed consistently. To ensure this consistency and strength of the manual, it is produced in three steps. First, the policy or procedure is decided and then sanctioned by management and counsel. Then it is organized and documented in the manual. Finally, the employees need to be educated on its contents and apply the rules in their relevant daily tasks.

Creating the manual is discussed in detail later in this chapter.

Training Manual

The training manual is a necessary tool often overlooked in Security Departments. Its purpose is not to dictate policy, but to detail the procedures of each task that follows a policy. The training manual follows the outline of the security manual, but details the steps of each policy. For example, a security manual might explain the policy of reporting employee accidents. The training manual would give the security officer step-by-step instructions for completing the paperwork, gathering evidence, and conducting the investigation.

CREATING THE OUTLINE

The best way to write any book, including a security manual, is to start with an outline. (Remember those term papers? Me neither). It is really not so difficult and you can use the example in this book to get you started. We will go through it systematically in order. You may add, delete, or modify certain parts of the example to meet the specific needs of your department. There is an outline at the end of this section for your reference.

Foreword

This first section of the manual, before section one, is not about policies or procedures, but is more of a warm-up to what the department and manual are all about. Naturally, it will start with an introduction. This is a brief summary of what the manual is about, how it is to be used and updated, and who the intended audience is.

Next might be the mission statement of the department. The mission statement was discussed in Chapter 2. Here it is placed in its official form as the guide to the department's policies and procedures.

Finally, I suggest a welcome to new employees. This should be in the form of a personal letter from you to them.

> This security team came together 10 years ago for the purpose of protecting the assets of the hotel. We hope you enjoy working here as much as the rest of us and if you should ever need anything, please do not hesitate to ask me or any member of the management team.

Or something like that.

Department Policies—Section 1

The first section of the policy manual is appropriately devoted to the most important policies of the department. These policies are critical enough that each employee signs them as part of his or her on-boarding process. These policies, probably already written, include your Guest Service Policy (hopefully this is your most important), your Confidentiality Policy, and others such as Sexual Harassment Policy.

Organization—Section 2

The next section outlines the organizational aspects of the department. You may want to include an overview of how the department is set up as it relates to reporting, accountability, and responsibility. The chain of command will be an organizational chart: department head at the top, and the succession down to the frontline officer. Be sure to include other branches, such as an administrative assistant, investigators, trainers, etc. Finally, each position or job will need a description. (Your Human Resources Department may have already written this).

Employee Policies—Section 3

This section includes every rule, procedure, and guideline relating to the conduct of your employees. This is where each employee learns what is expected of him or her. In the example, we start with new hire procedures—how new hires are selected, the interview and vetting process, and the training required in your department. This section will not include every training syllabus, but will include the requirements for each skill level (so many hours of classroom on these topics, so many hours of field training covering those topics, and so forth).

Appearance includes the obvious policies regarding dress code, uniforms, and hygiene. These policies become subjective and difficult to enforce when they are not in writing and easily referenced by supervision and officers.

Conduct is all of those rules that have been passed on verbally and in writing by email, meeting, and memo, and are flying around all over the place. These are technical policies like accepting gratuities, how to behave in court, and dealing with guests.

Discipline is probably already a company policy, but very necessary to include in this document. A good policy manual will be the first place a supervisor will look to find out how to discipline an employee.

Termination is coincidentally after discipline in our outline. This section may include the final step of discipline, but also the procedural aspects of how to give notice, where to obtain the final check, and clearing out desks, files, and computer logins.

Scheduling is the final section in this chapter. Included are rules on attendance, call-offs, which holidays are paid, how payroll corrections are handles, breaks, and light duty. Any rules associated with an employee's schedule or paycheck should be included here.

Posts/Patrol Areas—Section 4

As we will learn in Chapter 8, posts are any place you have an officer assigned, whether it is a fixed post or a patrol area. This section will list each post with a description and the post orders for each. This may be the longest part of your manual, as it will include posts that are not covered all of the time.

Systems/Procedures—Section 5

These are the "operations manuals" for each system used in your department: reporting systems, CCTV, and everything else technical. You also will describe and explain how to perform various procedures in detail, such as lost and found and locker assignments.

Laws Pertaining to Security—Section 6

Arrests

Types of crimes (misdemeanor versus felony)—The textbook definition of the different elements of the two (or three) crime types and the differences in when to arrest.

Searches—The Fourth Amendment, case law, state law, and company policies on when to search, how to search, and the associated liability and safety issues.

Holding room—How it is used, when it is used, conduct therein, procedures for use, etc.

Use of force—How officers advance in the force continuum, when force is justified, how it is applied, and the consequences for doing it incorrectly. This is the most important part of the manual.

This section includes a list of the common laws associated with hotel security, such as trespassing, burglary, theft, robbery, theft of motor vehicle, etc.

Officers need to know and understand relevant laws before they can make arrests.

Laws Pertaining to Guests and Employees—Section 7

Other laws, such as smoking ordinances and Americans with Disabilities Act (ADA) that officers may need to enforce, are listed here.

Emergency Procedures—Section 8

These procedures are not for all employees to follow. Officers will follow these procedures if there is an emergency. Housekeepers may be told to evacuate, but our procedure might be to check guest rooms.

Each type of emergency (fire, accidents, illnesses, active shooters, earthquakes, etc.) is listed with the appropriate departmental response.

Incident Response—Section 9

The procedures for how security officers handle all nonemergency incidents on the property are outlined here. These may include intoxicated persons, panhandlers, sleepers, water leaks, property damage, etc.

Everything from first response to investigation and report should be outlined.

Documentation—Section 10

Documentation is what Security is all about and here is where it is all explained. Procedures for writing incident reports, daily logs, and other reports are included.

Also, list your rules for records retention, the revisions of the security manual, etc.

Following is a sample outline for a security manual.

Manual Outline
Foreword
Introduction
Mission Statement
Welcome New Employees
(Other Items)

1. Department Policies
   1.1 Customer Service (Read and Sign)
   1.2 Confidentiality (Read and Sign)
   1.3 Other Important Policies
2. Organization
   2.1 Overview
   2.2 Chain of Command
   2.3 Job Descriptions
      2.3.1 Director
      2.3.2 Investigator
      2.3.3 Shift Manager
      2.3.4 Assistant Shift Manager
      2.3.5 FTO
      2.3.6 Officer
      2.3.7 Etc.
3. Employee Policies
   3.1 New Hire Procedures
      3.1.1 Interview
      3.1.2 Testing
      3.1.3 Training
      3.1.4 Etc.
   3.2 Appearance
      3.2.1 Dress Code
      3.2.2 Uniforms
      3.2.3 Hygiene
      3.2.4 Etc.
   3.3 Conduct
      3.3.1 Guest Service
      3.3.2 Off-Duty
      3.3.3 Confidentiality
      3.3.4 Gratuities
      3.3.5 Court Demeanor
      3.3.6 Liability Admission
      3.3.7 Removal of Property
      3.3.8 Etc.
   3.4 Discipline
      3.4.1 Progressive
      3.4.2 Coaching/Training
      3.4.3 Work History
   3.5 Termination
      3.5.1 Resignation Procedures
      3.5.2 Clearance
   3.6 Scheduling
      3.6.1 Attendance
      3.6.2 Call-Offs

3.6.3   Holidays
3.6.4   Special Events
3.6.5   Payroll
3.6.6   Overtime
3.6.7   Breaks
3.6.8   Light Duty
4. Patrol Areas
  4.1   Hotel
        4.1.1   Post Orders
        4.1.2   Key Assists
        4.1.3   Noise Complaints
        4.1.4   Etc.
  4.2   Restaurants
        4.2.1   Post Orders
        4.2.2   Steakhouse
        4.2.3   Coffee Shop
  4.3   Retail Stores
        4.3.1   Post Orders
        4.3.2   Kiosks
        4.3.3   Jewelry Store
        4.3.4   Lobby Store
  4.4   Basement
        4.4.1   Post Orders
        4.4.2   Storage Areas
        4.4.3   Locker Rooms
        4.4.4   Restrooms
        4.4.5   Exits
  4.5   Valet
        4.5.1   Post Orders
        4.5.2   Concourse
        4.5.3   Valet Office
  4.6   Lobby
        4.6.1   Post Orders
        4.6.2   Front Desk
        4.6.3   Bell Desk
  4.7   Other Posts
  4.8   Etc.
5. Systems/Procedures
  5.1   CCTV
  5.2   Lost and Found
  5.3   Lockers
  5.4   Radio
  5.5   Etc.
6. Laws Pertaining to Security
  6.1   Arrest

10.4   Records Retention
    10.4.1   Archiving
    10.4.2   Storage Locations
    10.4.3   Duration
10.5   Manual
    10.5.1   Updates

This is a somewhat generic outline. If you have a pool or a nightclub, you can add them. If you run a bed-and-breakfast, or an amusement park, or some other destination, keep the same format, but customize it to fit your property.

WRITING THE MANUAL

Now that we have an outline, all we have to do is fill it in to create some content.

3.3.5 COURT DEMEANOR

Security Officers will often be called to give testimony in court regarding situations that occurred during the course of their employment. Officers also may be summoned to meet with legal counsel for the company and to provide information.

- Officers shall arrive to court or legal offices on time and in appropriate business attire.
- Officers shall provide information, answer all questions truthfully, and cooperate fully with authorities.
- Officers will provide any evidence or documents requested by our counsel or government agency. Altering of evidence or changing of testimony is grounds for termination in addition to any criminal charges.
- Officers will not disparage the company, its management, or employees.
- Upon completion of the court appearance, the officer shall provide a written summary of the appearance and outcome.

The above textbox has an example of a completed "page" of the manual. Take each subheading in the outline and make it a title of that page. The first paragraph is a summary explanation of the procedures: why the policy exists, what it protects, its background, etc. Then each subsequent paragraph or "bullet point" is one procedure or rule for that heading.

In the example, Court Demeanor is the subheading and begins a new page in the manual. Note the numbering system used allows you to add and remove procedures without changing every consecutive number. After the heading, a short paragraph explains why court demeanor is important to the department, when it would apply, and so forth.

After the opening paragraph, each rule is listed separately with one or two brief sentences until all procedures for Court Demeanor are covered. Note that the format is important in that it follows the outline and is consistent across all sections.

Other Sources

Without a doubt, you do not have time to write a few hundred manual pages as described previously. Nobody expects you to do that because you are a director. So let's get some help, and we will direct them. Start by looking at your outline and see what information has already been written for you.

The Human Resources Department probably already has policies such as Sexual Harassment and Confidentiality in written form. See if you can get the electronic version so that you can format it the same as your manual.

If there is a company manual or corporate manual, these documents may also contain some of the generic policies you want.

You have saved all of those policy memos for a reason. Now is the time to pull them out and convert them to policy. I hope that it is just a matter of changing the format.

If you have another department that is on the ball, it may also have these policies written for their folks and would be happy to share them with you. This lends consistency to all departments if everyone is using similar policies.

Finally, many of these generic policies are available on the Internet. As you gather written pages, cross them off your outline to show your progress.

Delegation

The next step is to delegate some of the writing. Your supervisors and managers can do much of it. If they shy away, it is because they are lazy or lack confidence, not because they are incompetent. This is barely different from writing incident reports, which they should be very good at if they are in positions of leadership. You may even have some above-average officers that are up to this task.

Start with your outline and go through it, assigning sections to your list of delegates. Give each of them five sections or pages to write. They can choose the ones they want, or you can assign them based on where you think their interests or experiences fall. As you assign them, make sure they have the format and a deadline.

You can email them a sample, such as the one we wrote previously on "Court Demeanor" and allow them to cut and paste their paragraphs into your format. If their format does not match yours perfectly, accept it, congratulate them for a job well done, and then modify it to make it consistent with yours.

Make sure you give them a deadline. The deadline should be reasonable because they do have other things to do, and you do not expect them to do all of it at home. Perhaps two or three workdays per section are adequate for most. Most will not object to the idea of writing policy, but are more likely to freak out about writing anything. This is a work assignment and it is in their job description. If they cannot compose a few sentences for you, it is time to rethink some things.

You also may find some people in other departments willing to write policy for you. Those who enjoy writing—and there are a few of us—will do it with a smile.

Compiling

As you start to receive everyone's homework assignment, it is time to get organized. You can print the pages and start sorting them by section using the outline as your Table of Contents. You also can do this in your word processor by naming each section as its own file using the numbers as the naming convention. This way, they will be in order in your computer and missing entries will be easy to spot.

Once the manual is complete, you can print it out and compile it into a three-ring binder. If you want to save paper and you have the resources, save it to a PDF or some other form that cannot be edited. You do not want anyone making unauthorized changes. Make sure you have several backups on different servers and media.

Updates

The manual can, and should, change often. The property changes, management style changes, and local laws and procedures change. Try to avoid stuffing memos into a book and expecting anyone to understand your intent or take it seriously. In a hard copy, remove the outdated page and replace it with a new one that has the revision date on it.

Save the old policies, even if they were a mistake or irrelevant now. If you have to defend a policy that was in place when an incident occurred, you need to have it available. I suggest filing these old polices in a binder in their same order and note the effective date and the replacement date.

Your manual will accompany you to your first deposition. Your integrity increases when you are prepared. An organized, complete, and current manual shows everyone how confident you are.

EMERGENCY MANUAL

Emergency procedures and response are covered in Chapter 10, so we will not argue procedures here, but will discuss how to write them. The emergency procedures manual is actually a controversial issue in most Security Departments. Most directors can find many more reasons not to have one.

First, we do not want to take the time to write one. Second, writing one will probably make us aware how unprepared we really are for most emergencies. Third, and most compelling, is, "Why should we create a book that will sit on a shelf and become outdated?" We will not have the time or the presence of mind to refer to it during an earthquake or fire anyway. Sound familiar? This is explained in Chapter 10, so either read that now, or take my word for it and let's write this manual.

Make sure we are clear that the emergency procedures manual is for the response to emergencies and does not include business continuity, continuity of operations, or any of the stuff that happens *after* the emergency is over. This manual will cover procedures that save lives and property.

Hazards and Threats

Before we can write procedures, we need to know what our potential emergencies are. Yes, we did some of this in Chapter 1 for the Risk Assessment. Not every emergency was listed there, but those are a good start. Add to that list any other hazard or threat to life or property that can happen at your facility. I like to separate them into "Natural" (Hazards), "Fabricated" (Threats), and Technical.

Natural emergencies are weather-related events like hurricanes, tornadoes, floods, and blizzards. Earthquakes, lightning strikes, and "Acts of Nature" are also included. If you live in the mountains, you can probably exclude hurricanes, and so forth.

Fabricated threats make up most of our emergencies. Fire, active shooter, bomb threat, explosion, gas leak, bioterrorism, robbery, medical emergency, drowning, and vehicle crashes are some of the incidents you might include on this list.

Technical emergencies are not always emergencies and do not always involve security, but there are some for this list. Power failure, server failure, electrocution, elevator and escalator mishaps, and other machine malfunctions may be emergencies that require a security response.

Starting the Emergency Manual

This manual can follow a similar format as the security manual, but it needs to be simple, easy to read, and succinct. We are not going to add a lot of narrative and extra stuff. This is our nuts-and-bolts manual used in emergencies, so stick to the necessary facts. The simplest layout for this manual is to make each chapter a different emergency procedure. Having already determined what those emergencies are, create your outline by listing those events: fire, earthquake, power failure, active shooter, etc.

Some emergency response measures are common to many different emergencies. Evacuation is one that is used for a majority of incidents. Evacuation procedures will be their own section in our manual.

Under each heading (each emergency event) list the steps to be taken and by whom. You may find it easier to list responsibilities by department or position. Security Officers do A, B, and C. Engineers do X, Y, and Z. Bell persons do 1, 2, and 3. Once you have worked this out, your manual is essentially finished.

Testing the Manual

You are not finished! The biggest mistake planners make is printing up a well-written manual and placing it on a shelf in their office. Some go an extra step, and send one to every department and feel satisfied. You have heard the problems with this many times. First, you are not going to remember what the manual says a year later when an earthquake hits. Second, nobody you send it to will ever read it. Third, departments change, management changes, and the building changes so the manual has to live and breathe.

Most importantly, the testing and updating of the manual are necessary. See Chapter 10 for emergency planning processes. This is how the content of the manual is tested and upgraded. Your manual, if used in this manner, will never sit on the shelf and collect dust. Everyone will already know what is in it.

INCIDENT ACTION PLAN

An incident action plan (IAP) is used for special events or unusual security functions. (Some of these are discussed in Chapter 2.) A progressive security department will create an IAP for every one of these events so that there are no questions or uncertainties as to how the event is handled, how contingencies are mitigated, and what everyone's responsibilities are. A sample template of an IAP for a hotel is included at the end of this section and is explained by line next.

Incident Overview

This is the name of the incident and a brief summary of what it is, who is sponsoring it, and its purpose, for example, "New Year's Eve fireworks and party for hotel guests sponsored by the Marketing Department." Included here are estimated attendance numbers, staff numbers, and other departments involved.

Location

The location of the event, including all convention rooms, lobby, offices, etc.

Date/Time

Date or date range of the event including start and ending times.

Workforce—Management

List each rank beginning with the Incident Commander, their title, and name of person assigned.

Workforce—Posts

List each post, its location, primary duty, and person assigned. Note that we avoid the shotgun approach of putting 10 officers on the perimeter. Each officer needs a post and post duties, even if they overlap. Posts might include dispatcher, door host, perimeter bike rover, etc.

Special Assignments

This includes outside companies like ambulance services, police, and other contractors. Also, include your own people that have special assignments like undercover, investigators, etc.

Special Procedures

List only those procedures that are not normal for your property. In other words, do not list fire evacuations, as those procedures do not change. But you may include riot, crowd control, missing children, special money drops, or whatever is relevant to this type of event.

Other Department Procedures

List those responsibilities of other departments relative to this event. Perhaps Engineering has a Fire Watch on the roof for a fireworks show, Marketing is responsible for posting certain security signs, and Housekeeping cleans up empty glass containers for safety reasons.

Miscellaneous

You can customize this template however you want and add to it those sections that meet your company's needs.

Use the IAP so that everyone, including your supervisors, dispatchers, other departments, and even police and fire departments know how to manage the incident and what you will be doing for contingencies. Another advantage of using this form is to save it and when you repeat this event, you will have a record of your staffing and procedures. That will help you budget and plan for it next time.

Incident Action Plan
Incident Overview
Location
Date/Time
Workforce
    Management
    Shift manager (IC)
    Assistants
    Additional managers
Posts (Assignments)
    (Dispatch)
    Post 1
    Post 2
Post Duties
    Dispatch
    Post 1
    Post 2
Special Assignments
    (Investigators, etc.)
    Special Procedures
    Riot
    Code Adam

Other Department Procedures
    Engineering
    Marketing
    Internal Maintenance

5

Staffing

It is the still, small voice that the soul heeds, not the deafening blasts of doom.

William Dean Howells, author

People are the core of the hospitality business. I have found that hiring security officers is hard enough, but it is even more difficult when you consider that we need a candidate who is physically and mentally capable of dealing with problems. Compound that with our requirement for the officers to be pleasant and welcoming to our guests. This is quite a task and as Mr. Howells alludes to above, one person can have a huge impact on the business.

HIRING

Some may consider the hiring process the most important component of building a good security staff. There are several steps of the hiring process and if any one of them is weak, you are going to end up with the costly mistake of hiring the wrong person.

Recruitment

Most employers mistakenly post some minimum qualifications and hope they find qualified candidates out of a sea of applications that do not meet these qualifications. When you consider how much time you spend on this process, it really seems backward. You already have the profile of the perfect candidate in your head, so post those qualifications, and require applicants to disqualify themselves based on this list or certain application questions.

Before you start looking for a new recruit, establish a perfect candidate profile and the qualifications and experience needed. If you want military or law enforcement experience or a certain educational level, post it. If you are not going to consider certain criminal history, post it. Of course, check with your HR department to make sure you are legal.

Many security departments seek prior security or law enforcement experience. Ask yourself if these are your best candidates. We usually like this experience because they

73

may need less training or acclimation to our type of organization. Usually there is a tradeoff of skills for attitude. I would argue that a corrections officer, an army sergeant, or even a homicide detective is not necessarily suited for the hospitality environment. They may be better at handcuffing or dealing with violent suspects, but do not lend themselves to the customer service environment in a private business. I have found that it is easier to train a former restaurant host how to handcuff and deal with hostile persons than it is to teach a drill sergeant how to provide great service to a family in the hotel. Now, this is not to say that I discourage hiring anyone from a paramilitary organization because many of our best security professionals are from these fields. All I ask is that you not use this experience as your primary qualifier or even a prerequisite. You can train skills, but not attitude.

If you have a good team in place already and you want to add more just like them, have your team help with recruitment. A good portion of their friends and colleagues probably shares their attitude, work ethic, and experience. These referrals take some of the unknown out of hiring. It may be worth the cost to offer a finder's fee to your employees for these referrals. Another good source of recruits is employees from other departments. If you see an employee who possesses a great attitude and customer service skills, see if he wants to transfer. Most of the time, they have already considered it, but never imagined you would hire someone without security experience. Actually, they do have hospitality experience and you have already had a chance to watch them in action. This employee is not an unknown and you can easily train him or her technical stuff, but you cannot train attitude.

Application Process

Chances are your HR department has a good application process in place already. They use the same application for every department and it asks questions that maintain the very minimum requirements for employment like minimum age, criminal history, etc. If that is the case, you will have to have someone cull the applications for those that meet your department's slightly higher minimum standards. You can train the HR staff to do this or you may have to do it yourself. Some HR departments use more advanced application software that asks the applicant different questions based on the position. This automates the process for you as a first step in the hiring process.

Someone in your organization needs to have some training on reading applications. Besides the obvious legal limitations, there are several nuances in every application that can be gleaned if you know what you are doing. Reading between the lines is the best way to describe how you can disqualify applicants based on the words they use, the questions they answer, and their experience. You do not have time to interview every single applicant and even if you did, you would not learn the things you learn from an application in one tenth of the time. I would not presume to generalize or profile someone based solely on things they write on an application or résumé. When someone says he left his last job because of a "personality conflict," he needs to explain that in the interview. Make notes on the application of questions to ask.

Interview

Once again, whoever does the interview should be trained in interviewing skills. There are certainly legal dos and don'ts to adhere to, but many things can be learned from a 30-minute chat.

Start with start time. If you want your employees to be on time for work, then don't expect anything less for an interview. Someone who really wants the job and has prepared will do so by arriving early enough to find your office. The prepared ones will scout it out well in advance and do some "recon" of their own. This is another topic of conversation for an interview.

Before the interview, we can already start to evaluate our prospective employee. I like to have my candidates meet me at a different location on the property, such as the bell desk. I may watch them on camera, checking their body language, their interactions with others, and their demeanor. How enlightening it is to see someone paste on their smile and handshake when they see you coming, but were unenthusiastic and grumpy-looking up until then. You can also arrange with a trusted employee, such as a bell-person, to engage the candidate in conversation or test them in some other way before you arrive. A simple thumbs up or down when you arrive might save you some time or give you some more conversation topics. Remember that a candidate is on stage and giving his or her best performance during the interview. Attitude and answers are not always genuine, so any intelligence you can derive beforehand is valuable. In fact, in my personal experience, I have found that some candidates who are pleasant and courteous in an interview will treat the HR or other administrative personnel very poorly. This is a better indicator of future attitude with guests and employees. If your HR people tell you that an applicant was rude to them, cut your losses.

Traditionally, we expected an applicant to wear a suit to an interview. That may not be practical for a frontline employee, but that does not mean she wears jeans or a mini-skirt and sandals. Expect them to dress appropriate for the position: shirt tucked in, belt, well-kept shoes, and hair combed, clean, and presentable. From my experience, if they wear their pants sagging in the interview, they will wear their uniform in the same way.

You may learn much more from this preinterview than you will from hearing their prepared answers in the interview. How did they find their way? Did they introduce themselves to other people in the office? Did they make eye contact or look at the floor? There is so much information here.

One more thing before we start talking. If your security job involves report writing, have them write a paragraph for you. Look at penmanship, spelling, grammar, and sentence and paragraph structure. These are things you are not prepared to teach and will not have time to do so. If someone cannot form and write a paragraph, maybe you can recommend them for another position in the company that requires less writing. Writing is too important in our department. If everything you do is paperless, have them create a document on a computer.

> Please open Word and write about 25 words on why you want to be a security officer, or how you traveled here today, or about your last vacation.

Look for computer skills. You don't have time to teach officers how to use a mouse and keyboard.

You should prepare your interview questions in advance. Some will be standard, but others may be unique questions that probe the application.

Standard Questions
The objective of the interview is to learn about your candidate's history and character. This is not to say we care about their history or their personal life, but those things may be an indicator of job performance. Keep this objective in mind as you write your questions. Your HR team may be able to help you with this as they have had experience and can keep you from violating laws and policies with the wrong questions. Security may be a little different from cooks and housekeepers in that we are looking for people who can multitask, are quick thinkers, leaders (and followers), and so forth.

Situational questions may be the best way to learn how a candidate thinks and makes decisions. "What would you do if . . ." is a great way to develop an idea of their decision-making process. The answer to the question may be less important than how they come up with the answer. See if they consider options, consult supervisors, place the guest and the company before everything else, and are flexible. Make sure they know how to find answers they do not know and can admit when they do not know the answer.

Make sure you cover the obvious questions like can they work varying schedules and holidays, get to work on time, wear a uniform, walk and stand, lift 20 pounds, pass a drug and background check, etc. Remember that standard questions must be given consistently to everyone to avoid the appearance of discrimination.

Specific Questions
The questions that came up when reading the application need to be asked here. Common inquiries include reasons for leaving a prior job, what did you do between jobs, how was that job similar to what you will do at our hotel, etc.

Aptitude and attitude are the things to look for in an interview. Your successful candidate must have the aptitude to learn your skills, culture, and mission. He or she must also have the attitude you want. If they do not display it in the interview when they are at their best, they will not learn it later. One cannot learn attitude. They have either a positive attitude or a negative attitude.

Second interview

A second interview is a good idea if you can do it. Use one of your supervisors, investigators, or even someone from another department. Use a different format for this interview. Make it more casual, less of a questioning, and more of a discussion. If done right, this will put the candidate at a comfortable level to speak freely. "You survived the interview with the big boss, let's have a Coke and talk. How do you like our department so far? What would you change? What position would you aspire to?" This type of questioning puts you on the same side and extracts attitude and feelings the formal interview will not bring out. If you do not like the candidate from the first interview, do not bother with the second interview.

Group Interview

The group interview is difficult to manage if only one department does it. If your HR department is interested in doing this, please participate, as you will get candidates with a great attitude and team spirit.

BACKGROUND

Several years ago, the FBI decided that the integrity of their agents was of the utmost importance. They continue to this day to spend tens of thousands of dollars to check the background of each employee. Their unwritten slogan regarding recruitment is: "Don't hire a problem." While every group of people will have a few bad apples, this policy seems to have worked for the FBI. They maintain an image to this day of clean, responsible, honest agents.

Does it make good business sense to spend an amount equal to an employee's annual salary on their background? Probably not for a security officer. But in this age of having information at our fingertips, it is negligent of us not to make some simple inquiries. Criminal history is a given, but what about job stability, violent history, drug use, and personal character?

If you do a background check (if you do not, then start today), this is the time to do it. Some of the nicest guys you will ever meet in an interview can turn out to be bank robbers, physical abusers, embezzlers, or alcoholics.

We have all seen guard companies that do a criminal check and a drug test and let the insurance cover the rest. That just does not work in the hospitality industry. We cannot afford to expose our guests and their property to an unknown personality. Look at the last five employees you fired for stealing. On how many of those did you file criminal charges? How many of those were convicted? Answer: Less than five. How many of your applicants may have stolen from their last five jobs? Answer: You have no idea because they are rarely a criminal case. If you do not check elsewhere, the criminal history check will not do it.

We have to look at the business picture here. A common business reaction to an employee stealing is fire the employee and reimburse the guest or try to recover the loss. What does this do to the reputation of the hotel? That guest might admire you for making it right, but deep down he or she is wondering what kind of people you hire and how many are bad that you don't catch. The background for a security officer just became important to every employee on your property and to the reputation of your hotel. Some background checkers will do job history and references and some will not. If yours does not, you should do this yourself.

Everyone is afraid to check prior employers because nobody wants to give out job information for fear of being sued. There are two things to do to deal with this. One is to check them anyway. Even if the former employer just gives dates of employment is a big verifier. Someone who was trying to hide a job where they were fired, or a period where they were in jail, would fudge on their employment dates. A simple check of prior employers would create a nice timeline. Second thing to do with prior employers is call them personally. Do not just call HR; call their former boss. During the interview, you may have

77

asked the candidate: "What would your former boss say if I asked him about you?" You should actually ask the former boss if he or she would hire the person again. This does not violate any policies and it is off the record. This will take away all doubt, or add to it. Never disclose to the candidate what you found in the background check.

I think many employers are also afraid to call references because they fear the candidate has primed them. This may be true, but you can still learn a great deal from a couple of phone calls. First, do not ask them the obvious questions. Ask them about a previous job on the application or about a gap between jobs. If they have known the applicant as long as they claim, they will know what he was doing for those four months between jobs. If they say he was in school and the candidate says he was overseas with the Peace Corps, you have a problem.

Many privacy and credit reporting laws, most of them federal, put severe restrictions on what you can find out in a background check. Be sure you use a licensed company or that you are following these regulations and using proper waiver of privacy forms. More information on background checks is in Chapter 11.

DRUG TESTING

I know of few companies not using drug testing for preemployment screening. The ones that do not are probably thinking that what people do on their own time is their own business. You can resolve this question for yourself by asking your decisionmakers these questions: If they break drug laws, will they break any others? If they use drugs at home while they are taking care of their family, why wouldn't they take them at work? If their decision process between right and wrong did not pass the simple "Just Say No," then how will it work for other important decisions? Will drug use at home affect their attendance, performance, and even medical insurance costs?

Speak to a Workers' Comp physician or other companies in your area about the type of testing and testing facility. Many use blood and urine tests, but fail to realize that many drugs only stay in the system approximately four hours. Most applicants can hold their habit for a few hours to get a job. Another method is hair testing. Chemicals stay in the hair for days, weeks, and months. It will not show today's drug use so it is not good for postaccident testing, but it is great for showing a history. Be sure to ask the testing facility about prescription drug abuse. This problem is on the rise and is easy to explain, such as having chronic back pain.

BEFORE HIRING

One final thing before making the offer, or even if you have already made the job offer. If you find out they lied on the application or during any part of the interview process, fire them immediately. Nobody lies just once and if the person lied during this process, it was to keep you from uncovering something that would disqualify him or her. Integrity is the most important nontrainable skill your officers will have.

ORIENTATION

News flash: New hires do not remember anything you tell them or show them on the first day except where to pick up their paycheck. Keep this in mind as you devise your hiring process. It is probably better to receive information from them than it is to ask them to start absorbing your information. So, have them fill out payroll forms and get fitted for uniforms and such rather than ask them to study a manual or memorize sexual harassment policies.

Put yourself in your new recruit's place. She needs to go home, celebrate with family, buy some new uniform shoes, and dream of being your boss. Have her start work the next day or in a couple of days. This way her head will be clear when she starts and you will have her full attention.

The training process is discussed in Chapter 6. Whether or not you provide classroom training, it is unlikely that every new recruit will start his or her new job in a classroom. They are more likely to go directly into field training with another officer. This is a good day to do orientation. Review new policies, go over the geography of the property, tell them where to take breaks, and where to find the equipment and supplies needed for the job.

DEPLOYMENT

I hope that you or your predecessor has not used the "shotgun" deployment method. This method, more common than you think, consists of someone, somewhere who decided your hotel needs "X" number of officers. Then the officers were sent out and told to evenly cover the property. This force tends to become lazy, ineffective, and reactionary.

This is why we developed the Security Plan in Chapter 2. There, we calculated the amount of officers needed based on posts and patrol areas. Most of the work is done; we just need to contend with some variables—volume, shifts, and other duties. I suggest that even if you have staff and a schedule, you do this exercise. You may find some areas to make your staff more efficient or cost-effective.

Start with your minimum staff by listing your posts (fixed and roving)—hotel patrol, outside patrol, common area patrol, other areas, dispatcher, lobby key check, nightclub, etc. Do this for every block of time in a 24-hour period and for each day of the week. You do not need to do it hourly unless your posts change every hour. It might be 4-hour blocks or 8-hour blocks. We do the blocks because some posts are not staffed all hours, such as the nightclub. You may also want to add roving officers based on guest volume. More people up and around might require more security during those hours.

Next, add to this number a breaker for every 4, 6, or 8 posts depending on your total break time. (Six officers who get 30 minutes of break time in your 4-hour block will get about one breaker officer.) Also, decide if you want to add any extra staff for report writing, emergencies, administrative duties, covering call-offs, and so on.

Now that you have this spreadsheet, create 8-hour shifts (or 6- or 10-hour shifts if you prefer). Do not hesitate to use staggered start times if that is how your shifts work out. You should end up with variable staffing levels that change with need and volume rather than the shotgun. You may have even justified that dreaded 10-hour workday that you have been trying to pull off.

In the next section, we will work on days off.

SCHEDULES

There are several ways to work out a schedule. I will show you an easy way to do it. Suppose you need six officers on the weekdays and eight on the weekends. Each officer works a 40-hour workweek with consecutive days off. We will work on just one shift to make it easy. You can change these numbers depending on how many you need on each day.

In Figure 5.1, I used a piece of graph paper (or scratch paper with a table drawn like this one) and created a draft schedule. Days of the week go across the top and the rows are left blank, but indicate the name of each employee being scheduled. I made nine rows. Make several more if you are not sure how many positions you will need. I then start creating position schedules. Since everyone has consecutive days off, I start on Monday marking an "X" for each day off. Line 1 is off Monday and Tuesday, line 2 is off Tuesday and Wednesday, and so on. When I got to Saturday on line 6, I knew I probably would not have two officers off on Saturday, so I skipped and gave that line Sunday and Monday off. At that point, I did a quick count of each day (counting blank boxes in each column) to see what my officer count was for each day.

That quick count told me I was running about four each day and five on the weekends. Since my goal was six and eight, I was on the right track and just needed to add a few more positions with the days off evenly dispersed. The next three positions were added with different days off, giving nobody Saturday off. This schedule worked out almost perfect. I have six on weekdays, eight on Saturday, and seven on Sunday. If that is acceptable, great. To fill that spot on Sunday, I could use overtime, part-time, or hire one more position and over-staff on other days. If that works for your budget, I would do it, because there will be sick calls, vacations, and extra days off that will decrease much of that extra payroll.

This simple exercise can be expanded to any number of officers. Those who use the "shotgun" approach mentioned in the last section can do this scheduling method, only

Officer	Mon	Tue	Wed	Thu	Fri	Sat	Sun
1	X	X					
2		X	X				
3			X	X			
4				X	X		
5					X	X	
6	X						X
7	X						X
8		X	X				
9				X	X		

Figure 5.1

backward. Start with the number of officers you have in the left column, and then do the same process, filling in the days off as you go down the line until days off are equally dispersed.

Do your staff a favor and create a schedule that you can stick with and not change every week. I am sure you have a restaurant manager who creates a weekly schedule with split days off, and does not tell his employees until the Friday before the week starts. This is not considerate of employees' lives and does not promote loyalty or positive morale. Inconsistent scheduling with split and different days off will not benefit the company either. You will have more sick calls (to get their consecutive days off), employees who are not properly rested, and in the extreme you may have those who will join unions to get better work conditions.

WAGE STRUCTURE

Wages are the most important thing to your employees and your management. Employees want them to be higher and management wants them as low as they can be to increase profits. Whether you are establishing a new department and a new wage structure or need to modify your existing one, here are several elements of a good wage program.

Survey

Competitive wages are important to morale and vital to recruiting a competent staff. Before starting the survey, you need to determine with whom you will be comparing salaries. Like the Risk Assessment, we have to compare to the local market, the national market, and the industry in general. However, if you live in Houston, Texas, you should not expect to pay as much as in New York City.

A good HR department will do a wage survey for you, but you can probably do it easier yourself. Your colleagues at other properties should be more than willing to participate in a survey, especially if you share the results with them. A survey should be done once per year.

Base Wage

Naturally, you would like to be at the top of the market in pay. This attracts better applicants (well, more applicants) and can promote longevity and morale. The survey will help you appeal to your boss for a competitive wage for your staff. Where you place—and where you want to be placed—in the survey is dependent upon several other factors. These include the amount and frequency of raises, training provided, experience required, specialized positions, benefit package, and the reputation of your organization.

Raises

Most companies provide a cost of living adjustment (COLA) and possibly a probationary increase. I recommend a structure based on experience and training. This recommendation is outlined later in this section. As for determining the base wage, you may want to start a bit below the highest payer, if you have a substantial probationary increase. Or, you might start highest if you have no such type of raise. Another consideration is if you pay more for armed officers, experienced officers, EMTs, etc.

Training

Providing compensated training is rare in our industry. If you provide it, then that is a benefit and should be included as such when you publicize an open position. When you calculate your starting wage, consider this paid training. (Lower starting pay is more attractive if you pay training and other hotels do not.) By the way, I would never recommend providing training without compensating the employee, but some organizations do it and get away with it.

Experience

Many businesses base the starting salary on experience or education. This is a double-edged sword. You may attract better candidates, but as mentioned earlier in the Hiring section, experience is not always a plus. If you do provide this added pay, your base pay should be lower than the competition. This goes the same if you offer pay right off the bat for those specialized positions mentioned previously.

Benefits

Human Resources will tell you that the benefits that the company provides are worth $4 per hour. If you provide these benefits and the other hotels do not, that is plenty of reason to have a lower base pay. If everyone has similar benefits, but you start them at four months and others start them at six months, for example, then you also have an advantage.

Reputation

Finally, the reputation of your department and your hotel may affect at what pay you start your officers. If you have an iconic brand name, or your security department has a reputation for being good to its employees, you can afford to start at a lower pay because your applicants are not drawn to you for money, but seek prestige.

OFFICER DEVELOPMENT PROGRAM (ODP)

I now propose to you the Officer Development Program (ODP). Although not unique, it is certainly an unusual way to organize, motivate, train, reward, and pay your officers. It was developed by officers for officers and I have seen it work quite successfully.

The premise of the ODP is to compensate officers based on their skills and to allow them to give those skills back to their fellow officers through training. This plan has four levels of officer: Officer Trainee, Level I, Level II, and Level III.

An officer starts as a trainee at the entry-level wage. (For the sake of this example, let us say $10 per hour). To advance to the next level (Level I), the trainee needs to earn a minimum number of training points. Points earned during the normal course of work are less than those earned off-duty. For example, a mandatory CPR class might be worth 2 points, but a seminar taken at a local college might be worth 15 points. After spending at least six months in the trainee position and earning at least 25 points, the officer advances to Level I. He or she gets a raise of 50 cents.

In Level I, the officer is encouraged to continue taking classes provided by the company, outside opportunities, and classes taught by other officers. Once again, he or she must earn 25 points and spend six months or a year at this level, before advancing to Level II. Another 50-cent raise is earned.

Level II changes slightly, as the officer is encouraged to complete advanced or specialized training, such as bicycle patrol, medical, dispatch, investigations, or training officer. The Level II officer must attain at least one specialty, earn the required points, and spend the minimum time at that level before advancing to Level III. A raise of 50 cents or $1 is earned.

In Level III, the learning cycle is completed as officers start to give back to the department. Officers in Level III now earn two types of points. They still have to earn their minimum training points, but also have to earn instructor points. To do this, they can create their own class or use an existing syllabus provided by someone else. This develops your senior officers into instructors and mentors while creating a training-rich environment that is also economical.

The minimum months of service required to reach the next level, the percentage increase in wages, amount of points to be earned, and the point value for each class, are variable and at your discretion based on your situation. After the first year, and in order to sustain the program, you will have to develop a test for each level. The test will not be necessary for the first year, but at the end of that year, the officers will have to prove proficiency in that level to maintain that level.

Remember that level increases are not promotions, but advances. This may be semantics, but your HR people are more likely to buy into this program if you are not creating layers of supervision. You are better off comparing levels to kitchen workers, who have been using levels for years. Their system is a little different, but the first level workers might be prep cooks, who then advance to line cooks, fry cooks, chefs, and so on. It is important that you do not create supervisors with these levels.

You can add some bells and whistles as well to this system by creating a rank insignia, such as chevrons on the uniform. You also may want to adjust the wage increases to match your local wage survey. I also suggest a pay differential for those specialized positions mentioned previously.

As for the 20 percent of your employees who just want to come to work, do their job, and go home, let them. Some people will just want to stay at Level I. That is fine because you actually need a few of those people who will do the basic work. Soon, they will see the newer officers pass them by, making more money and they will jump on board. You also will have those who will race to the highest level and then go back to stagnation. This makes the test and the annual renewal of points essential.

Ideally, you will end up with staff that are smarter and more motivated to learn and share their knowledge with their co-workers. Morale should improve and sustain itself with the program. The best part of the ODP is your Level IIIs. These senior, more experienced, and better-trained officers now make up the bench strength for your next generation of supervisors and managers. You can even start training them as such and watch them work in that capacity.

Feel free to use all or part of the ODP and customize it for your own use. The cost of the increases is negligible, most of the training is free, and it is more rewarding than your average wage structure or COLA raises that you are using now.

PROPRIETARY VERSUS CONTRACT

Personally, I prefer proprietary security staff—as you can gather from most of this book. I think hiring, training, and managing your own staff outweighs any cost savings you can get from using an outside service. Most of those agencies are quality companies that strive to recruit and retain qualified officers. The ones that do not, do not last long. However, a staff that you develop and manage is more likely to serve guests as if they are in their own home and protect assets as if they are their own.

Having a proprietary staff is entirely dependent on your motivation to hire and train such a staff. If you do not, then contract is the way to go. Many reputable companies actually train officers to work in the hospitality industry. This is a question to ask when interviewing these companies. You do not want the same "guards" used to secure a warehouse serving your guests in a hotel.

If you have at least one staff member that you can devote full time to hiring and training, then you can run your own security officers. Even though there are a few variables and a couple of minor details, this is the easiest way to break it down. Determine how many officers you need, including supervision and breaks. Get your bids from outside companies, making sure to account for costs that they will cover, such as hiring costs, benefits, uniforms, equipment, and liability insurance. Then make your own bid for the same thing—wages, benefits, equipment, etc. Be sure to account for that one extra training position. If it is less for you—or close—then it is probably worth doing it yourself.

There are some exceptions to this equation. First is liability. Find out if a contract security company assumes all liability for its officers as well as any losses incurred. If not, to what extent are you responsible? Some put this right into their contract and the reality is the deepest pocket may be held liable. Check with your attorney on this, especially if you are self-insured. Workers' comp insurance is also a consideration. Second, check with your HR department. They may or may not be willing to provide hiring services for you. They also may not want your staff on their benefit plans. Alternatively, they may welcome having more employees on the rolls because it gets them a discount on group plans. Finally, you may have an owner or manager who is already set on having proprietary or contract. You may be able to prove your case in the opposite direction, but this will be dependent on your research. (See budget proposals in Chapter 3.)

Many hotels and tourist destinations find it necessary to augment their proprietary staff with contract security during special events. I find this to be poor judgment for the same reasons as mentioned previously—and more. As I mentioned several times in this book, do a little Risk Assessment in your mind. Determine the probability of a contract officer doing something that will put you both in a position of liability (false arrest, excessive force, etc.). Then determine the severity of that incident to your company. In other words, if one of those things happens, who will be sued and who will be defending it? Chances are that even if there is a contract in place limiting your liability, your deep pockets will be a target.

To put it another way, will a security officer from an outside source handle even minor situations with the same discretion that an inside officer would? Think about these situations: An intoxicated hotel guest wanders into the wrong party and causes a disturbance; a man walks into an event and starts shooting; 25 women show up at a conservative political rally and start heckling the speakers about abortion; a 16-year-old is caught drinking alcohol provided by her father at a wedding party. These are all difficult scenarios for any security officer, but more so for new or outside officers.

A woman who walked into a drugstore in California to return some items was accused of shoplifting by the store's contract loss prevention agents. (The agent did not witness the alleged crime.) The agent put his hands on the woman's shoulders and forced her into a back room. When she tried to make a call, the cell phone was knocked from her hand. The agent also made sexual advances toward her. The woman sued the store, the contract security company, and the agent. She was awarded $3.45 million.

Though small businesses, including hotels, cannot always have proprietary security, there is some risk involved in using those who have no loyalty or direct oversight from management.

You may find it less expensive, both operationally and legally, to pay overtime to your current staff for special events.

MANAGEMENT

Managers and supervisors are a very important part of your team and are integral to the success and efficiency of your staff. They play several roles and some of them are described here.

Responsibility

Any team or organization needs one person at the top to take responsibility. For the department, it is the director. For a shift or other group—depending on how the team is organized—it is the manager. This responsibility cannot be shared, so if the group is large, there may be supervisors running smaller teams that report to the manager. Several managers can report to a higher manager like an operations manager.

Responsibility provides for accountability, which means that each person has a job to do, ensures that it is done correctly, and is held accountable for it. The manager holds his or her officers accountable for their actions, and is in turn accountable to his or her boss for his or her actions. Accountability includes job supervision, training, coaching, and discipline. It also provides for delegation.

Supervision

The difference between a supervisor and a manager is the level of responsibility. Supervision is also something that both managers and supervisors do. Because managers are responsible for the actions of those persons on their team, they need to oversee all of the work being performed by those persons. Other steps in the supervision process are discussed next, but first, we must observe. Managers tend to be caught up in administrative tasks, such as reports, schedules, and meetings. These are all important duties, but a good manager knows he cannot take responsibility for the performance of others if he does not witness it for himself. Guest interaction, technical duties, patrol techniques, and confrontational skills are a few of the skills that a manager should be observing for all of his team members.

Training and Coaching

Training does not conclude after initial training is complete. Officers (and managers) will be constantly learning as they encounter new situations. It is the manager's job to organize and conduct this training. Some of this education comes in the form of group meetings, such as briefings, pullout training, and scenarios. Other opportunities for developing officers come during and after each incident. As the officer is collecting evidence or witness statements, responding to a domestic disturbance, or after a medical call are all good times to evaluate and coach officers on their performance.

Discipline

Also a form of coaching, discipline should be designed to correct behavior, not to punish for it. Either poor performance can be corrected or it cannot. If it can be corrected, we retrain, coach, and evaluate the new behavior. If it cannot be corrected, then discipline is used as a progression toward termination. This function—discipline—falls upon the manager when accountability fails.

Delegation

Delegation is the process of passing responsibility to the lowest level where it can be satisfactorily handled. Managers often confuse delegation with slavery. "Everyone else can do all of the work while I do other things I want to do." Giving officers new responsibilities develops them professionally, gives them better job satisfaction, and prepares them for more responsibilities. Delegation needs to be done carefully so as not to overwork officers who are already busy and not to exceed their capabilities. For example, if you have an officer who has mastered her other job duties and wants to learn more about the business, it would be prudent to have her start working on break schedules for the other officers. The manager would have to supervise this to make sure it is done fairly and correctly so she does not make new enemies. Managers err when they delegate too much work and do not follow up to make sure it is being done properly.

Managing Managers

As mentioned previously, managers usually get into trouble when they try to delegate too much. The opposite can be said for some managers who feel they have to do everything themselves. Therefore, this is a fine balance between tasks and responsibilities. If the manager delegates too much, he or she is likely overworking the staff and proving that the job may be unnecessary. On the other hand, handling all the calls, doing all the breaks, and writing all the reports is even worse because then the manager cannot supervise, evaluate, and coach as we discussed before.

A manager who is doing a proper job is one who is everywhere at once, knows everything that is going on, and has a competent and well-trained staff. This is simple for a director to observe. Start by observing the activities of the team. Do they handle routine situations without assistance? Is the manager consulted or advised on the resolution of all situations? Is there chaos during an emergency or order? Next comes some questioning. As we will discuss in Chapter 12, the director should work alongside officers and ask them how their manager is doing. Finally, test the manager and hold him or her accountable. Randomly check logs and reports and see if the manager is informed. Observe an emergency, or create a mock emergency scenario, and watch the manager's participation. Managers can make your job easy or difficult, but it is up to you to hold them accountable.

6

Training

Planning is bringing the future into the present so that you can do something about it now.

Alan Lakein, writer

In Chapter 5, we discussed the differences in using proprietary and contract security. Whether you have your own training program or you rely on the program of someone else, you should read this chapter. Either way, you want to have some input and oversight into those who will be protecting your assets.

FUNDING TRAINING

Training is going to be the foundation of your department. It is also the biggest expense in hospitality security and the hardest to sell because it is perceived to offer little or no return on investment. Remember, here in the private sector we have to justify expenses as necessary for the operation of the business or as a revenue generator. Our executives in the C-suite do not necessarily understand training for its own sake, or training, because that is how the other guys do it. Fortunately, there are ways to articulate the need for training, its advantage to the business, and even its return on investment.

Liability

Properly trained security officers actually save money in several ways by reducing and preventing exposure to legal action. For example, at hotel ABC, officers are provided an orientation and issued handcuffs on their first day. At hotel XYZ, officers go through a week of classroom training on laws of arrest, provided eight hours of handcuffing and defensive tactics, and a week of field training with a training officer. The differences are obvious and so are the potential results. If each of these officers gets into similar incidents on his/her second day of work, here are the probable outcomes.

ABC officer responds to a fight in a room. He enters the room with his master key and sees a woman crying in the corner and a man sitting on the edge of the bed. He attempts to take the man into custody. During the altercation, he tears the rotator cuff in the man's shoulder, but is successful in arresting him. Then the woman jumps on the officer and tries to rescue her husband and, in the process, bites the officer's earlobe clean off and scratches his face bad enough to require stitches. The officer fends her off, backup arrives, and the suspect is taken to the security office to await the arrival of the police. After the police arrive, they determine that there actually was no fight, other than arguing, and the arrest was false. The man with the injured shoulder wants to press felony charges for battery, false imprisonment, kidnapping, and anything else he can. Your officer attempts to press charges on the female for battery and she convinces the police she was just defending her husband who was wrongfully attacked by your officer. You decide to terminate the officer on the spot. Eleven months later, after the others involved have moved on to other positions, you and the hotel are named in a lawsuit from the male guest and his wife. They claim negligent hiring, inadequate training, negligent security, and seek millions of dollars. Your risk manager says it is not winnable and settles for $100,000 plus medical bills. Meanwhile, the former security officer, who was denied unemployment, sues for wrongful termination. He claims he was told to provide security, was given handcuffs, and sent to a call where he thought someone needed help. He wants back pay, medical bills, and $50,000 because his facial scars and loss of earlobe have left him deformed. Your risk manager reluctantly pays this one as well. Other costs associated with this incident are the other guests who left the hotel due to the unprofessional conduct of the security officer, the others who will never return after reading this incident in the newspaper, and all of the friends and associates of the original guests who will never patronize such a dangerous place.

The same incident at XYZ sends an officer with two weeks of training to the same type of incident. This officer goes to the room, determines there was an argument and that nobody wants to press charges. Finding no reason to arrest anyone, he gives them a warning about disturbing other guests and says the police will be called the next time. This incident costs about $1,000 for the extra training given to the officer. Spread that cost of training over the career of the officer who will handle at least 100 similar incidents and it is only about $10.

These are extreme examples of how training saves money. Your boss will understand this, especially if you show him examples of real lawsuits and the monetary awards.

The example of false arrest in this chapter is fictitious and used for the purpose of illustrating the point. The best illustration is an actual event that resulted in a large payout.

One of the greatest and most abused responsibilities of private security is arrest. The company has a responsibility to ensure that every officer is properly hired, trained, and tested on powers of arrest and use of force. The company also has a responsibility to protect arrestees with proper procedures, safe holding rooms, and adequate supervision of its officers. Awareness of and compliance with the laws in your area are also paramount to avoiding possible negligence or litigation.

Reduced Turnover

We can save money on attrition in two ways with a good training program. The first way is to use the initial training as the observation period for your new officer. Putting an officer right into his duties on the first or second day does not give you a chance to watch his interactions, behavior, and other opportunities he has that could put you in a position of risk. A substantial training period will give you a chance to model correct behavior with a qualified officer, and to observe poor attitude, violent behaviors, and learning types. If you have to let an employee go, it is better and cheaper to do it in the first few days during training than to wait for months until you actually observe a costly mistake.

The second and more positive way to prevent turnover is by producing qualified, professional, confident officers. These employees historically take more pride in their job and company, produce more, and are thereby more honest and likely to stay longer.

Quality In Is Quality Out

You would not hire a cook who never worked in a kitchen, and even if she had experience, you would have to teach her how to use your kitchen equipment, the menu options, and ingredients to all of your signature dishes, and how they are displayed on the plate. The same goes for the guy who repairs your air conditioning and drives your shuttle. Whether you manufacture widgets or provide a service, the better-trained worker makes a better product in less time. In security, our product is protection of assets, and a better-trained officer is going to identify problems before they occur, prevent criminal behavior, and, therefore, better protect those assets and save money.

When security officers escorted some unruly guests from a private party at a hotel in 2010, one of the guest's friends started a fight with Security to get them to release his friend. A struggle ensued and the original offending guest was struck by one officer with a bottle. The injured guest sued the hotel for negligent hiring, training, and retention because the officers did not know how to handle intoxicated patrons. The court sided with the plaintiffs after a security expert explained that proper background checks and training relevant to their jobs would have prevented the officers from losing control.

Too often, "bouncers" are hired more for their appearance and size rather than their training or expertise. Make sure the hiring and training process is relevant to the skills required to perform this particular job. Guest relations, use of force, and de-escalation techniques are training programs often overlooked, but are necessary in any hospitality security program.

It is tempting and sometimes seems necessary to fill the open position with someone as soon as possible. Establish your training program and stick with it as if you have no other choice. It is just a cost of doing business. Your business will have proven positive success because of a more professional, better-trained security force.

In Chapter 5, we mentioned that skills can be taught but attitude cannot. It is a common mistake to hire for experience and hope to save money by not having to train someone who was trained elsewhere. This may or may not work out for you, but you need to weigh this risk and decide if it will work in your favor. A police or corrections officer may be able to effectively arrest bad guys, but have they ever had to worry about making a false arrest? When they learned to quell riots, did they get training on dealing with a bunch of drunken conventioneers? Maybe you will get lucky, but you cannot design your training program around luck. Documentation and consistency are the two keys to training, and the previous examples will not satisfy either.

Consistency

In the previous section, we talked about the importance of training for reducing risk. Even though risk was used as the justification for selling the program to your boss, it is the absolute primary reason that you have to provide training. This training, whatever it is, must be applied consistently across the entire staff. If two officers receive different amounts or types of training, you may be found negligent when one takes a different action than the other.

This is also why we cannot rely on an officer's prior training as being adequate for our hotel. If all of the hotels in your community used the same training program, then that gets you part of the way there. But there are still policies and procedures unique to each hotel that would require consistent training by the hotel. This especially applies to contract security if used at your hotel. Make sure they receive basic training from their company, but also ensure they have specific, consistent training on your hotel's practices and techniques.

TRAINING PROGRAM

We have established why training is important: consistency. We have also determined that its cost can be justified: liability. Next is the implementation of your program.

As discussed earlier, training is a full-time job. Therefore, our first step is to fill the position of training coordinator. This person will write and present various training programs, evaluate trainees, coordinate the timing and schedule of the different training programs, and maintain the records of all of it. Besides being able to do all of those things, you will need someone who understands learning and teaching styles and techniques and who can develop and modify training programs as policies change. In addition, this person should be able to monitor and research current events and case law while keeping abreast of how risk is managed within the company.

There are three components to a complete training program. All three are necessary for a successful security department that reduces liability while protecting assets. Those components are classroom or academy training, field training, and in-service training.

Academy

You should never put an officer into service without a minimal amount of orientation to their new job, the company's policies, and relevant laws. Much of this can be taught in a classroom setting. Many security companies choose to contract this service. There may be someone in your area that can teach security basics for all of the hotels or other security functions in town. Whether you use a service like this or create an "academy" of your own, here are some suggestions of what to include in this training.

Basic laws—A security officer needs to know the laws for crimes she may encounter. These include crimes against persons, such as murder, rape, robbery, theft, etc., and crimes against the company, such as embezzlement, fraud, vandalism, and "defrauding an innkeeper." Some laws, like that last one, vary from state to state and even among municipalities. Many of those are specifically designed to protect hotels and guests.

Laws of arrest—In this segment, we would explain the difference between a misdemeanor and a felony and the requirements to arrest (committed in your presence, reasonable cause, etc.). States also differ in their requirements for a private person arrest. Some give special powers to security, but most do not. This is where many officers get into trouble, so this distinction is important.

Use of force—This issue is often neglected in officer training, but also can lead to trouble. Officers should be very clear on every step of the force ladder from verbal all the way to deadly force. It is ironic that police officers spend days and weeks on this training and they have the same ability to apply excessive force that we do. So, spend that amount of time required for your staff to understand it.

Company policies—Even if your company provides new-hire orientation, there are many policies that pertain specifically to security officers. Confidentiality, accepting gratuities, sexual harassment reporting, evidence handling, lost and found, and rules of conduct are examples of these policies.

Documentation—Report writing procedures are probably the most difficult to teach new security officers. This is, unfortunately, mostly a high school English class (paragraph structure, grammar, spelling) with some company report procedures thrown in.

Emergency procedures—Evacuation plans, medical protocols, robbery, and active shooter procedures are among the procedures discussed in this part of the academy. These still require physical exercises, but we will come to that later.

Guest service—This not only includes your company's policies of meet and greet, but also includes conflict resolution, de-escalation, and even ADA (Americans with Disabilities Act) rules.

These are what I would consider the minimum requirements to be included in a new-hire academy. You can add your own unique classes to your academy to make it more rounded and definitive of the style of your department and company.

Classroom training should use various media and learning platforms. PowerPoint® slides, videos, guest speakers, role-playing, exercises, and written and verbal testing are all proven methods of increased absorption. If you are going to introduce an academy to your existing training program, work out a schedule to put all officers through it. The veterans can be put in class with the rookies at a pace that does not tax your staffing levels. Consistency and documentation are the names of the game in training, so you want everyone to go through the same training.

Field Training

Postacademy training or "on-the-job" training needs to be more extensive and structured than what you may be used to seeing. Without being able to prove through documentation that training occurred, the training is useless in court. Following a senior officer around and being "shown the ropes" is good, practical training, but we need to support it to make it more valuable.

In 2010, a national retail store chain was sued by a Sri Lankan man for violation of his civil rights (discrimination based on race in places of public accommodation). The man had been speaking to a woman in the store and was asked to leave by Security. The plaintiff claimed that the security officer acted inappropriately, that the police were summoned to question him, and that he was unnecessarily "86'd" from the store. The court ruled that the plaintiff fell short of proving that the store employee's conduct was "outrageous and extreme" and dismissed the case.

Even though the store "won" this case, the lesson to be learned here is that professional conduct, courtesy, and discretion might have prevented this case from going to court. This trial was, without doubt, very expensive for both parties.

Before we start field training, we need some field-training officers (FTOs). FTOs are selected based on their experience, aptitude, and attitude. Your new recruits are going to spend a lot of time with FTOs, so their attitude and ability to teach is very important. Teaching skills can be taught through an instructor development or similar program. Here, FTOs learn how to make presentations, identify learning styles, and use the "explain, demonstrate, observe" method of teaching tasks. They also learn how to give constructive feedback and correct unacceptable behavior.

Rather than just selecting the most knowledgeable officer to be an FTO, make sure he or she is going to be able to "sell" the job to the new employee. The last thing you want is someone who will teach bad habits or badmouth the company for eight hours. You may want to have tryouts and some sort of testing process to make sure you get motivated employees to take this position.

Task List

Once you have your trainers trained to train trainees, you need an organized training process. To structure the training, it is best to start with a task list. The task list is made up of every job that a security officer does, no matter how insignificant. Everything is listed from common patrol procedures to fire extinguisher inspections to guest interactions to report writing. The task list may be several pages long. If you get writer's block on this, try using your daily logs as reminders or have your FTOs make notes of their activities for a week or so. Once the list is compiled, create a form where the FTO and the trainee initial each task as they show proficiency.

The task list may determine the length of your field training. In a large hotel, two weeks is probably adequate. If you are not sure, look at other comparable hotels and make sure your training is at least equal to theirs. If that is not helpful, you may have to run a few trainees through your new field-training program and see how long it takes them to feel comfortable and confident on their own. The daily reports will help you make that determination.

Evaluations

Daily observation reports should also be created for use by the FTO. This one-page evaluation form lists several categories in which to observe each day. These categories include guest service, knowledge of property, officer safety, knowledge of procedures, etc. Next to each category, place a 1 to 5 or 1 to 10 scale in which the FTO circles the number corresponding with the trainee's performance. Each substandard and each above-standard rating is explained with a comment. The FTO reviews the report with the trainee at the end of each day to let him know what he did well and where he needs to improve. Trainees are kept in training until they meet standards on every category.

Weekly observation reports are identical to the daily reports, except a supervisor completes them. This gives an extra set of eyes to the evaluation report and ensures that training is being administered fairly and consistently. The supervisor reviews his observations with the trainee just as the FTO did.

These three forms of documentation—the task list, the daily observation report, and the weekly observation report—show in a very detailed fashion exactly what was trained and how it was trained. If all aspects of training are covered in your list, it will be difficult for a plaintiff to accuse your company of having inadequate training. There are also some training classes or modules that will be too intensive for a task list. These include CPR, weapons, defensive tactics, bomb awareness, etc.

In-Service Training

In Chapter 5, I offered the Officer Development Program as one way of doing your in-service training. Whatever your method, there are three reasons to keep training current after the new-hire training is complete. First, there are several required programs to be taught that were not covered in the initial training: CPR and defensive tactics, for example. These classes are also difficult to pile onto a new hire who is absorbing so much in a short period. They are not needed during the field training anyway. Second, procedures change and are added constantly, so we need to keep everyone updated. These include emergency procedures and various specific incident responses. Third, in-service training keeps officers fresh on various procedures that we do not want them to forget, but may not happen very often. Defibrillators may not be used very often, but, on a regular basis, we need to make sure officers can show proficiency. This covers us for those lawsuits that claim we do not adequately train our staff.

There are several methods of providing in-service training to your staff, and I recommend you use all of them.

Classroom—Officers need to be pulled away from their duties on occasion for a class. Lecture or workshop classes are good for teaching CPR, first aid, defensive tactics, and other intensive multihour programs. Make sure officers are paid for these classes, that the instructors are qualified, and that attendance is documented.

Briefing/pullout—If you are fortunate enough to have a preshift briefing for your officers, there are many topics that can be covered in a few minutes. Handling agitated persons, working oxygen regulators, or handcuffing refreshers are good topics for these short presentations. During shift, pullout training can be done with minimal disruption. This type of training can be discussion/tabletops or actual exercises. Fire drills, active shooter scenarios, CPR practice, and many other topics can be covered on a daily basis. Make sure each officer gets a chance to participate and that it is always documented.

Tabletop—A tabletop exercise is the best way to train officers without disrupting business. Officers gather around a table in a workshop format and run through a scenario. Upon being given a scenario, each officer relates what actions he or she would take. More information is provided and then officers continue updating their actions until the situation is resolved. This is a great way to train, but also to test procedures to see if they work and if anything was forgotten. Emergency procedures can be developed or tested using this method and then modified as necessary—all while providing training to those who participate.

Debriefings are another type of tabletop exercise. After a significant event at your property or even one that you hear about in the news, officers discuss their actions or the actions of those involved and observe lessons learned. They decide what could have been done better, what worked well, and what did not. Debriefings are an emotional release for the ones who experienced a traumatic event and a learning moment for everyone.

Drills—A drill focuses on one component of a procedure, such as an evacuation drill or a response drill. These take a bit of planning and coordination. You can include other departments and select a time where you do not disrupt business or guests who are relaxing. However, do not be afraid to let guests see you practicing. Get a big sign that says, "We are practicing to keep you safe," or something like that and let people watch you do CPR on a mannequin or handcuff a fellow employee. I see this when I go to my local water park and it is very reassuring. Remember documentation.

Exercises—An exercise is training that involves all of the components of a plan. For example, an active shooter exercise may include the response, setting up a perimeter, dealing with phone calls and upset guests, and triage of injured persons. This training can be as large and as complicated as you want. Full-scale exercises are discussed more in Chapter 10.

Now we will look at some specialized training that you might use at your facility.

Defensive Tactics

Any incident that becomes physical with security officers is "defensive." We should not be taking any action with anyone where we are "offensive." Our physical actions are to protect ourselves or someone else from harm. Because we do not arrest people for warrants or something they did outside our presence, even an arrest is made in our own defense. It also sounds better to a jury that your officers are trained in defensive tactics rather than offensive tactics.

Defensive tactics includes everything from officer presence to deadly force. Because consistency is one of the keys to training, we must teach everyone the same tactics in the same manner every time. Use of a qualified instructor is the only way to do this physical training. Many police and military training programs employ a form of martial arts for their defensive tactics training. This does not mean you should go over to your local dojo and hire sensei Bob. It does mean that you find an instructor who not only knows the moves, but also the legalities, liabilities, and medical dangers.

Sudden in-custody death syndrome is a term given to deaths of uncertain reason following an arrest. The cause is often (but not always) drug-related and can occur during, immediately following, or days after a violent struggle. Researchers are still investigating ways to prevent it medically, but in the meantime, there are precautions we can take and responsibilities we have to those in our custody.

Besides the consistent, strict adherence to training and procedures, arresting officers should have a protocol for tending to persons in handcuffs. First, ensure that the fight is over. Once someone is restrained, it is no longer necessary to apply pain or restrictive holds unless those moves are defensive. Second, prisoners should be monitored closely for abnormal breathing and other signs of stress, shock, heart failure, or injury. Third, any signs of anything unusual should be reacted to immediately. This includes first aid and calling emergency medical services. It is better to be safe than sorry.

I cannot tell you how many times I have seen security directors provide handcuffs to their officers on their first day with no training. You might as well give them the keys to the company safe. I cannot think of a more costly mistake than to give an untrained officer handcuffs—except maybe giving him or her a firearm. Even an untrained officer with a gun would probably not be as bad because most people realize the seriousness of pulling a firearm. Instead of speculating what is worse and what are the risks, let's just agree not to provide those things without proper training.

Handcuffs are a necessary tool for security, but dangerous legal exposure comes from depriving freedom especially by force. This liability is discussed in more detail in the next section.

USE OF FORCE POLICY

The use of force posture for your property is a very important decision that will take into account the company reputation, insurance, training, staffing, budget, and legal ramifications. Some properties take the simpler route to save money and keep their employees safer. As we learned in the Seattle bus terminal incident, and many other incidents all over

In an effort to save money on police protection in a Seattle bus terminal, the city decided to hire security guards whose policy was "observe and report." Their orders were to be observant, watch for potential problems, and alert police to intervene. In 2010, a girl was attacked by several others in a beating and robbery that was caught on video. Two security guards watched the incident as it unfolded and appeared to be using verbal commands to stop the violence, but were obviously unsuccessful. The entire world watched as a girl was severely beaten while two uniformed security guards did nothing to help her. The litigation is still pending, but the security company was fired and the "observe and report" policy revised.

If the method of "observe and report" is going to be used at your facility, it does not mean you are immune to responsibility and the associated liability. Society does not expect anyone, even untrained security officers, to stand helpless while a preventable incident occurs in their presence. Make sure officers understand the "observe and report" philosophy and know the exceptions when to use discretion under unusual circumstances.

the world, a cautious reaction to violence often puts employees in more danger and may even cause you more money and legal troubles in the end. Many companies who invest in comprehensive force training, including weapons, have found that they prevent and deter more incidents and can safely and effectively resolve most violent situations. For those who would argue that the police are better trained, equipped, and legally protected to deal with violence, I would agree with them that the police are the best response. However, there is an important few minutes where a guest or employee is getting his butt kicked on your property while you await the arrival of the police. You have a duty to protect that person from harm, within reason. So, ask your lawyer and general manager where they feel that duty falls on your officers.

Don't forget to see what your neighbors are doing. If the 300-pound linebacker from the local college football team is trashing your bar, and an innocent patron suffers brain damage from a flying stool, what is your response? What is the security response at your neighbor's property? I want my guests, employees, and all the lawyers in town to know that if there is a violent situation in my bar, there is no better trained and equipped security department to deal with it.

Whatever you decide, make sure the appropriate tools and training are provided so your officers can carry out that duty effectively.

Use of Force

Use of force policy is necessary to provide guidance and boundaries to your staff when using force and to justify your actions in court. The amount of force we use is generally organized into a scale from least force to greatest force. This scale is also called a ladder or a continuum. It is sometimes visually displayed as a staircase or pyramid as well. However you want to characterize it, the objective is the same. I will explain each of the steps on the ladder. Some are always included, and some—like guns for unarmed officers—may not apply to you. Force usually includes anything physical, but at least two types of force are not physical.

We use a rising scale, ladder, or continuum to illustrate "escalation of force." Because it is not acceptable to use excessive force, we teach officers to "climb" the ladder until they reach that level of force that is the same as their opponent's. In other words, you do not use deadly force to overcome the resistance of a man waving a rolled up newspaper, and you would not order someone coming at you in a speeding truck to "Stop!" When officers are being accused of using unnecessary force or unreasonable force, it is because they may have skipped steps on the ladder or climbed it too high for the situation.

The science of use of force seems very straightforward to those of us who use it regularly. However, juries are having a hard time, in the last few years, applying this concept to police officers who are accused of using excessive force. The ladder, escalation, or continuum is difficult for laypersons to understand because they assume that you must start at the bottom of the ladder. Because our options are even more restrictive when it comes to force options, security officers should always be trained to use that amount of force that is reasonable under the circumstances to defend themselves or someone else. In other words, even though we use the ladder of force to train our officers, a jury will only care that the force used was "reasonable."

To keep yourself out of trouble in this unpredictable arena of litigation, use an experienced, proven, certified tactics instructor; test, drill, and exercise your staff in scenarios on a regular basis; and consult your legal counsel on this and any other policy you mandate. Following are the levels of force in order.

Officer Presence

Surprisingly, just being present is a use of force. A professionally attired and equipped officer standing in a certain area can prevent trouble. Just her arrival at the scene of a violent incident may be enough force to stop a fight or prevent an argument from escalating. Officer presence is the basic and first step on the use of force continuum. There are many training programs available for this level as it is the most common, most preferred, and even the only level available to some officers. (See the previous box about the Seattle bus incident.)

Verbal Commands

Use of an officer's voice is the second step on the ladder. When presence does not work, the officer climbs to the next step, issuing verbal commands. "Place your hands behind your back," "Drop the magazine," and "Get out of here" are all examples of verbal commands. This training is often combined with the previous level and may be as far as many officers can go. It is also as far as we let our nonsecurity personnel go, so this is training to consider for other departments.

Soft Hand Controls

Most continuums include this intermediate physical step. Soft hand controls are those where there is no pain compliance used. This may include guiding someone by the arm, pushing someone's back to get him or her to move, and pushing down on one's shoulders to get him or her to remain seated. In the upcoming subsections, we discuss why security officers hardly ever use these types of controls.

Chemical Spray

Pepper spray, foam, stream and aerosol, mace, and other chemical irritants are placed in various levels of the continuum. I place them before hard hand controls because they are not lethal and can do no serious or permanent injury. Many departments place the Taser® at this level and use it as an alternative to going "hands on." I do not disagree with this practice, but I think in the coming years, the courts will decide this for us. As with most of these levels and tools, their place in the ladder depends on the type of training. If an officer was taught to use a Taser as the first step in an arrest, then it would fall here. If the Taser was taught to be used as a defense of a violent aggressor, it would fall in the next step, or even after that.

Hard Hand Controls

Hard controls are those that use pain compliance like arm bars or wristlocks to overcome violence. You learn this in your defensive tactics class. Every officer, regardless of his or her duties, needs to learn these techniques because in the absence of training, officers will make up moves. Worse, they will resort to prior training, which may be inappropriate and excessive for the current application.

A chokehold is a common name for either of two holds called the Arm Bar Control and the Carotid Control. The Arm Bar Control is one arm around the front of the neck, using the other hand to pull back on the arm bar. The effect is to cut off the windpipe and decrease oxygen to the heart and oxygenated blood to the brain. The Carotid Control places one arm around the neck (from behind) with the elbow at the front. The other arm pushes against the other arm, creating a vice. This cuts off blood flow in the carotid artery and the jugular vein, decreasing blood to the brain.

Between 1975 and 1982, the Los Angeles Police Department included a chokehold as part of their use of force policy. Sixteen people died as a direct result of the chokehold and it was finally restricted to use only in life-threatening situations. Physicians deduced that the desired effect of compliance and loss of consciousness were often preceded by the undesired "fight or flight reflex" where the prisoner actually resisted more because of the fear of death. The desire to escape—which is a conscious decision—is overcome by the will to survive—which is instinct. During this resistance, the suspect uses his instinctive final breaths and energy trying to stay alive rather than complying with rational commands.

Anytime you put your hands on someone, it had better be to make an arrest. Except for catching someone from falling or helping in a medical situation, any time you touch someone you are stepping into a legal situation. Placing someone in a wristlock, pushing a drunken patron out the door, or placing handcuffs on a possible shoplifter all constitute false imprisonment and are subject to legal consequences, unless they are pursuant to a lawful arrest. The scenes you see in the movies where the two bouncers throw the bad guy out the door are for Hollywood and have no place in our business.

Remember that police officers can use hard hand controls to modify behavior. They have legal authority to lay hands upon people where we do not.

Impact Weapons

Ancillary devices, such as stun guns, Tasers, batons, clubs, and ASPs (expandable batons) are all considered less-than-lethal force alternatives. For security, these are defensive weapons, so they would not be used on fleeing suspects, or in threatening ways. Many police officers and security officers place these items on the wrong level in the force continuum, causing allegations of excessive force. Because most of these weapons *can* be lethal, they are often introduced too early in the escalation of force.

Deadly Force

This is obviously the top of our ladder/continuum. We generally associate deadly force with firearms and that is largely true. Impact weapons also can apply, or be used to overcome, deadly force (e.g., a monkey wrench, drill motor, or vehicle). Other weapons need to be realized as deadly so that your officers can justify their actions. Deadly force and each of these levels apply not only to the force being encountered, but also to the force being exerted to meet the threat. Good guys carry guns, impact weapons, and pepper spray. Bad guys also have guns, use impact weapons, and even pepper spray. Both good and bad guys use soft and hard controls. The level of force is comparable—the only difference is that we have to justify ours and cannot exceed what is reasonable.

The use of force continuum can be used in two ways. First, it helps us to determine and justify what level of force is appropriate. If someone is using a certain level of force against us, we make an instant decision, based on our knowledge of this continuum, what level of force we will use to counter the threat. We can use the same level to meet the threat or we can use the next highest level to overcome it. Someone coming at you with a baseball bat in a batter's position would have to be countered with the next highest level, which is deadly force.

Second, because situations can escalate and de-escalate rapidly, we use the continuum to adjust our level of force accordingly. If we point our gun at the person with the bat and he drops it, we no longer need to use deadly force. We may drop down to a hard hand control to arrest him. If he resists the arrest, perhaps we push him away and use pepper spray, Taser, or baton. On the contrary, if we are trying to awake an intoxicated person in a lounge (using verbal commands or soft hand controls) and he rises up swinging, we might immediately escalate to counter the new threat. The fluidity of changing levels to meet new threats is why we call it a continuum.

SPECIAL TRAINING

Bike Patrol

Bicycles have been used for patrol for over 100 years, but organized training and policies did not really become part of the program until the late 1980s. Many police departments claim to have originated the official training style that has permeated security and police departments all over the world. My first experience was in 1993 with two Seattle police officers who developed a training program for police that included safety, coordination, riding techniques, and equipment selection. The training program I developed evolved from that one after I modified it for the armed security officer.

Equipment

Twenty years later, many manufacturers sell mountain bikes designed for urban patrol. The primary difference between these and a regular mountain bike is their durability. Weight is sacrificed for strength in the frame and components. Since patrol bikes will be ridden almost entirely on concrete as opposed to dirt, this durability absolutely prohibits buying a bike off the rack at a bike shop. Just as a police car is modified for constant use and abuse, so should a patrol bike be built for bumps, jumps, and maybe even a heavier rider. Rather than custom building a bike, find a manufacturer that makes "police" bikes.

Helmets and gloves are basic, but apparel must have the attributes of a security uniform and the comfort and flexibility of bike shorts and shirts. Lighting, reflectors, and other safety equipment are standard.

A qualified mechanic and a bike shop should make repairs. You can try to create your own shop, but by the time you count labor and the cost of inventory and special tools, it is faster and cheaper to have repairs done by a professional.

Training

A certified bike patrol instructor should train bike officers. Many renowned organizations certify training and they offer classes for instructors. Some hotels rely on their local police departments for this training. Ensure that the training includes the following components:

Bike patrol policies—These include use of force with the bicycle. The bicycle can uniquely fit each of the levels in a use of force policy from presence to deadly force. Other policies include where it can be ridden, pursuit policies, and sidewalk or road-riding laws.

Repair procedures—Training should include basics like minor adjustments, flat repairs, and safety inspections.

Control and coordination—Bike officers need to be shown how to control the bike at slow speeds, ride through crowds, use pedal straps, ride with one hand, etc.

Riding techniques—Speed-shifting, emergency braking, obstacle avoidance, curb and stair climbs and descents, and even falling are important parts of the overall training.

Dismounts—Patrol officers learn to use the bike as a tool and even a weapon for apprehending criminals.

Training for bike officers should be at least three days and include long-distance and strenuous rides to evaluate endurance and stamina of the riders.

Other specialized patrol functions are discussed in Chapter 2.

DOCUMENTATION

I am not sure I mentioned documentation enough times in this chapter. If training is not documented, it did not happen. All that work is a waste of time if it cannot be proved to have happened. Keep training files for each of your officers separate from their personnel files. Track every piece of training they receive. These records will be subpoenaed when you are sued for inadequate training and that is great. Most lawsuits due to training inadequacy are lost by hotels that did not have documented training. You want the most well-trained, well-equipped security officers in the world and with some work you will meet that goal.

7

Safety

Two things are infinite: the universe and human stupidity; and I'm not sure about the universe.

Albert Einstein, scientist

In most organizations, the responsibility for the safety function rests on the shoulders of the security director. This is a logical fit because Security and Safety are very similar jobs. Security's function is to protect assets and Safety protects the two most important assets: guests and employees. Actually, the Occupational Safety and Health Administration (OSHA)—the primary safety regulating agency—exists to protect employees, not guests. Fire departments and other business codes protect all occupants, including guests. It is good business—and to everyone's benefit—if you apply all safety-related programs to guests and employees.

Whether the safety responsibility is yours or under the umbrella of another department, you can still work very closely with that other department toward the common goal of protecting employees and guests.

PROGRAM

In most cases, the government requires you to have a safety program in place. You will find that if you do certain things, you will exceed the level of being compliant. Because some safety codes and regulations differ by jurisdiction, this chapter will address the general setup and organization of a good safety program.

The program consists of four components: compliance, awareness, training, and communication.

Compliance

The safety manager is responsible for tracking regulations, codes, and recommendations and applying them to the operation of the company through the establishment of policies. The safety manager is also responsible for coordinating outside and internal inspections.

105

In most court cases, the plaintiff (usually the guest who slipped and fell) has to prove that the defendant (the company and its employees) knew about the hazard and failed to act or that they should have known and had time to clean or repair the hazard. On one extreme, a guest who spills his drink in front of another guest who slips and falls is an example of a case the company could win. It is not reasonable in that case for the company to be held liable because there was no time for them to be aware of the hazard or to clean it before the accident occurred. The other extreme is when a guest spills a drink on a main pathway and it remains there a very long time before someone slips and falls. The company should have known of the spill through regular patrol and activity and should have cleaned the spill to prevent accidents.

Most facility managers realize it is much easier to find hazards and correct them than it is to defend their procedures in court. Every employee should receive training on being aware of spills and other hazards and taking action to clean them immediately. Some facilities have clean-up stations throughout the property. Others use regular documented patrols by certain departments to look for and correct hazards. One famous retailer makes regular announcements over its public address system that "it's time for a safety sweep."

Outside inspections are those made by a government or regulatory agency not affiliated with the company. Inspections you may see in a hotel on a regular basis are Fire, Health, OSHA, and others depending on the jurisdiction. Private insurance companies generally inspect their client properties as well. The safety manager should accompany inspectors to take note of violations or recommendations and explain dubious practices or equipment. The safety manager will communicate these exceptions to the correcting department, and document the infractions that may require a policy change or employee corrective action.

Internal inspections are those that you establish or possibly those made by a corporate entity. If you belong to a chain of hotels, corporate may have its own inspectors to see that you are complying with corporate policy and protecting the brand.

Awareness

The safety manager's job should be focused on employee involvement. It is not feasible for you to be responsible for the safety of the entire property. Instead, you should coordinate the efforts of all employees to be aware and focused on safety. There are several traditional methods of coordinating the employees and some less traditional ones.

Safety Committee

We all know that if you simply write memos and manuals and pass down information, there will be no buy-in and little or no compliance. You need to get the stakeholders—which are all of the employees—involved in the process. Safety committees are mistakenly believed by many to be an OSHA requirement. OSHA cares less how you achieve safety and more with the result. A cross section of employees is a good way to get a safety committee started.

So, what is your biggest exposure to loss? A car stolen out of valet? Maybe a robbery of the day's receipts? Try this: In 2007, a truck driver was delivering a load of food to a retail store that had a deli. The store's grease interceptor clogged causing a slippery grease spill on the loading ramp. The truck driver slipped and suffered serious spinal injuries. She was awarded over $15 million for her fall.

Every employee has a responsibility for safety. Many stores and hospitality environments maintain very strong safety programs for this reason. Spill stations, wet floor signs, immediate reporting procedures, and equipment inspection programs could have prevented this fall and this huge loss to the store and the driver.

Set a monthly meeting date with an agenda. The agenda should include a review of inspections (discussed later), new safety rules, safety suggestions, and a review of accidents or noted safety violations. Allow the committee to discuss safety suggestions that will benefit employees and reduce accidents; for example, a suggested covering for a slick walkway to avoid slip and falls.

Safety committee members will be responsible for bringing forward information from their departments, suggestions from themselves and other employees and taking this information back to their department meetings. Many consider this topic dry and send their least energetic employees. It is up to you to make the format interesting and relevant. Show the cost of accidents for the company. Pass around photos and evidence that makes the accident personal. Show the employees the effects of their recommendations and how they have prevented accidents. Prizes and awards for great suggestions or cost savings is an inexpensive motivator.

Consider bringing guest speakers like the fire marshal to speak to the committee about safety hazards and life-threatening safety problems he has seen. This goes toward that networking skill we develop and discuss further in Chapter 12.

Departmental Inspections

As I said before, the safety manager cannot do it all and would not be effective if he did. Let the employees have some empowerment over their own work area. Create an inspection form for each area so that any employee can do a regular walk-through and look for daisy-chained power strips, blocked fire exits, supplies stacked too high on shelves, etc. This provides a preinspection for officials, but more importantly, brings the awareness to the inspecting employees and all of their colleagues. These inspection forms are brought to the safety meeting and exceptions are discussed with the group to make changes.

Training

Some training is safety related for almost every department. Since this training is subject to verification by regulatory agencies, the safety manager should coordinate it. Security is one department that has a lot of safety training, like CPR. Your facilities department has even more safety training. Lockout, tag-out, welding, safety harness, and CPR are some of the classes required for your engineers. Depending on how many employees you have, this can be quite a job for you. Most managers find it easier to set up a matrix of required classes and schedule them over the year, spread out so the training is constant, but not a burden on the workforce of that department.

In early 2008, an outside contractor was hired to build a steel catwalk on the roof of the Monte Carlo Hotel in Las Vegas. During the welding, a spark landed on the exterior foam facade of the structure. The foam, which is highly flammable, was a popular product used to create different textures and shapes on most hotels in that area. The resulting fire was mostly contained to the roof, but damaged the 32nd floor suites and caused evacuation of the entire building. Costs of repair and loss of revenue were reported at over $100 million.

OSHA requires that nonmovable flammable structures be protected against sparks and flame during any hot work, including welding. As you might imagine, several persons and entities would be blamed for the cause of this fire.

You may be tempted to learn each of these training programs yourself and to do all of the training alone. As admirable as this is, it is not fair to the company. If something happens to you, the company will be stuck without a trainer. Spread this training over the employees who need to learn it. Have the welder teach the hot work safety class, the fountain maintenance person teach the SCUBA class, and so forth. If someone leaves, you just have to worry about that one person and that one class. Keep in mind that many agencies and even your own insurance providers provide many classes for free.

Communication

Safety policies and procedures are worthless without a way to communicate them to the entire staff and sometimes guests. The Safety Committee is just one form of communication; here are some others.

Safety Newsletter

A safety newsletter can be a very informative way to get employees involved in safety. There is never a shortage of information that can be included in a monthly or quarterly communication. Many of the items discussed in the safety meetings can be included. Here is a list of other ideas for content:

1. Safety suggestions and rewards
2. Safety tips for employees
3. Department of the month
4. Safety tips for employees at home (weather, robbery, disaster, etc.)
5. Monthly themes for the property (October is Fire Prevention week)
6. Games that highlight safety
7. Photos of safety hazards

8. Articles from guest writers (fire chief, company doctor)
9. Safety training and class schedule

Safety Wall
At least one display or bulletin board in employee areas should be devoted to safety. Items from the safety committee and from the newsletter can be included with training class information and a place to receive suggestions.

Safety Suggestions
If given an opportunity to submit privately, many employees will be motivated to become engaged in safety in their own manner. A traditional suggestion box is just one way to encourage suggestions. Perhaps a page on the company website or a safety phone hotline will get people to become involved.

Insurance Company

Your workers' comp, business, or general liability insurance companies may be willing to provide training classes or written material, posters, and presentations on the subject of safety. Anything to make the employee more involved is of help.

Workers' Comp

We sometimes are so caught up in compliance that we forget that the objective of a safety program is to reduce accidents. I hope that you can achieve compliance while promoting safety, but the follow-up with accidents at your property is usually the forgotten step.

Workers' Compensation is simply an insurance program for employees injured at work. Sometimes it is administered by the state, but usually there is a third-party administrator or insurance company to pay medical bills and compensate for lost work time. Most hotels have a claims administrator to act as the liaison between the employees and the insurance company. This position probably falls under your Human Resources department or benefits, but there is a close relationship with the safety coordinator.

The first part of this chapter discussed prevention programs. In this next section, we will look at how accidents and claims are used as metrics for the success of the safety program.

ACCIDENTS

If not already done, there should be some level of investigation for every employee accident. This process is discussed in Chapter 11. The report should include the supervisor's statement, which answers the following questions regarding the employee's actions leading up to the accident. Has this type of accident happened before? Was the employee acting in the normal course of his or her duties? Were any policies or safety procedures violated while performing the task? Was personal protective equipment used correctly? Was other equipment used correctly? How could this accident have been prevented? Has this employee been involved in any other accident reports?

The report should also include a statement by the Engineering Department, which answers similar questions and information regarding the accident scene: hazards noted, equipment operating properly, measures that might have prevented accident, etc. Witnesses, photos, and other evidence should be included as well.

Once the report has been completed, it should be reviewed by the safety manager or coordinator. She should review all the facts to determine what action should be taken. Possible action steps include: disciplinary action against the employee for abuse of safety practices or other policies (i.e., running in the hallway); repair order for damaged or faulty equipment (i.e., loose handrail); recommendation to management for safety upgrade (i.e., replace tile floor with nonslip tiles); or recommendation for new safety procedure (i.e., carts must be pushed and not pulled).

The safety manager or, better yet, the safety team should review all accident reports (omitting personal medical information) to look for trends that might indicate a safety issue. For example, several employees have slipped in the same spot in a certain area of the kitchen. The team then comes up with recommendations where applicable, such as ergonomic training, better lighting, different flooring surface, spill stations, etc.

Other factors may lead to rises in accident reports. Some employees fake or exaggerate accidents just to get off on a busy weekend, hoping they will be paid for their time. There may be attention-getting reasons or contention with a supervisor or co-worker. The most serious reason may be insurance fraud. It is not uncommon for an employee with a chronic back or knee problem to fake an accident so he can get the needed surgery and time missed covered by the company. A good investigator should reveal these, but the safety team should be aware that no matter how good the safety program is, something like the previous examples could still lead to issues.

Your claims administrator, in an effort to reduce costs, will be very aggressive with return-to-work programs. Most employees would rather work their regular job than peel carrots or fold towels on light duty.

Documentation

OSHA requires certain reporting of accidents and other statistics related to safety. If you are tracking accidents as described previously, this should be no problem. You will not be able to accurately measure the success of your safety program unless you are tracking these incidents. Do not even think of covering up accidents or falsifying the numbers. Smaller companies do that to fly under the inspection radar, but you do not need to do that. You will not have an inordinate amount of accidents if you have a program in place, and your company would not have you in your position if it wanted to keep this information from the government.

RISK MANAGEMENT

Somewhere along the line, safety programs were tied in to risk management in hospitality venues. When you look at a brief history of guest accidents, hotels were not a very lucrative defendant for most plaintiff lawyers through the 1970s. While hotels had relatively deep pockets, accident claims were considered more of the bottom of the barrel for trial lawyers, so they were left for the struggling law firms. Insurance covered most of these cases. In the 1980s, mega resorts like the ones in Las Vegas, amusement parks, and overseas monstrosities came on the scene. With these huge facilities came more escalators, elevators, marble (slippery) floors, and the proportional increase in accidents. However, these large corporations also brought highly paid and experienced lawyers, modern video surveillance systems, and increased staff training to monitor and reduce accidents. Most importantly, the insurance deductibles for large facilities are now in the hundreds of thousands of dollars. Entire departments were devoted to the settling of accident and criminal claims.

The down economy has affected law firms as it has everyone else, and they too are struggling for business. So, now we are seeing expensive, aggressive, and successful lawyers come after hotels for accidents that were settled relatively inexpensively before.

The moral of this history lesson (subjective as it is) is that the hospitality industry is back in the "deep pockets" category and we are up against a better adversary. We have more cases and most fall under our deductible. This makes our safety program one that is not only for compliance, but also for reduction and defense of risk. Some examples of safety programs or policies that reduce risk are discussed next.

Note: Of course, just about every policy mentioned in this book is designed to reduce risk. The ones here are specifically aimed at safety, but not necessarily at security. Other departments contribute to safety as well.

Restroom Logs

You have seen them in fast food restaurants, retail stores, and just about every public restroom—The Restroom Maintenance Log. These appear to be evidence that the facility is concerned with the cleanliness and stocking of paper goods. Rest assured that this is a risk reducer. A log of restroom cleaning provides several things. First, it shows the guest that someone is checking the restroom every X minutes. Second, it provides your defense that your cleaning staff cleaned up spills and other safety hazards every X minutes. Third, it provides a security defense that a set of eyes and ears entered that restroom on a regular frequency to prevent crime and violence.

You do not have to have a log on the bathroom wall, but you should have a log or schedule somewhere. If you assign a porter to clean three bathrooms all day, then you know he is in each one about a third of the time. That covers it as long as he goes back and forth to each one on his route. Be sure to assign male and female porters equally and consistently. Having a male responsible for a female restroom is not efficient, as he would have to close the restroom on each visit.

Safety Sweeps

I mentioned previously that a large retailer announces its safety sweeps on its public address system. That is a great policy (the announcements), but not necessarily for our industry. You should have a regular program of employees checking their areas for spills and safety hazards every few minutes. An employee calling in a spill to the cleaning staff is not good enough. Each employee should be trained to stand by the spill while cleaning help is called to prevent accidents.

Spill Stations

Spill stations are displays set up around your property that contain the equipment for resolving a spill or safety hazard. Generally, a broom, mop, towels, and cleaning solution with a warning cone or sign complete a spill station. The more convenient you make it for employees to take care of a hazard, the fewer accidents you will have.

Escalator Shutdown

Escalators invariably have some sort of minor issue that can lead to major injuries if not addressed. Shoelaces are caught, luggage is caught, people trip or lose their balance, and some with wheelchairs even attempt to ride them. Since escalators are not staffed by an employee, all employees need to be trained how to deal with an escalator emergency. Working the emergency stop, notifying engineers, and keeping guests off the stopped escalator are the important elements of this training. This policy will reduce accidents and keep accident severity to a minimum.

SECURITY AWARENESS

We have all heard the suggestion that "Security Is Everyone's Job." Well, maybe that was "Safety," but it still applies. Whether you have a separate Security Department, it is still a good idea—in fact it is necessary—that you involve every employee in security. There are several ways to engage the rest of the staff. This becomes a force multiplier for you, increases the number of eyes and hands assisting you, and provides a safer and more efficient operation for the entire business. Most employees will even enjoy the extra work if it is presented properly.

The first step to engaging other departments is to increase awareness. Most non-Security individuals have no idea what Security really does. They may think you are there to spy on them or just to deal with unruly guests. Many are amazed at all of the functions we have in a hospitality environment. Awareness, therefore, starts with an overview of what Security does and the types of things for which we watch. This can be done at a new-hire orientation or a visit during department training. Here are some of the things you can talk about and programs you can develop to increase awareness on your property.

Terrorism

Many government agencies and private corporations use a version of the "See Something, Say Something" campaign. This slogan simply reminds employees that it is everyone's responsibility to report suspicious activity, no matter how trivial or incomplete it may seem. This, and any awareness program you may use, needs to be constantly reinforced through training, media, and follow-up.

Training can be a simple PowerPoint® presentation on the types of activities or things that may be important. You also can use professionally made videos, such as those produced by the Department of Homeland Security just for hotel employees. Media can be as simple as articles in the company newsletter and signs placed throughout the property with your company's slogan on reporting suspicious activity. You may want to provide an anonymous tip line within your internal phone system voicemail. This could be used for any crime or internal reporting and answered only by you or your delegate.

In August 2009, a housekeeper found some suspicious documents in the trashcan of a guest room in Columbia, Maryland. Police were called and they uncovered a ring of identity thieves and the personal information from dozens of victims. After a high-speed police chase, four suspects were arrested and charged with credit card and general theft.

This is just one example of hundreds of incidents where regular employees see something suspicious and say something to the authorities, which results in arrests.

Emergency Response

Emergency response is more than just awareness. It may become necessary for employees to participate in the response to certain major incidents. Fire alarms, active shooters, earthquakes, and hurricanes involve every occupant of a building. In most of these and other situations, security staff will be overwhelmed and will need as much assistance as possible.

This should be incorporated into your emergency procedures. Security officers will perform the critical functions, such as responding to the scene of the fire or cornering an active shooter. Bell persons can lockout elevators and evacuate the lobby. Food servers can clear restaurants. Housekeepers can check hotel rooms for stragglers.

Most employees, when presented with the idea that they are necessary and part of the team during emergencies, will respond eagerly and proudly. For those employees who might resist new job duties, it may be necessary to remind them or their department head of the gravity of these situations. If someone is injured or killed during a disaster or violent incident and he could have been saved if it was not for the inaction of an employee, your company may be held responsible. Besides that, most normal operations, such as delivering luggage and serving food, will cease during an emergency, so employees' regular jobs are suspended until the emergency is over. They may as well help with the emergency until it is resolved.

Workplace Violence

As discussed in the next section, workplace violence prevention is an important way for employees and supervisors for every department to keep everyone safe from harm.

WORKPLACE VIOLENCE

Workplace violence is one of the biggest issues facing the business world today. The hospitality industry is not immune from criminal acts that range from bullying to mass murder. Many of the incidents that have occurred over the past 30 years have taught us how to prevent them. All we need is a strong prevention program. Before we outline that program, we will look at the history and types of workplace violence.

OSHA defines workplace violence as any physical assault, threatening behavior, or verbal abuse occurring in the work setting. This includes a lot of different violence, so it is further divided into four types.

Type I—Criminal Acts

Violence resulting from criminal acts committed by strangers is by far the most common. In this type, the perpetrator is not an employee and has no relationship with the business or the employees except through the criminal act itself. This type includes robbery and even terrorism. As you might guess, taxi drivers are the most common victims of Type I violence. This chapter will not review prevention methods for robbery and other Type I violence as it was discussed as part of the Security Plan in Chapter 2.

Type II—Customer/Client/Patient Violence

Type II violence includes any type of violence where there is some sort of business relationship between the perpetrator and the company. Patients who commit violence in hospitals are the most common Type II violence. Mental patients assaulting doctors, disgruntled customers attacking salespersons, and even a guest attacking a prostitute in a brothel would be examples of Type II violence. This type is not discussed in this chapter, as violence from outsiders (guests) should be addressed as part of our Security Plan and there is no way to prevent it using the techniques to be discussed here.

Type III—Worker-on-Worker Violence

This type of violence is the one we most commonly associate with workplace violence. The term "Going Postal" (discussed later) derives from this type and includes any type of violence between current employees. It also relates to violence caused by a former employee or even a contractor or vendor. This type of violence is preventable because we know or have known the employee and we have some control over his or her behavior. We at least have the ability to monitor the behavior before it becomes violent.

Type IV—Violence Stemming from a Personal Relationship

Type IV is another type commonly associated with our image of workplace violence. In this type, the perpetrator is an employee, a former employee, or is involved with an employee in a personal relationship. Because we may or may not know the aggressor in this type of violence, we need to identify the victim, who is our employee. This is not so difficult, and we will discuss this here as well.

History

In 1986, a postal worker named "Crazy Pat" walked into work in Edmund, Oklahoma, shot 14 co-workers, and then shot himself. In a few minutes, Pat had changed our view of workplace violence forever. He had been described as odd and a loner and had been involved in several confrontations with other employees. In fact, management was preparing to fire him for that behavior, but they never got the chance.

There were several similar shootings at postal facilities (and other businesses) up until 1993. In retrospect, the term "Going Postal" was earned by the United States Postal Service (USPS), which had a work environment that was ripe for violence. In the 1980s, the USPS employed over 900,000, so statistically it was bound to have a large percentage of workplace incidents. It also had the largest and one of the most powerful unions in the world up against a huge government bureaucracy, which made it easy for individuals to feel insignificant. As new companies like FedEx and UPS emerged, it became apparent that the post office had competition for the first time ever.

As a result, this bureaucracy started focusing on productivity and timelines more than ever and worker stress rose sharply. From 1986 to 1993, 1 in 12 postal workers had filed a grievance against management, which likely raised the stress levels even more. These grievances and other employee issues and morale were secondary to the timely delivery of mail. Right about that time, email changed everything.

Meanwhile, other companies had their own issues with Type III violence. Several current and former workers committed more mass killings. Background checks, which were previously reserved for security officers, money handlers, and managers, had to be completed on employees of all disciplines in any size company.

In 1993, after five more mass murders at postal facilities, management started to take notice. The first solution was to establish a toll-free hotline for postal employees to report management abuse and other unfavorable work conditions. It was shut down a short time later because there were too many calls. Later that year, a new position called Workplace Environment Analyst was created to focus on the prevention of workplace violence. This may have had some limited success because there were no more mass shootings at postal facilities for several years.

In 1998, the U.S. Postmaster created the Commission on a Safe and Secure Workplace. This study did not receive much attention because "Going Postal" had kind of left the post office, but it created some prevention methods that are still in use today. Those will be discussed later.

Meanwhile, the late 1990s had several more mass workplace shooters. Many criminologists attempted to create a profile of the potential workplace killer, but were unsuccessful. The physical characteristics of these murderers were of all races, ages, nationalities, and both genders. Some were blue collar and some were professionals. We even saw teenagers get into the action at a Jonesboro, Arkansas, middle school and later at Columbine High School in Colorado.

As workplace homicide entered the twenty-first century, it finally became apparent that there were two things that contributed to this type of violence: difficulty dealing with anger, and the "end of the line" feeling. But most important, more than 80 percent of these killers left visible signs of their violent behavior—and not one of them "just snapped."

Conclusions

The 30 years of history did lead us to some conclusions. Most attackers had no criminal record, but they almost all had poor job performance. As mentioned previously, they crossed all economic and social levels, were either current or former employees, and were of almost every race and gender. About half of them committed suicide. Almost all of them were motivated by anger, usually at the supervisor, and either had been terminated or were facing termination. About half of the murders occurred the same day as the termination and the other half occurred up to a year later. One postal worker waited three years to kill her co-workers. Very few had undergone a background check or their violent backgrounds were ignored.

Two of these factors are screaming for attention. One is the previously violent behavior, as noted by warning signs. Two, is the pending termination. We can deal with these two tangible subjects. Before we extrapolate those into some prevention methods, let's have a quick look at anger.

Anger

You may have learned in your college psychology class that there are two personality types: A and B. Anger is normal to each of them, and that anger can turn to violence in some people.

Type B personalities tend to be very passive. As they get angry, frustration builds until it turns to aggression. That aggression can turn to physical violence in some persons. This is not to say that every type B personality becomes violent; it only shows us how they could become violent. I like to think of a character like Darth Vader in the movie *Star Wars*. He started out as a happy, passive child, until his mother was murdered. He started displaying signs of aggression and violence that some noticed and some did not. His anger built up to the point where he turned to the "dark side" and became a mass murderer. This type of person faced with losing his job might appear to "snap."

Type A people are generally aggressive in their daily routine. The angry ones tend to be mean and are the ones we consider bullies. They have to show their superiority by making others feel inferior. Imagine someone like that being fired from his or her job. "You are firing me? I will show you who's boss." The embarrassment and loss of control become overwhelming to them and they decide to end everyone's life including their own.

These personality descriptions are very general and overly simple. We all understand that human emotions are very complicated and it takes years of education to get a grasp of them. For our purposes of developing a prevention module, the simplified version should suffice.

Workplace Violence Policy

The first step to prevention of workplace violence is to establish a policy. You may already have one, but if you do not, get some help in writing it. It is the Human Resources Department's job to write employee policies. Your labor lawyer or general counsel may have some input and there are plenty of samples on the Internet.

The policy should have three elements. First is your company's definition of workplace violence. The policy we started with might suffice, but make sure it includes threats, bullying, harassment, and intimidation in addition to physical violence. Second, it should include the duties of management and the duties of employees. For example, all employees have a duty to report workplace violence even if they are not sure whether it actually happened. Management has a responsibility to thoroughly investigate all reports and to report violence to HR and Security. Third, it should outline consequences. Define what will happen to those found in violation of the policy and what will happen to those who make false reports.

Make sure the policy includes the company name. It is important to make the company the victim rather than the employee. This will make some perpetrators realize that if they attack an employee, they are attacking the entire organization. This is a subtle scare tactic to potential offenders and it shows your employees, and any potential victim of such behavior, that you have their backs. Avoid using phrases like "zero tolerance" and defining specific penalties for violations. Part of the prevention process is a negotiation with a potential killer and we need to leave some wiggle room to do that. Also, avoid promises of confidentiality. You cannot guarantee that a witness or victim will remain anonymous. You may need them in court or a police report.

Developing the Program

There are several components involved in developing the program. First, review your company's pre-employment screening. Work history should be thoroughly checked. Interview questions should be designed to provoke responses that will reveal violent tendencies. Consider using a second interviewer or a team interview to get a valuable second opinion of personality. Always drug screen every new hire. Also, consider running contractors and vendors through a similar process. These methods are discussed in more detail in Chapter 5 and Chapter 11.

According to the State of Wisconsin Department of Administration, "firings are the cause of most violent, rampage attacks in the workplace." Actually, that is like saying guns are the cause of most murders. Terminations are the *motive* for most of these mass murders. Knowing that, we can train our supervisors and managers, in all departments, how to discipline and terminate employees. It is possible to avoid that "end of line" feeling when firing someone, but it takes some tact and it takes more time. Supervisors should also be taught how to properly discipline employees so that it is a positive coaching experience rather than one that will leave an employee angry and vindictive.

Managers and supervisors also can be taught how to identify the behaviors that indicate a tendency toward violence. Employees who make threats or react irrationally to trivial matters should be identified and the situation resolved as soon as possible.

Employees usually know the signs before anyone else and can be extra eyes and ears to future problems.

If your company does not have an employee assistance program, you should look into getting one. If you have one, make it more than a brochure in the Benefits office. This is a valuable employee benefit that can be used early in the escalation of violence. Use it to get help for employees before they become a violent problem. Sometimes this program and others can be used in lieu of termination. If you have an employee with an anger management issue, order him or her to seek counseling as a condition of employment. This defers their anger back to themselves. If they drop the program, it is on them and not the company. Other negotiating can take place to avoid violence. If you want to get rid of someone who you fear is going to be violent, why not buy them off? Maybe you allow them to resign, or you promise not to contest their unemployment benefits, or even give them a severance. A few thousand bucks to have someone leave with a smile will go much farther for your peace of mind. I did not believe this until I tried it.

> We had an employee who was a loner. He did his work for the most part, but was mediocre at best and did not get along with others. One day, his co-workers teased him about some less-than-great work he did. His response was: "One of these days, I am going to come back here and mow all of you down with my AK-47." This was a union employee and if we had fired him, it definitely would have come back as a grievance. Instead, we got together with his department head, the union leader, and our labor counsel. We all agreed we were scared to have him on the property and equally worried that he might actually come back and make good on his threat. We got the union representative to buy in to a deal where the employee resigns, collects unemployment and all his accrued vacation time, and we put nothing in his file. I cannot express the relief on everyone's mind when that employee shook everyone's hand as he left and bragged about all the fishing he would be doing. It cost us about $5,000 and was worth every penny. He left without an "end of the line feeling." He had hope and optimism.

Another useful tool is the exit interview. A good exit interview can be used just as the hiring interview to identify violent emotions. Ask questions to find out about his state of mind regarding revenge, anger, and whether he has any hope for future jobs, where to live, income, bills, etc. This is not necessary for every employee and not everyone will do it, but most angry people want to vent to someone. The venting alone may be enough to avoid a problem later.

Related Policies

Besides having a workplace violence policy, there are other policies important in preventing it. Drug use and possession, in some cases, go hand in hand with violence, theft, and other misconduct. It has no business in the workplace and your policy should reflect that. A strict drug testing policy for cause or postaccident should be in place. Most lawyers do not recommend random testing because it is difficult to make testing truly random. I support it, but I suspect your lawyer will not.

Weapons should be prohibited on property. The last couple of years have seen many conservative states guarantee the rights of individuals to carry guns in their cars, whether the employers permitted it or not. Whatever the laws in your state, you do not have to allow weapons on your property. If you are in a right-to-carry state, provide a safe place and method for employees to secure their weapons at work so they are not stolen from their cars.

Anonymous tip lines have been addressed in a couple of places in this book. Workplace violence prevention is a perfect reason to have an employee tip line. If someone is worried for their safety or does not want to be directly involved, they should have a mode of communicating directly with management. One way to do this is setting up a voicemail box that is only accessible by Security or HR.

Training Program

Once we have our policies in place, it is time to train everyone. Training needs to start at the top. Executives are trained first to get their buy-in and support. Supervisors and managers need training in leadership, prevention, and awareness. Leadership training includes proper counseling techniques, terminations and layoffs, hiring and interviewing, etc. Prevention includes how to intervene in a violent situation, de-escalating a violent employee, and avoiding mistakes that create a violent or uncomfortable atmosphere. Awareness training is most of the information contained in this section of the book. All employees should know what causes violent behavior, how to recognize it, and how to report it.

Conflict resolution training is not only good for guest services and handling complaints, but supervisors and co-workers can use it to maintain peace in the work area. Employee assistance programs should be made clear to every employee so supervisors and co-workers can see the value in this free service. Active shooter training and response to other emergencies should be given to all employees so they know what to do in the event there is a dangerous episode while at work. Finally, communication should be included in this training. Where do employees go to report violence? What type of violence do they report? Who has to be notified? What if there is an incident off-duty?

As I mentioned before, *document* all training.

Threat Management Team (TMT)

Also called Threat Assessment Teams (TATs), this is one of the solutions I mentioned earlier that was developed by the Postal Commission. The TMT or TAT is made up of HR, Legal, Safety, Security, Employee Assistance Program (EAP), and even medical professionals from your company or from outside. When a report of violence or a potentially violent person is identified, this team is assembled to review the case. They can come up with alternatives to termination and a comprehensive course of action that is in everyone's interest. Some of their options are to recommend medical or psychological treatment, to require a fit-for-duty evaluation, reassignment of the offender, anger management training, and many other clever ideas.

This team manages the prevention program to keep it current by making changes. In the event of a major violent incident, this team would communicate with staff, the media, and police to control information going out.

DOMESTIC VIOLENCE

Most of the prevention methods we discussed previously are related to Type III Workplace Violence—the disgruntled employee. Type IV, as you recall, was violence from a domestic situation involving an employee. In that type of violence, we often do not know the aggressor and certainly do not have any control over him, so our first step is to identify the victim. First, here is a very brief history.

Domestic violence in the workplace does not always get the same headlines because there is generally only one victim. But, as we all know, everyone in the workplace can be traumatized or even injured or killed as a result of this type of violence. Over the past 30 years, society has taken a very strong stand against domestic violence. Restraining orders are handled as a matter of routine, and friends, neighbors, and relatives of victims tend to be more aware and more willing to assist someone who is being abused. Unfortunately for us, the aggressor has learned that it is much easier to abuse the victim at work than at home. There are no family members, dogs, or alarm systems to protect the victim and the aggressor knows right where to find her.

Here are some statistics: 74 percent of domestic violence victims are harassed at work, 64 percent of domestic violence victims report that their job was adversely affected by their attacker, 83 percent of EAP referrals are for domestic violence, and 15 percent of women who die on the job are killed by their abuser.

Relating back to our risk assessment in Chapter 1, we need to do something to mitigate this type of violence. Our first step is to identify the victim (because we do not know the aggressor in most cases). Most people have been exposed to domestic violence enough to know that a victim experiences unexplained bruises, absences, and anxiety. Their lack of concentration or disruptive phone calls and visits affect their job performance. The best way to identify a victim is to just ask them. What? HR always says we cannot ask about someone's personal life. Of course you can. If there is something affecting a person's job performance, you can certainly ask what it is.

Once we identify a victim, we need to help them help themselves. As mentioned before, this is not only for them but also to protect our other employees. We can help someone get a restraining order by walking her through the process, going with her to court, or giving her work time to go to court. If a regular restraining order does not suffice, some states allow companies to get a restraining order. This takes the heat off the employee and puts it on you.

Other options include the EAP or other counseling, increased security such as escorts to the vehicle, panic alarms, and special parking arrangements. HR can consider temporary reassignment of the victim to get her out of public areas or even relocation to another property.

As a last resort, there is termination. That's right: termination. If you have a victim who is being beaten at home, receiving threats that her boyfriend will kill her at work, and she is doing nothing to help you prevent the problem, you may have no other choice but to terminate her. This is better than putting all of your other employees in danger and disrupting the business. Tell a victim that this is an option, and that may solve the entire problem.

Our final safety topic in this chapter is not related to violence or accidents because it is environmental. Natural hazards, like weather and bugs, are hardly preventable, so awareness, preparation, and reaction are keys to keeping everyone healthy.

BED BUGS

Bed bugs not only make the occasional appearance in hotel rooms, but also they have recently been infesting news reports and blogs. Although no one has come out and reported an epidemic or widespread infestation, the perception is clear. Sometimes in the tourism business, perception is more important than reality. And the perception now seems to be that it is a big problem. One recently published list of the 15 worst cities for bed bugs seemed directly proportional to population, with New York at the top, so it is difficult to see any trends.

Provided here are some facts about bed bugs that do not come from the people paid to eradicate them or from the agencies that spread the news. I hope that you will be able to use this reality at your facility to change the perception and deal with this issue.

Bed bugs are tiny flat insects that resemble a small version of a cockroach. They feed on the blood of mammals. They do not fly but tend to travel on humans and in their luggage. Their small, flat shape allows them to crawl into mattresses and crevices so that they are virtually invisible until they come out to feed. They gorge on humans much like a mosquito, digging their elongated beak into the skin, and drawing blood for as long as 10 minutes. The "bite" is usually not felt and occurs at night when they prefer to come out of hiding. Although they draw blood, they are not known for carrying disease.

The insects are usually found in and around mattresses and are distinguished by their small dots of brown excrement or reddish blood smears. They do not have nests or colonies but will congregate in those dark places near their feed. Due to their size and hiding places, they are best discovered by a trained professional.

Bed bugs have been around for centuries and were almost completely eradicated in the early 1950s with the use of DDT. This did not apply to other parts of the world where they have continued to breed. The recent resurgence may be due to increased world travel. Bed bugs spread just like a virus by piggybacking onto a traveler or his luggage. They can be found in hotels, airplanes, and other tourist locations. However, bed bugs also are prevalent in households and, unlike cockroaches that are attracted to filth, they just want blood, so they can be found in the cleanest of environments.

Prevention of bedbugs is almost impossible, but the best method is finding them and destroying them before they move on. Once again, a professional exterminator who knows where to look and how to destroy them does this. Besides poison, bed bugs can be killed by exposure to heat over 120° for at least 10 minutes. Clothes can be washed in hot water or even just dried in a hot clothes dryer. Other items such as electronics that cannot be exposed to water or a dryer can be placed in a plastic bag in the sun or a hot car.

Hotel managers should consult their professional pest control company before they have a bed bug complaint to devise a plan that eliminates the problem while caring for their guests. The exterminator may recommend destroying items such as mattresses and furniture that are infested as they are difficult items to treat. The hotel should make arrangements for the guests' belongings and other items to avoid spreading the problem. And don't forget that if bed bugs are in one room, they are likely in adjacent rooms. This may mean treating or inspecting as many as nine rooms (the infected room, one on each side, and the rooms immediately above and below those rooms).

Section 3

Physical Security

8

Patrol Procedures

HOSPITALITY, *n.* The virtue which induces us to feed and lodge certain persons who are not in need of food and lodging.

Ambrose Bierce, writer

This chapter will look at the different types of patrol or posts you will use at your facility. Then, we will look at techniques and procedures for situations that you may encounter in just about every area of the property.

POSTS

Every area (see textbox) of the property will have a committed officer on post, a regular patrol, or it will be part of some patrol route. As discussed in Chapter 2, some areas will have other layers of security as their primary protection, but we still have to physically check every nook and cranny of the property on a regular basis. Any fixed post or patrol route is called a Post.

Is there some place on your property that is not patrolled by security? I hope not. While some public areas are more prone to risk, every square foot of the building and landscape could potentially have a problem. Basement areas, boiler rooms, electrical closets, roofs, storage sheds, catwalks, offices, and walk-in refrigerators should be on some patrol schedule, even if it is once a day. Let your imagination run for just a minute as to what could happen in these areas. Some examples of things that happen in these unpatrolled areas are safety issues, such as leaks or cracks, unauthorized sleeping areas for employees, drug labs, sexual assault hiding places, hiding stolen property, and other illegal or risky activity. If you can think of it, someone else already has. Employees who know Security may stop by at strange intervals will not take the risk.

A fixed post is a guard shack, a security podium, a desk, or someplace where an officer is assigned all the time. A modified fixed post might be one that is manned at certain times and left to regular patrol at others, such as at a swimming pool. Fixed posts are used for high-risk areas or others where the risk can only be reduced by having constant attention. Access control is the most common reason for a fixed post. Of course, modern technology allows for using remote cameras, card swipers, and a myriad of high-tech devices. The company and the Security Director use the Security Plan to decide which is better based on cost, effectiveness, and image. The cost of a technological solution can usually be justified with labor savings, but sometimes loses to the more subjective live human. Thus far, there is no technology to replace reasoning, evaluation, and the welcoming nature of a friendly face. We have to keep in mind it is a hotel for leisure, not a storage site for nuclear weapons, so the hospitable human may be more appropriate even if more expensive.

Regular Patrol is an area that is part of a fixed route or group of posts that are visited by an officer on a regular basis. Random Patrol is not a good term to use because it denotes that the area might be patrolled only if randomly selected. The frequency of the patrol might change from one round to another, but on average, it should remain constant. While the fixed post requires one person to cover it, the patrol point is one of several posts covered by one officer. So, once the determination is made to make it a patrol point, the next decision is how many points and what type of frequency are necessary to mitigate the risk. This is discussed further in Chapter 2. One floor of a hotel is an example of a patrol point. It would be inefficient to make a hotel floor a fixed post (unless a dignitary staying there increases the risk). However, one officer might patrol all the floors or a group of floors on a regular basis. This is called a patrol post.

Patrol frequency is subjective and should be decided based on a couple of factors. First, check the patrol frequency being used by hotels in the same market or even across the country. Second, consult counsel to find their comfort level. They will be the ones defending the patrol frequency in court, so they should have an idea of what judges and juries find acceptable. Most hotels will use a one- or two-hour patrol interval; that is, if there are no other factors such as high crime areas or lack of other security measures. You definitely do not want a patrol frequency that is less than the competition.

Random Patrol is a term that I discourage using in your Security Plan, manual, official memos, or even in your vocabulary. "Random" denotes that there is no regularity or consistency. Imagine yourself on the witness stand answering this question: "Why did you decide to randomly patrol the area where my client was assaulted rather than patrol it regularly?" You and I both know by "random" we mean "without a pattern," but the meaning can be used against you.

Another phrase I like to avoid is "short-handed." I hear this in every security department I have ever visited. Once again, imagine yourself explaining why you were short-handed when my client was raped. Is it because you put money above the safety of your guests? There is no right answer. Get your staff and yourself accustomed to saying that you are properly staffed. Put yourself in the habit of explaining every decision you make while on the witness stand. You might just change your perspective.

POST ORDERS

Post orders are a set of instructions for each post. (Remember that a post is a place or area that has an officer assigned to it.) Post orders are included in our Security Manual (Chapter 4) and are meant to be given to officers who work a post so that they know what their duties and responsibilities are.

Post orders should be written for every post, even if that post is not always manned or is sometimes combined with other posts. For example, you may have a patrol area that covers the perimeter, valet, lobby, and restaurant. That patrolling officer would adhere to the post orders for each of those posts. It is less complicated if your post orders are individual to each of those areas. There is no reason to get too lavish or long-winded when writing a post order. One page generally does it, and the format looks something like a job description—with bullet points. Start with a description of the post. A post order example is included in the textbox below.

POST ORDERS—HOTEL LOBBY

The lobby post includes the area commonly referred to as the "lobby," which is the main entrance of the building, the elevator foyer, front desk, bell desk, and associated back work and storage areas.

- Maintain high visibility walking and standing patrol of all lobby areas.
- Greet and assist guests.
- Observe, identify, and remove those persons not authorized or engaged in undesirable activity.
- Identify and correct unsafe conditions.
- Observe that employees are properly performing their duties and report issues to the contrary.
- Observe that the assets of the company are not exposed to unnecessary risk and are protected.
- Ensure that queue lines for front desk and elevators are neat and organized.
- Address all guest concerns and needs.

PATROL PROCEDURES

Many security officers are assigned to a post or sent out to "rove" or "randomly patrol" on their own without knowing what to look for. They may have had some training, but have they ever been told what exactly they are patrolling? In the last section, I introduced post orders, which are the specific assignments or duties to be performed at a specific post. Later, we will also talk about certain situations and how to handle them.

As for patrol techniques, they can and should be discussed in the classroom setting, but you will need to devote some field time to these practices. Without a consistent, documented training process for patrol procedures, you are likely to end up with each officer doing his or her own thing. Ask yourself if you have these officers working for you or if you have seen them working elsewhere.

Officer Stare stands at his post with a fixed gaze into the distance. He is making eye contact with no one, watching nothing, and probably thinking about his big date coming up or the poker game he lost last night. *Officer Miner* walks through the building looking at the floor. She is probably looking for money, but maybe she has poor eyesight and the carpet is the only thing in focus. Perhaps she is thinking about her date with Officer Stare. Each of these officers is working at about 50 percent because they are being seen, which is good, but they are seeing nothing.

Officer Rookie is walking through another part of the building, one hand on his shoulder microphone and the other on his radio volume control. His head is moving around in circles like a ship's radar. He stops each time someone says something on his radio because he cannot walk and listen simultaneously. He is so preoccupied trying to see everything that he is not seeing anything. If there is a guest looking for an elevator, he will never know it and has no time to stop anyway. Finally, there is *Officer Cool*. He is so slick, walking through the building, that nobody dares try anything on his post. His John Wayne swagger leads him to every pretty girl in the building and he will make sure they get his undivided attention. Somebody needs to unlock the trash dock? Officer Cool will wait for Officer Rookie to answer that call because he has to keep his rhythm going.

These are exaggerations, but I see the same officers just about everywhere I go. Without established patrol procedures, you will get results like these and your staff will be operating at about 50 percent—being seen, receiving calls, but initiating nothing. Security officers need specific tasks to stay focused. They need to be looking for something. When you provide expectations for patrol, you can measure the results. Here are some examples of patrol techniques employed by effective officers. Use as many as your staff can handle.

Safety—This is one of the primary duties of security officers. Each department in your organization may or may not do safety inspections, so the security officer needs to incorporate this into his or her regular patrol. The obvious things to check are fire extinguishers, blocked access, broken equipment, water leaks, water spills, etc. More subtle things to check are locks and pressure gauges on wet standpipes,

A common defense to injury claims is the "open and obvious" doctrine. This means that if a hazard is open and obvious, there should be no fault on the property owner for injuries suffered in an accident. For example, a light pole in the middle of a parking lot is in the open and obvious, so if you run into it, it is your own fault. However, if there is no lighting in the parking lot and a pothole is obscured by darkness, a fall into the hole might be blamed on management.

Part of a Risk Assessment is to inspect each area for hazards, both obvious and discrete, and take reasonable measures to prevent accidents around them. Light poles, although visible and obvious, sometimes have reflective tape at eye level or brightly painted poles around them just to be sure. Daily inspections of every area should be conducted to find new hazards, such as potholes, spills, or broken tiles, so that they can be repaired or marked to prevent injuries. Defense of these more-than-reasonable measures is much easier than admitting you were not aware of them.

house phones, auto door closures, loose handrails, broken floor tiles, etc. Officers should be encouraged to use facilities that guests and employees use so they can be checked and properly patrolled.

Parking—After some time patrolling a parking lot, officers get bored and lazy and ultimately get tunnel vision. They turn into one of those 50-percent efficient officers. Cars start to look the same and a broken window or suspicious person would hardly be noticed. Try assigning specific tasks to officers to force them to get that neck moving: counts of cars, checking for sleeping persons in vehicles, inspecting permits or license plates for parking authorization, and checking for abandoned vehicles. This is not busy work, but good supervision. I had a supervisor that used to hide a purse near a car or in a stairwell to see how long it would take an officer to find it. The officer who found it would get a reward. Others would compete and the result was a more thorough patrol.

Headcounts—As I mentioned previously, counting is a great way to ensure officers check every public area as well as make eye contact. Guests who see officers looking at every single guest assume that they are very diligent and are giving everyone their full attention. One of the men at my church used to walk up and down the aisles of pews, very slowly, looking at every parishioner. For several weeks, I thought he was some self-appointed church security officer. I finally realized he was performing a headcount. I don't think he intended to look so vigilant, but I figured if anyone got out of line, he would be the one to deal with them. He was providing security and probably did not know it.

Purse advisories—Most guests (not just the ones with purses) travel with a false sense of security. I think they feel that they are on vacation and they have left their personal security in our hands. This is evident by most guests' carelessness in the most basic situations. People walk away from their luggage, leave their doors open, and forget to lock their cars—things they would never forget at home.

In casinos, nightclubs, restaurants, and other crowded venues, it is common for thieves of opportunity to patrol the area looking for unattended purses or easily distracted persons not holding their purse. It is amazing how easy it is to distract someone on one side, while another grabs the purse on the opposite side and leaves without being noticed. In restaurants, the purse always goes on the back of the chair or on the floor—easy pickins'. A great prevention effort is to have officers who notice the unattended purse remind the guest to hold it. Write this in your daily log to show how many crimes you prevented. This also guarantees your officer is doing more than wandering through the restaurant aimlessly. The careless guest is left with a comfortable feeling that this place really cares about safety.

Loiterers—Persons hanging out with no business are opportunists, vagrants, or both. Of course, we encourage our guests to hang out with lounges, sofas in the lobby, and benches scattered here and there. These are guests, they are welcome, and we are happy to have them. The loiterers are taking up space, making the environment look bad, and will not pass up an opportunity for theft if it presents itself. As we discuss in Behavioral Recognition, later in this chapter, these folks need to be challenged. We always start friendly because it may be a guest. Create a culture

among your staff where guests are welcomed enthusiastically, and vagrants are
expelled with equal exuberance.

Eye contact—There is nothing as powerful as eye contact. A good hard look in the eye
will comfort a guest and dissuade an undesirable. Remember, we looked for this
trait during the recruitment process because you cannot train it. The officers who
do it well enjoy it and will not be ones who give you 50 percent. Encourage this
practice with everyone every time.

Greeting—The greeting is also part of that behavioral recognition and is just good
customer service. Encourage officers to greet everyone within a certain proximity.
I am not too fond of the retail stores that require that every customer be greeted
because it does not seem genuine. However, if you can have a general policy that
requires it, your staff will appear friendlier and your patrol more efficient.

HOTEL POLICIES AND PROCEDURES

This section looks at each area of the hotel property and examines the risks, threats, and
other guest issues and how they can be mitigated or addressed through policies and
security actions. Hotel policies require some collaboration between Security, Front Desk,
Housekeeping, and other departments. Sometimes they may be the policies of one department or another and even enforced by any of these involved departments, but the common
goal is security. The following recommendations are made with this in mind.

Room Entry

We could easily devote an entire chapter to this subject and still walk away from it confused and arguing. Therefore, our purpose here will be to keep the Security department
out of trouble while still respecting the guest's privacy. There are many situations for hotel
personnel to enter rooms. They should always either be business-related or for emergencies. Probable cause and the Fourth Amendment are for police officers and crime investigations, so focus on common sense and ordinary business purposes. Here are some
scenarios you may encounter and how to deal with them.

The housekeeper tells you that she saw a white powdery substance on the armoire
while cleaning the room. The guest is out and the housekeeper has already closed the
door. Consider locking the room so that you can inquire when the guest returns as to the
nature of the substance. It might be baby powder or an illicit substance. Your concern is
that it might be a dangerous substance and you don't want your staff being subjected to it.
The guest can convince you it is harmless, make it disappear, or you can ask the guest to
leave for refusing to satisfy your safety concerns.

A security officer smells smoke coming from a particular room. You have knocked
and received no response. There is a Do-Not-Disturb sign on the door. You can absolutely
enter this room by whatever means necessary because you are concerned for the safety of
the guests and hotel property.

A neighboring guest says she heard a child screaming from a room and it sounded like he was in distress. Now you hear nothing. Of course, you can enter this room after knocking and calling the room.

The front desk clerk says he heard two guests checking into a particular room talking about killing someone at a political speech the next day. There is no reason to enter the room, as there is no emergency in the room. This situation might be better handled by notifying the proper authorities.

The bell person says she has seen a female who continually brings different men to her room. She suspects the woman is a prostitute and is using the hotel room for this activity. Once again, we are not police officers, there is no emergency, and there is no business-related reason to speak to this guest about the accusation. Depending on your local police department's policy on prostitution, you may want to contact them.

A police detective contacts you and says that a guest in a particular room has set up a check-printing operation and is engaged in forgery crimes from the room. He asks that we find a reason to enter the room and verify if the equipment is there. This is a criminal matter and you acting as an agent of the police will not only violate the guest's rights, but may nullify any evidence that comes from your warrantless search. Kindly remind the officer that he needs to follow his department's procedures and obtain a warrant.

The local fire department calls you and says they received a call from a relative of a guest in a certain room. They said they received a text message from the room occupant that he was going to take an overdose of pills to commit suicide. This is an emergency and entering the room is reasonable.

You find the above room empty, except for the guest's luggage, so you decide to search the drawers to make sure there are no weapons or drugs. This is violating the guest's privacy and is not an emergency. Do not search anyone's room without permission.

Note that we avoid acting as agents of the police and searching for criminal activity. Our concern is always safety.

Housekeeping

Guests cannot refuse service for more than three consecutive days. Housekeeping will need to enter the room for a visual inspection on the third day. Housekeepers are looking

In 2011, a couple of high-profile housekeeper assault incidents caused everyone to look at housekeeping procedures. Housekeepers being assaulted or harassed is not a new problem, but when something garners that much attention, the company needs to address it to prevent litigation of foreseeability (discussed in Chapter 1). These in-room assaults are easily prevented with strong procedures that are followed consistently. Develop safety programs and policies that will keep your housekeepers out of trouble. Some of these are not using a master key to allow entry to a guest; not cleaning a room or bringing in supplies while the guest is present; not entering a guest room alone when the guest is present, etc. These procedures will not only protect a guest-room attendant, but also will protect the guest from a bad employee.

for damage, health hazards, and criminal or suspicious activity. Some guests are a bit strange about this privacy, so let them have the three days, but let them know in advance that it will not be longer than that.

Marijuana

Marijuana is a controversial substance and its legality depends on your jurisdiction. (Although, to date, the federal government still considers it an illegal substance.) Whether or not it is legal, the odor is offensive to most people and difficult to eradicate. An easy way to resolve this issue is to make the smoking of marijuana or any similar substance against hotel policy. When guests are caught smoking in a room, the options are eviction or the payment of a deep cleaning fee. The threat of calling the police and tying up resources is eliminated. Remember, it is not our job to enforce laws. As a hotel, our aversion to marijuana is not its legality, but its offense to our guests and the damage it causes to our carpet and drapes.

Service Animals

Laws on service animals are not very clear. Unfortunately, interpretation of HPPA (Healthcare Patient Portability Act) makes it illegal to ask a person about their disability that requires an animal. The best advice I have seen on the subject of animals on the property is to ask the guest if the animal is a service animal. If they say "Yes," then the conversation ends and they can have a nice day on your property with their service animal. You cannot ask what service the animal provides or why the guest needs the animal. Just leave it alone. Now, if an animal causes a disturbance, such as excessive barking, uncontrolled soiling, or biting persons, then you can absolutely have the owner remove the animal because the hazard trumps the need for the service. Note that I mentioned animals instead of dogs. All kinds of animals are trained to be service pets these days.

As for other pets, this is a policy decision of the hotel and I am sure that carpet cleaning, damage to furniture, and excessive noise will be taken into consideration if animals are permitted in the hotel room.

Wheelchairs or Other Mobility Devices

This policy should be handled very similar to the service animal. If someone is riding in a wheelchair, it is best not to even inquire as to his or her need for the device. Just accommodate it. The exception, just like the animals, is if the device is a hazard. Riding a wheelchair on the escalator or speeding through your property on a Segway are hazardous activities. Use caution when dealing with these situations. A warning is more reasonable than kicking someone out on the first offense.

Parties in a Room

It is better to have a policy that prohibits excessive noise than one that prohibits having a good time. We want people to enjoy themselves and we even provide the ice. Parties, then, should not be forbidden. If there are 10 people in a room and there are complaints from the neighbors after midnight, then that is something you do not want. A good policy is the Three Strikes Rule. First strike goes like this: "I see you are enjoying yourselves, but the noise is disturbing the other guests. You can go to the lounge downstairs, or perhaps call it a night." Second strike is sterner: "Folks, I asked you nicely the first time. Now I must insist that everyone except the registered guests leave immediately. If I have to come back here tonight, you will all have to leave." Depending on the cooperation of the guests, time of day, and type of party, you may only have two strikes (one warning), or even no warning. This is a discretionary call by the security or hotel manager.

Underage Drinkers

It is too common to see persons under 18 drinking in a room. It may be that an adult rented the room for them or the adult is actually hosting the party. This situation is full of ramifications and you do not want the responsibility of intoxicated minors. As soon as you enter the scene as the responsible adult, they are your responsibility and you need that "monkey" off your back. If you do nothing, you are now contributing to their delinquency and guess whom the parents will go after when something bad happens? You need to notify the parents or police. Get one or the other there and document everything. If a minor does not want to stick around and wait for the police, hold on to them (more on minors later in this chapter). You are far more reasonable to make a good faith detention of intoxicated minors than you would be in letting them go on their own.

Domestic Fights

Next to parties, your most common disturbance in a hotel may be the domestic fight. These are difficult situations with which to deal, so keep it simple by keeping our objective in mind: protecting our assets. Police officers have extra concerns when dealing with these because they have to enforce certain laws created just for domestic violence. We do not have that burden, so our response is simpler. First, remember safety for your staff. Make sure at least two officers respond to this type of call. (If you are not adequately staffed and trained, call the police, observe, and report.) Second, go to the room and listen for fighting, screaming, yelling, physical contact, etc. If nothing is heard, check with the reporting guest and find out exactly what was heard. A phone call to the room may be in order before knocking: "This is hotel security. Can you please meet our officers at the door?"

The aggressor usually opens the door. Remember your intentions. You are checking that nobody is in danger and other guests are not disturbed. Inform the guest that neighbors reported a disturbance and you need to make sure everyone is okay. You do not need to do any investigation. You are not going to enforce any laws or take anybody to jail. This will befriend you with both parties. Ask both parties if they want to call the police. You can ask the "victim" in private if you think necessary to get an accurate response, but if he or she is an adult they can decide for themselves. Yes, even if there are signs of a physical fight. Many security officers are under the mistaken impression that they have a duty to arrest or call the police if one party shows signs of a battery. With no police being requested, we just want the disturbance to cease immediately. If we have to come back to this room, all parties will be evicted and the police may be called.

This call, and all disturbance calls, requires a follow-up. After terminating your conversation with the guest, stay near the room for a minute or two. If it starts back up again, that is your eviction right there. If all is quiet, wait about 15 minutes and return to the room to make sure it is still quiet. This is done for the safety of the guests, but also because if a disturbance continues after you have been there, the reporting guest and other neighbors are going to assume that you are taking no action and they will be very dissatisfied with their hotel stay. In fact, a phone call (not direct contact) with the reporting party is a good guest service. Let them know that everyone is okay, you gave the other guest a warning, and that they should call if they hear anything else. You may want to offer them a different room.

Cooking and Other Unsafe Practices

Many guests prefer to bring their own food and prepare it in the room. It is common to see guests "smuggle" in rice cookers, toasters, and even microwave ovens. Whether or not you provide these items or a full kitchen in the guest room, you should discourage guests from bringing and using these items. Safety hazards, such as overloaded electrical circuits, inadequate extension cords, and faulty heating elements, are a fire hazard. Guest rooms are not properly ventilated to deal with smoke and especially an open flame or accidental fire from burning the toast. Of course, the odor of cooking may be offensive to other guests and is difficult to get out of carpets, drapes, and linen.

I have seen guests use their rooms as a laboratory, a machine shop, and even a methamphetamine lab. These practices make for a difficult mess and involve chemicals and substances that might be toxic and are definitely offensive to other guests. Prohibit anything involving chemicals from tuning up bicycles to waxing surfboards. These odors would be a reason for security to enter a guest room without permission.

Door Ajar

The most common hotel crime is burglary. Theft from rooms is not always an "inside" job as most guests think. It is usually a result of the guest leaving the door open and rarely by lock-picking or forced entry, as they will allege. You may have (and should have) spring hinges that automatically close a door that is opened more than 45 degrees. Guests still leave doors ajar accidentally when they leave the room. The hinge may be faulty, or the guest is walking out, holding the door for the rest of the family, or hesitating to make sure he has his keys, and the door closes and the latch hits the strike plate without catching. Housekeepers may be guilty of this as well, either accidentally leaving the door open or intentionally leaving it open so they do not need their key.

Door pushers are folks who cruise your hotel hallways looking for doors left ajar. The amateurs will see a door open, go in, grab what they can, and flee. The more refined burglars will work in teams. The scout walks the halls, maybe under the guise of sliding coupons under the door, and leaves a signal for the actual thief. The signal might be to leave the coupon sticking out into the hallway, or a mark on the door. There may even be a third member of the team that picks up the stolen merchandise after the burglar leaves it behind that big potted plant in the elevator lobby or the vending machines.

There are three effective ways of dealing with these thieves. One is the key checkpoint at the elevator lobby on the main floor. This is not a foolproof method, but has its advantages. Two is Hotel Patrol. Security officers patrolling the hotel need to be on the lookout for doors left ajar and act accordingly to secure the room. Third is employee awareness. Housekeepers should be made aware of this problem and make sure they secure all doors and keep watch for guests leaving doors open. Housekeeping, Engineering, and Security should work together to inspect spring hinges regularly and at every opportunity to make sure they close at an acceptable opening.

> In the early 1990s, a woman returning to her hotel room from a night in the casino inadvertently left her room door open. As she entered, she let the door close, and it did not latch. Two men, who had followed her from the casino, saw that the door did not secure, entered her room, and raped and robbed her. The lawsuit that followed probed every aspect of security in the hotel. Door hinge springs were examined and compared to hinges in other hotels, security staffing in the hotel was scrutinized, overtime and call-off policies were examined, and minimum staffing for the entire property was criticized.
>
> Besides having regular patrol that looks for open doors, a routine maintenance or inspection schedule of doors is recommended.

Welfare Check

Requests for Security to enter a room are numerous. The room may be locked from the inside and Housekeeping cannot enter. A relative may be unable to find or contact their loved one, or the police may have received a call. Call the room first just to be sure. This will cover you in case you walk in on someone in a compromised position. Take a witness (or a backup if it is a possibly dangerous situation like a suicide). Knock loudly and announce "Hotel Security." Open the door and announce again. Keep announcing as you slowly enter. Remember why you entered the room and leave once you have concluded that there is no emergency. We have no right to open drawers or search luggage. Remember, it is reasonable to expect Security to enter a room to check on someone's well-being, but not to search for contraband.

Privacy

A guest's room is his castle. It really is. As far as the law is concerned, people are protected in a hotel room as they are in their house. That means you cannot just enter a room for no reason. In fact, it has to be one of certain reasons.

Danger—Smelling fire, hearing gunshots, screams for help, etc.
Housekeeping—Guest has not answered phone or calls for service after a preset amount of time. The first time is not good enough. It has to be long enough where a reasonable person would be worried for the guest's safety.

Eviction—You already have a reason to remove the guest, such as the Three Strikes rule explained in this section.

Lock-out—Explained in this section.

Reasons you cannot enter a room are:

Police request—If the police are looking for someone and they think he is in that room, it requires a warrant and the police should not even ask.

Suspected criminal activity—You think a guest is printing bad checks. There is no danger to anyone. Call the police and let them figure it out.

Unknown Guest

The more guest rooms you have, the more chance there is for errors with reservations and check-ins. From time to time, the Front Desk will question if a certain room is occupied, where they put a certain guest, or why an unoccupied room has luggage or persons in it. The rack clerk or hotel manager will generally resolve this with a phone call and some research. On rare occasions, they may ask Security to enter a room to determine who is in there or to read the name on the luggage. As mentioned in the "Privacy" section, a guest's room is his castle and a hotel error is not reason enough to enter a room. Here are some policy suggestions to resolve this problem.

1. Determine your hotel's night privacy time: a period each night when you will not disturb a guest with phone calls or door knocks unless it is an emergency (9 p.m. to 8 a.m., for example). During this time, if the Front Desk asks you to bother a guest to determine his or her identity, remind them of this policy and leave the guest undisturbed until morning. The worst that will happen is someone gets a free night out of you. Otherwise, you disturb a sleeping guest, possibly lose a customer for life, and look like an idiot.
2. During business hours, start by asking Housekeeping. The Front Desk has likely done this already, but maybe they did not ask the actual maid on that floor. They may have seen the guest or belongings in the room.
3. Call the room before making contact. The Front Desk likely did this already, but security should always do this before entering a room.
4. Knock on the door. If someone is there, you certainly have the right to identify him or her. Remember, the person is probably not a criminal. Treat him or her like a valued guest.
5. Do not enter the room. If it is normal housekeeping hours, let the housekeeper enter or enter with him or her. Do not go through anyone's belongings. Looking at a luggage tag should suffice. If you cannot determine identity from anything in plain sight, leave the room with everything intact and lock the room. This will force the guest to call for assistance when he or she returns. At that time, the guest may just think the key is malfunctioning. Verify the person's identity, okay it with the Front Desk, and let the person in. No harm—no foul. Alternatively, you can tell the guest exactly what happened. That may make the hotel look inept, but most people would understand.

6. If it is not housekeeping hours (swing shift), and nobody answers, you do not have a legitimate reason to enter the room. Of course, you could enter the room to see if someone is incapacitated. Rather than doing that, it is safer to just lock the room and await the guest's return as mentioned previously. This beats walking in on Mr. Smith's collection of panty hose and sexy lingerie.

Room Inventories

It is common for the Front Desk to have you lock out a room in which the guest has not paid. This procedure, if done consistently, is harmless and painless. Generally, a guest is due to check out in the morning. Housekeeping will report to the Front Desk sometime before they go home that the room is still occupied. The Front Desk will generally wait until early evening and if they have not heard from the guest they will ask Security to lock the room out.

This is best done with a witness. A second Security officer or even another hotel employee will suffice. Follow your room entry policy. One of three things will be apparent upon entering the room. It will be empty of personal belongings. In that case, it can be left as is and Housekeeping informed of its availability. If there is luggage or belongings, but no people, we generally lock the room. If there are people in the room, call the Front Desk for their advice. They will ask the guest to pay for another night, to leave as soon as possible, or apologize for a bookkeeping error made by the hotel.

The hotel, depending on the need for the room, will ask Security to remove the belongings from the room. This is called a room inventory. Room inventories should be done by two persons, properly documented, and the property secured. Lost and Found is the most logical place to secure these items, not at the Bell Desk where everyone has access to them. Belongings are kept for a reasonable amount of time—30, 60, or 90 days and then sold or given to charity. Keep in mind, the guest may be in the hospital, in jail, or dead. I have seen people return up to 6 months later. If a guest returns in the next day or two, the Front Desk will negotiate payment for the room and have you return the items to the guest. Have the guest sign for the items and retain this documentation.

Weapons

Occasionally, guests will bring weapons to their room for a variety of reasons. Normally, we will not even know about it unless they are careless enough to leave them out and the housekeeper finds them. There are a few valid reasons for this and they are both legal. One reason might be that your guest is a police officer and carries the weapon as part of his or her normal routine. A good cop will not leave a gun in the room, but there may be an exception like going to the pool. The second common reason for finding a gun is that many people practice their Second Amendment right to bring a gun into a hotel room for personal protection. As with most rights, there come some common sense obligations such as preventing someone like a housekeeper from finding it. The third possibility is that your guest is a criminal intending to use the gun for some unlawful activity or already has and is running from the law.

137

Whatever the reason for the gun in the room, the response is generally the same. First, do not touch it. Leave it in place and lock the room. When the guest returns, explain your concern for having a firearm in plain sight in the room where the maid has access to it. Suggest (insist) that the gun be placed in the room safe, the hotel safe, your security fire-arms storage (yes, you should have one just for this situation), or their car. If they really want to keep it in their room, they should place it out of sight in their luggage. Remind them of your hotel policy that weapons may not be carried on the premises. (You can have a rule like this on private property.)

Make sure housekeepers know this policy, and always tell you about guns in rooms and never touch them. If you have some feeling or reason to believe that the gun is unlaw-ful, stolen, or the carrier is a criminal, there is no harm in notifying the police. They can certainly run the name you give them, or come out and speak to the guest and inform him or her of local laws regarding firearms.

As for other weapons, such as knives, pepper spray, impact weapons, martial arts objects, and the like, treat them like guns and have the guest stow them for the safety of your staff.

Room Thefts

Guests will report missing property on a frequent basis. It is generally blamed on Housekeeping. (Internal investigations are discussed in Chapter 11.) There are two addi-tional common explanations for these losses. They are both caused by guest error.

First is a theft by someone known to the guest—an "inside" job. Children, boyfriends, or roommates all occasionally steal from each other. Alternatively, it may be that they don't actually steal it at all, but pack it in the wrong place or lose it. It is difficult to control or know the actions of third parties, which is why you cannot accept blame for these losses. You can help them to prevent these losses by offering room safes or safe deposit boxes. Some jurisdictions actually require this as a condition of limiting your liability.

Many hotels issue safety tips with the room keys or in the room reminding guests not to leave their room receipt with their keys, not to be followed or fooled into giving out their room number, and so on.

The second common reason for loss in a room is the door pusher as described previously.

Violent Crimes

Throughout this section, we have looked at some of the problems that occur in a hotel. The most severe is violent crime. In fact, most of Chapters 1 and 2 and many other parts of this book are about preventing these incidents. If you are sued, it will likely be a result of an assault, robbery, or other violent act that you should have prevented. We have already looked at several measures that prevent crime in the hotel, such as locks, lighting, cameras, and certain policies. By far, the most important is human patrol. Your hotel should have some type of regular patrol, hopefully with an associated tracking system.

Security officers on patrol serve two purposes, as they do in other patrol areas. First is visibility. A known, visible, uniformed officer patrolling guest-room floors is a deter-rent. I refer to this as "passive patrol" and half of the job. Second is active patrol. Active patrol is the action of that roaming officer looking for problems and acting upon them.

This includes safety hazards, mechanical problems, and dangerous situations like smoke, screams for help, fights, etc. It also includes confronting strangers. This is really the heart of the entire hotel patrol: finding and challenging people in the halls. This is a way to catch door pushers, transients, and assailants lying in wait. A documented patrol of searching for and acting upon suspicious persons is one step closer to having adequate security.

> In 2011 at an Atlantic City resort, an elderly couple was leaving their room to go to breakfast. They were confronted in the hall by two robbers who forced them back into the room at gunpoint. The woman escaped the room and ran down the stairs. The two robbers went back to their own room and barricaded themselves inside until police finally apprehended them.
>
> It is impossible to prevent every incident like this in a hotel, but regular patrol, safety tips for guests, and even key inspections go a long way. (Note that the key inspection would not have prevented this crime because the suspects were actually hotel guests as well.)

Key Check Stations

Many hotels use a key inspection station to control access to the guest-room area. This is more of a visible deterrent and behavioral recognition post than it is a key inspection. The reality is that anyone can get a room key to show for entry and I guarantee prostitutes, drug dealers, burglars, and the pizza delivery guy already have them. The real intention is for the officer to give the impression of a secured hotel tower. It also allows the officer to make eye contact and briefly determine if the person with the key belongs in the hotel. As we discussed in Behavioral Recognition, more questions can be asked and information obtained.

If you decide to employ a key inspection station, ensure that the officers assigned are trained in these methods and not just looking at keys. Also, if you have these posts, ensure that you staff them regularly and put some thought into removing them. Removing any security feature because of cost will come back to bite you if something happens after you remove it. Document the success or failures of this post so you can justify removing it or keeping it.

Key inspection stations are a great show of security and an excellent opportunity to provide significant guest service. Like any staffed post, they can be expensive to operate.

RESTROOMS

Restrooms in common areas require a lot of attention from the Security Department. This is one of the few areas where we do not have cameras and our patrol of each facility is limited by the gender of our security officers. Threats we might see in our restrooms are graffiti, other vandalism, assaults, drug use and sales, and inappropriate sexual activity. (Some of these are also discussed in "Nightclubs" later in this chapter).

There are several tools we can use to defend against these threats:

Cameras cannot be used inside a restroom because there is an expectation of privacy there that cannot be invaded. One clever way of providing video coverage there is to mount cameras on the outside of the restrooms. This gives a clear image of those entering the restroom and not only enhances an investigation, but also acts as a visible deterrent to those who enter. Combined with regular patrol, the camera can be a valuable tool in catching vandals and other miscreants who think they are going unnoticed.

Patrol of the restrooms is essential whether you have cameras or not. Implement a well-documented regular patrol of EACH restroom. This patrol can be enhanced by your cleaning staff and your maintenance people by having them log their patrol of the restroom as well. Other staff members cannot replace uniformed security patrol, but they can certainly augment it. If you had an all-male security force, you would rely on these other departments to check the women's restroom for you. They can even be used to "clear" a restroom so a male officer can enter and do his own check.

Restrooms near bars or other areas where young adults and older teens congregate are prone to drug use and drug sales. Officers should be aware of what this activity looks like from the outside. Some indicators of drug activity in a restroom are: the same person entering and leaving the restroom several times in a short period; "locals" who you notice day after day using your facilities; lookouts posted at the entrance; contraband hidden beneath counters and in toiletry receptacles; two persons in the same stall. The only way to prevent drug activity is constant, vigilant patrol. When doing patrols of the other common areas, the restrooms are a good place for officers to stop and observe while they rest their legs.

Your facilities experts already know most of the anti-vandalism methods available today, but it never hurts to make sure. There are many types of wall coverings that resist graffiti and damage. If you are seeing etching of mirrors, there is an inexpensive clear film that can be applied to the glass so that it can be removed if it becomes etched. Etching is either done with a sharp tool or an etching acid available at craft stores.

The Lobby

In almost every hotel in the world, the lobby is the main entrance to the entire complex. Generally, the lobby includes the Front Desk, Bell Desk, Concierge, maybe a lounge, guestroom elevators and a connection to all of the other amenities offered on the property. This busy hub of the hotel probably does not see a fair share of violent incidents, crimes, or other undesirable activity because it is so well-patrolled by other employees and guests. However, because it is the main point of entry to the facility, it is where we can best apply our Behavioral Recognition skills. (See Behavioral Recognition later in this chapter). It also becomes an important guest service and high visibility. Even if you do not think it necessary to have an officer in this area because of the low rate of incidents, remember that it is this area which allows guests (and perpetrators) to actually see your security posture for the first time. This first time needs to make a good impression.

Patrol of the lobby, as just mentioned is primarily a guest service and "watching the front door" post. There are still many other things a security officer needs to be aware of in a common area. Safety hazards, unsecured doors, loiterers, and unattended property are some of the things a security officer will handle. These will be noted in your Post Orders for the Lobby. Post orders are discussed in detail at the beginning of this chapter.

LOST AND FOUND

Guests leave objects behind very often in hotels. Administering a lost and found program can be quite daunting. Remember the objectives—Guest Service and Protect the Assets. Make sure your lost and found procedures keep these objectives in the forefront.

- Administration—Decide who is responsible for the safeguarding of the merchandise and reuniting it with its owner. Security often handles this duty. This allows for a third party to be responsible rather than those who find the items. Housekeeping is another logical choice because they find the majority of the items and are already responsible for the guest rooms.
- Tracking—Depending on the size of your operation, you can use anything from a log book, to an electronic spreadsheet, to one of many software programs available for this purpose (see Chapter 9). Tracking information should include a description of the item, where it was found, date and time it was found, who found it, and where it is being stored. The disposition of the item should include person to whom it was returned, his or her address, ID (for verification), date and time it was returned, and whether it was returned to owner (RTO), given to finder, donated to charity, or sold.
- Found objects—The most important component of any transference of anything is to have an audit trail. This trail starts with the person finding the item. They need to begin the tracking process by completing a form or log with the item information mentioned previously. The policy needs to be clear on how they handle the item and where it is kept. Avoid allowing employees to keep items in their possession or to put them on maids' carts or storerooms where they are unsecured. Some hotels will have a runner available to transfer the item so the housekeeper can continue his or her duties. Remember, the runner and the finder both need to be identified in the tracking process.
- Valuables and cash—These items should be handled differently to avoid loss. It is best to have two persons take possession and transfer the items to safekeeping. Cash, cameras, jewelry, and electronics should not be placed into storage where any one person has exclusive access to them. Regardless of how much you trust the lost and found custodian, that is where the suspicion will fall if these items come up missing. Consider a two-department safe at the Front Desk for valuables. This is called dual custody.
- Storage—First, you will need to decide how long found items will be kept before they are disposed. Most guests will call the same day or within a week of losing an item to claim it. Thirty days is easy to organize and track if you have the storage space. You might want to save cash and valuables a bit longer just in case. Items should be organized by date found. Smaller items can be stored in something like a file cabinet and shelves in a storeroom will suffice for larger items that are left behind. (Many large hotels recover so many phone chargers that they do not even bother

logging them.) Chargers can go into a separate area because probably they will not be claimed. They can be used as an amenity for those guests who forgot to bring theirs on vacation. The storage area should have access limited to one or certain persons. Items will come up missing from this area and you need to limit the list of those under suspicion. Having one person responsible for this function is best. Access afterhours can be achieved with a dual-custody or management key.

Do the math—A 1,000-room hotel may average 10 to 50 found items per day. That is 300 to 1,500 items per month. If you have a mall, casino, nightclub, or other venue attached to your hotel, then that number could easily double. Do these calculations before configuring your storeroom.

Disposition of items—About 25 percent of items will be claimed the same day. Another 25 percent will be claimed within about a week and they will have to be mailed. Some hotels charge for this service and some provide it as an amenity. Shipping supplies and postage add up, but it should not cost a large hotel more than about $3,000 per year. You need a policy for this: who does it, and how addresses are verified. I recommend *not* blind-mailing items to the address on the registration or even calling the guest to claim the items. The address could be incorrect and either the item will be returned or you will mail it to the wrong person. Calling the guest could get a husband in trouble with his wife—or worse. You will have to be reactive on this matter and avoid complaints.

The other half of your inventory is going to be unclaimed items. You need another management policy decision here. You can donate them to charity, sell them for profit, sell them to employees, or let the employee who found it keep it. All of these options are very time-consuming and you will need to decide whether each one is worth the return. Donating to charity is a worthy cause and might be a tax write-off. Selling items on an auction or classified Web site might be lucrative, but may not be worth the labor involved. An employee rummage sale is good for morale, but also a lot of time and labor to organize. The finder will want some of the items. This encourages the employee to turn items in rather than stealing them, but it does not eliminate the theft problem.

RESTAURANTS

Security issues in restaurants are limited mostly to walkouts, employee food theft, customer disturbances, and problems associated with bars. (Bars will be discussed separately.) There is also a new concern with agro-terrorism, which is the intentional tampering with food.

Walkouts

In most jurisdictions, a walkout, or "Defrauding an Innkeeper," is defined as consuming all or part of a meal with the intent to defraud the restaurant (refuse to pay). We all have seen the tactics used in a "dine and dash." It may be a transient who never had any intention to pay and is not worried about the consequences. It may be kids who do this for a thrill and the challenge of if they can get away with it. The final offender is the person or group that does this professionally and makes a profit from it. Each of these situations is like shoplifting: You cannot prove that their intent is to defraud unless they leave the room. Chances are, even if you catch them outside, their defense will be that they forgot, they thought their companion was paying, they thought it would be charged to their room, etc. Therefore, an arrest should not be the objective. If you catch someone, working with them to make the payment will protect your assets better.

Employee Food Theft

Employees stealing food is common and comes in various forms. Employees picking food off the line, leftovers from guests, or just lying around in the kitchen must be mitigated by management and simple polices. No eating on duty, separate break rooms, and even policies about picking from the trash will solve this.

More serious is the wholesale theft of food products (and utensils) from the kitchen and storerooms. This is the sous chef's responsibility and can be controlled through proper documentation of supply use. A "backdoor pass" (a document signed by management authorizing removal of property) should be included with any food, bags, or packages taken out of the restaurant by anyone. Employee lockers should never be in the kitchen or near storerooms.

RETAIL POLICIES

Most hotels have some sort of retail footprint from a kiosk of sundries near the Front Desk, to a full-blown shopping mall. Retail has become an important revenue source for most hotels, surpassing some of the traditional generators. It is vital that you establish strong loss prevention policies in this area to protect the physical assets as well as the safety of guests and employees.

Shrinkage

Shrinkage is the amount of goods lost in a retail environment due to theft or breakage for which there is no reimbursement. Shrinkage generally counts for about 1 to 2 percent nationally, but varies widely depending on the type of store. In a hotel, the first consideration will need to be who is responsible for protecting against shrinkage. A store that leases space may be responsible for its own merchandise and employees. Or it may rely on Security to provide this function. Either way, it needs to be worked out in writing, in advance, because your officers will need to be acting as an agent of that company when making arrests or conducting investigations. If the store is owned by the hotel, then your umbrella will extend over that store as it does all the other amenities on the property.

Shoplifting

Shoplifting is what we commonly call petty larceny in a retail environment. (Theft by employees is different and is addressed later.) Petty larceny is defined by state law in most cases and is the taking of property with the intent to deprive the owner of that property. Both of these elements need to exist for a crime to occur. Larceny can be grand or petty depending on the amount of goods taken and that varies by state. There may be some other covenants associated with this crime, so make sure you are familiar with them. Some larcenies may be burglaries depending on whether you can prove the suspect's intent, certain tools used for the crime, etc.

Larceny, as mentioned previously, requires the intent to deprive. That is why you generally don't stop a suspect before he gets past the register or the door because of the doubt that the person intended to pay for the item. Most shoplifts are misdemeanors and in most jurisdictions, a private person needs to witness the crime in order to make an arrest. This makes loss prevention more difficult because you cannot stop someone just because you think he put something in his pocket or you are pretty sure he hid something under his jacket. Some states have created retail loss prevention laws that allow security to stop and question someone whom they have reasonable suspicion to believe committed theft. This is a touchy situation, as it does not necessarily allow you to arrest or search the person.

Catching Shoplifters

Because of the restrictions just explained, which are really an extension of the Constitution, it is difficult to catch thieves in the act. Prevention is much easier and is discussed shortly. Retail loss prevention officers are a special breed and they seem to have a sixth sense for knowing who is going to steal. You cannot watch every part of the store or every shopper, so it can seem like looking for needles in a haystack.

Profiling, or behavioral recognition, is the first step in identifying a shoplifter. Of all the people entering the store, who is most likely to steal? This depends on your hotel and the environment. The obvious physical characteristics might be someone dressed as a transient, a local resident in a tourist hotel, teenagers, and persons with heavy jackets in the summer. There is no physical profile that addresses gender, race, or age because shoplifters cut across all of these demographics, so concentrate on behavior more than appearance. Notice shoppers in any store. There are browsers and those who know what they want. Either way, both types generally focus on the merchandise. A potential thief concentrates on his surroundings. He may be looking for cameras, clerks, other witnesses, or his lookout. This is called "rubbernecking." Some will eye their target and immediately grab it, and some will position it on the shelf, try to appear disinterested, and then come back to it when the coast is clear.

Surveillance

A good loss prevention officer spends much of his time on surveillance. There is physical surveillance, which means walking the store undercover, and visual surveillance, which means using cameras or mirrors and blinds. A blind is a two-way mirror, catwalk, or hidden area. Loss prevention officers often work in teams with one officer at the entrance, profiling people as they enter or patrolling the store. The second officer will be working the cameras. Each officer communicates with the other, pointing out suspicious behavior. When a crime is observed, they will intercept the thief at the door.

Arrests

Whenever you put your hands on anyone, regardless of the justification, you have just exposed yourself to great liability. Besides the risk of making a false arrest, and injury during a struggle, you now are responsible for that person and anything that happens to them will be your fault.

In 2009, two loss prevention officers working at a well-known home electronics store chased a shoplifter out the doors and into the parking lot. The suspect pulled a knife after being tackled and threatened the officers to make his escape. He got away and the men were summarily fired for violating corporate policy on off-property pursuits. Most companies have strong policies on pursuits and arrests because of injury liability. The chances of the employees and even the suspect being injured running through the parking lot are extreme, and not worth the value of the lost merchandise. In this case, the employees could have been murdered, resulting in a much more serious loss for the company and the employees' families than some hi-fi equipment.

Nobody likes to let the bad guy get away, but we need to look ahead and think of the big picture when creating and enforcing policies like these that keep our liability at a minimum.

Many national retailers now have policies that forbid or restrict arrests for shoplifting. Others allow the arrest as long as it does not involve a pursuit. We hate to let someone get away with theft, but compare the cost of a stolen CD to the price of a lawsuit, even if you win. Your policy will need to weigh the value of the arrest—deterrence effect, hotel reputation, labor cost—with the value of letting the person go.

Preventing Shoplifting

Like everything else we do to protect assets, prevention is more effective and cheaper than trying to catch criminals. There are several things we can do in the retail environment to prevent shoplifting.

Retail Staff Training

Our best defense against thieves in a store is the clerk, cashier, stocker, and manager. These employees must be given basic training on loss prevention and guest service. They are actually the same training, if done right. The following are suggested training points that your retail manager will love.

Greeting—Every person who enters the store should be greeted and given eye contact. Besides the obvious service value, this tells the thief, who wants to go unnoticed, that he was noticed. The eye contact forces the clerk to remember the person's face and to unconsciously do some behavioral recognition of his own. Workers in a store know which visitors are going to steal.

145

Follow-up—This separates the two shoppers we identified earlier. The "browser" from the "targeted." The guy who wants a bottle of aspirin goes right to it, gets it, pays, and leaves. After the browser has passed a couple of displays, the clerk says, "May I help you find something?" or "Did you know these are on sale?" This reminds the shopper that we are watching, we haven't forgotten about him, and it is unlikely he will get away with stealing something.

Clerk patrol—The clerks should be walking the floor as much as possible. When there is no transaction, they should be cruising the store, providing that follow-up. During transactions, they need to be trained to lift their head from the register and make an occasional sweep of the store with their eyes.

Communication—There needs to be a method for the clerk to alert Security or Loss Prevention of a suspicious shopper. Maybe it is a silent alarm button, a discreet phone call, or body language that tells the manager to watch that person. There may be a different signal if they actually witness a crime. Remember, we cannot stop someone unless we witness it, so what do we do if the cashier witnesses it? Have a plan to act as their agent and make the stop, but it has to be a solid communication. You do not want to chase a guy down and stop him only to find that the clerk just thought he looked suspicious.

Store Layout

This is a conversation you need to have with the store manager. Remember our Risk Assessment? This is where it is used. Most retail professionals know how to lay out a store to maximize floor space, provide the best visual sales, and protect merchandise. But sometimes they forget that last one about protection. Once you have made your assessment, sit down with the manager and review your concerns. They should be willing to cooperate with this mutual concern.

Layout of displays needs to account for ease of shopping for the customer, but also for good sight lines between the clerk and the customer. Smaller, more expensive items need to be near the register; larger items should be toward the back and in the blind spots. Consider a layout where the register area has a clear view down each aisle. The retail manager can meet your needs as well as his own with this configuration. Convenience stores have definitely figured this out and are a good resource.

Cameras and Mirrors

In order for cameras to prevent crime, they need to be visible, but not obvious as to their view. Dark bubbles are best because it is assumed that a moving camera is behind the bubble. Mirrors can be used with cameras very effectively. Many retail shops use decorative mirrors around the upper walls of the store, angled down. These mirrors not only allow store personnel to see blind spots, but a skilled camera operator will use mirrors to expand his coverage of the store as well. Mirrors are a relatively inexpensive alternative to having so many cameras.

Antitheft Devices

Antitheft devices are those small tags that are now installed at the factory in DVDs, power tools, cosmetics, etc. These generally work as a radio frequency tag or magnetic sensor.

The types and choices are vast and varied, so just keep a couple of things in mind when installing or operating them. First, you need to justify this expense. Maybe you don't have a big enough shrinkage problem for this to pay for itself or your merchandise is lower value stuff. Second, is shoplifting the majority of the shrinkage problem? Many losses go out the back door with employees and you need to have an idea of what the percentage is.

Also, remember that these devices can be defeated by the shoplifter and by the employee. This will be just one layer of security and will not eliminate the need for other security measures.

FLASH MOBS

This is a relatively new gang activity brought to you by texting and the Internet. Groups of juveniles (usually) arrange through text messages or social networking to meet at a certain place and time to perform a flash robbery or theft. These mobs of kids will invade a store or other facility, grabbing everything they can and leave, knowing that not all of them can be caught. The store employees either are overwhelmed or stay back out of fear. Some of these groups have used the mob to commit violence like attacking a lone person and beating him.

This is such a new phenomenon that nobody has really studied it enough to figure out a prevention measure. Even if your facility is not a victim of one of these crimes, it may be the meeting place for a mob that will strike a nearby business or citizen. Here are some recommendations to prevent or minimize these incidents.

Intel—Monitor the Internet for the activity of organizing these mobs. A simple search for your property name or address and an RSS feed will send you these search results to your smart phone. Watch news and police reports for these incidents occurring in your area. Once the first one happens successfully, it will only be a matter of time before it happens again.

Communication—Take advantage of alerts sent out by other properties. Make sure the police are willing to contact you and others if they have knowledge of a mob gathering or planning. Let your employees know of the potential and to be aware of social media conversations so they can tip you off.

In-store—Make sure your retail staff is prepared for these types of thefts. They need to be trained to be good witnesses, but not endanger themselves. High-value items should be locked up separately. The exploding dye packs on some goods are a great way to dissuade and later capture thieves. Have cameras positioned to get facial shots of everyone entering and leaving the store or property. Apprehension of one—especially the leader—could lead police to the others later.

Perimeter—Discourage groups of juveniles gathering for any reason. Write down their names and descriptions for later use. Make sure cameras are positioned to see these groups gathering or approaching. Door cameras should be able to gather facial photos. If these mobs become a problem, consider posting an officer at entrances. Make paths to and from entry doors a bit circuitous so persons cannot run at the doors or run from them in a straight line. A revolving door is great for this purpose. Everyone slows down and gets their picture taken.

Parking areas – As in the textbox illustration, parking areas can be used as a gathering place just before a crime is committed. Deter this activity by prohibiting loitering of any kind in your lot or garage. Mobs need a place to meet and divide their loot. Watch for nearby rallying points and direction of travel of vehicles and those on foot.

In 2008, a "swarm" of seven or more black males attacked a landscaper at the MGM Grand Hotel in Las Vegas. The victim was white and the suspects were all convicted of a hate crime. They all belonged to the same gang.

This was not the first crime of its type, but was one of the first recorded on video. It brought national attention to the phenomenon, which became known as Flash Mobs. It was determined during the investigation that the gang used texting to coordinate the crime by arranging a meeting place and time. The meeting place was a nearby retail parking lot. Las Vegas and other major cities have seen the expansion of these events to include other types of venues. The proliferation of social media has aided these groups to the point of including any stranger who wants to attend as an associate.

SPAS AND POOLS

Spas and pools usually occupy the same space and are probably managed by the same person but have some different security issues. Pools (for recreational swimming) are a huge liability and need some specific measures to prevent safety concerns. Spas (where special treatments are provided) are more like a retail outlet and have those same security concerns.

Lifeguards

It is important to discuss the needs for having a lifeguard with your property risk manager. Many properties have gotten away from this service and chosen the "swim at your own risk" philosophy. This is partially due to cost and partly because lifeguards take on the entire burden of safety. If something happens, it will be the fault of the company whether it was or not. Other properties have taken the middle road and provide a towel attendant whose job is to control access to the pool without really taking responsibility for people swimming. Some properties still provide full-time lifeguards. These personnel must be trained and supervised and can protect the facility from the guests while protecting the guests from the water. The decision of which water safety posture, probably not made by you, will take several things into account: size and depth of the pool, type of clientele (families, children, elderly), and other safety measures in place (cameras, lifesaving equipment, gates, windows, etc.).

If you are going to have a lifeguard, this is going to be the most important person on your staff. Her training cannot be compromised and her performance must be 100 percent. Falling asleep, failure to act, and inattention to duty can lead to a tragic death, which could close a pool and maybe a hotel. Whatever certifications are in place for lifeguards in your jurisdiction, exceed them. Scheduling must be absolute. Will you have a hotel security officer cover breaks? What about his training? The lifeguard will have to enforce pool rules, have the proper equipment, and know his job and the security function very well.

Pool Rules

Most pool rules are standard and can be purchased on ready-made signs. These include no running, no diving, no urinating, etc. There may be other rules that are specific to your hotel. Depending on your lifeguard presence, you may want to prohibit unattended minors, alcohol, food, and toys. Make sure the rules are clearly posted and enforced. Remember that signs are not an enforcement tool, but a warning mechanism.

Safety Equipment

Make sure the basics are present and supplement wherever you can. The cost of safety equipment pales in comparison to a death. Recovery poles, life preservers, depth indicators, and CPR instruction signage are easily provided tools. Check with your local parks department and other public pools for ideas and standards. An emergency phone, panic button, or other instant alert device is advisable whether the pool is staffed or not.

In June 1998, at least one child who was suffering from an *E. coli* infection had a bowel movement in a water park pool in Atlanta, GA. The chlorine level was not high enough to kill the bacteria that infected the water. Twenty-six children became ill and one died from the infection.

Even though most of us feel that personal accountability should have prevented the parents from bringing their sick child to a water park, the blame is likely to go to the park operator. Maintaining proper chemical levels and monitoring guest behavior might prevent this type of crisis. Who is responsible for this maintenance at your facility? Who sets these standards and inspects their accuracy?

Hot Tubs

Hot tubs, Jacuzzis, whirlpools, whirling jet tubs—whatever you want to call it, these relaxing and therapeutic little pools are associated with many types of deaths and injuries. Besides the effect of the hot water on the bloodstream, there have been several bizarre deaths caused by hair getting caught in drain covers, the suction of the water inlet pulling elderly persons and children under the surface. A rare bacteria disease from the steam has caused enough deaths to warrant a good safety plan for your hot tub. Temperature monitoring and automatic cutoffs are vital to keeping the water temperature at a safe level. Manual emergency stops are also a necessity. Alcohol use in a hot tub increases drowsiness and decreases judgment. Sexual assault is another matter not related to your equipment and maintenance. Make sure the security plan for your hot tub does not overlook these threats.

Spa Treatments

If your hotel has an actual spa, then you probably provide massages and various other relaxation and cosmetic services. Unlike the other components of your spa, which are equipment-related, these amenities are service-based. Therefore, the risks associated with services are similar to those found in the Retail and Restaurant departments. Check those sections in this chapter for concerns that cross over into all revenue-generating departments: retail theft, fraud, etc.

There are also some risks uniquely associated with spas that need to be considered by Security. These include, but are not limited to, sexual assault and abuse, loss of stored guest property, health reactions to treatments, and sanitary health issues. These are not deal-breakers, but should be addressed in advance by legal counsel, Security, and spa management. Some simple rules that are enforced by Security can prevent most of these incidents.

Chemical Hazards

Sometimes we forget that pool chemicals are some of the most toxic substances in existence. Chlorine (sodium hypochlorite, or similar) used to sanitize pools is deadly if inhaled or ingested. Hydrochloric acid is used to balance the pH in the water. Large pools may have tanks with automatic dispensers. These should be perfectly safe, but are susceptible to earthquakes, tornadoes, and hurricanes, as well as terrorism and tampering. Make sure pool chemicals are secured in an OSHA-approved and fire-rated container or cabinet that is locked and away from guests.

In 2010, a major hotel was having its outdoor pool system repaired by an outside contractor. The valve controlling release of the chemicals was accidentally left on, so the pool was flooded with too much of the toxic substance. The chlorine was diluted enough to be less than lethal, but as it evaporated, the gas was inhaled by 100 of the 1,500 pool users. Twenty-six of those persons went to the hospital, the pool and surrounding area was closed, and the hotel paid out money to settle dozens of claims as well as being fined by OSHA. The hotel sued the contractor and is still in litigation. Although the hotel was not entirely at fault, it definitely suffered losses that it may or may not recoup.

Pool Parties

Pool parties have become big business in many larger hotels in cities throughout the world. These are not the pool parties you have at home for your child's tenth birthday, but are a successful way to convert an existing amenity into a lively venue at night. Many of the risks and concerns associated with pool parties also are present in nightclubs, so go to Nightclubs and Bars in this chapter and review it with your pool in mind.

Combining the risks of having a pool and the risks of having a nightclub will not cover the new and unique risks associated with pool parties. After all, during the day you probably do not allow alcohol or even glassware anywhere near your pool, but at pool parties they will be prevalent. Your security presence will drastically change. The pool may or may not be covered or open for swimming. Your beverage department will install new fixtures, cabanas, seating, electronic equipment, lights, and music. Make sure you do a thorough, and separate, Risk Assessment and Security Plan for pool parties. The plan for a family swimming pool is different from the one for pool parties. You will need new post orders as well.

Theft

Theft from lockers and of items left around the pool is very common. As in other parts of the hotel, patrol will help prevent these crimes. Officers should make sure lockers are secured and that items are not left unattended. Limiting pool access to hotel guests with keys helps, but does not eliminate theft. Hotel guests steal from each other, too. Signage is a common way to mitigate loss. Usually the signage will focus on how the hotel is not responsible for theft or damage. Go the extra step and offer tips on how to prevent it ("Please do not leave valuables unattended. Lockers are provided for your security and convenience.").

VALET

Your legal department has no doubt written a disclaimer that is printed on the back of every Valet claim ticket. "This contract limits our liability..." does not necessarily limit your responsibility to take reasonable care of the guest's property. This means you and your Valet department need to take reasonable precautions to secure guests keys, vehicles, and their contents. Like everywhere else, there needs to be controls in place for these safeguards.

Keys should never be left in vehicles. Establish a procedure where the attendant receives the car from the guest, completes the ticket, and secures the car and the keys. It is common for a thief to walk through Valet looking for the keys in cars and drive off, or worse to impersonate a valet attendant and take a car from a guest.

The valet office or key box needs to be secured every second. Combination lock key pads are popular, but easily thwarted by anyone watching. Valet attendants are in a hurry to take care of their guests so they tend to bypass locks and procedures that slow them down. Locked doors tend to get propped open. Keys in vehicles find themselves out of sight, but within reach—visor, floor mat, etc. Look into a card swipe or something similar that will allow fast access but keep our guests' property secure. Think of the value of all those keys and your hotel's reputation if you lose them.

The parking area should be as secure as possible. Fencing, lighting, controlled access, and patrol are very important here. Make sure attendants are securing vehicles by having security officers check doors and windows on a regular basis. I bet if you patrol your valet parking area, you will find at least one vehicle unlocked every day. Better you than a burglar.

Your parking area should have speed limits posted and Valet employees need to follow it. Security can help monitor this, but good supervision should catch offenders. Reckless drivers should be dealt with swiftly and sternly. Avoid putting time constraints on Valet drivers. They have enough incentive to hustle—tips.

Remember the pizza company that promised delivery in 30 minutes or it's free? That marketing campaign was ended in 1993 after several multimillion dollar lawsuits claimed that pizza delivery drivers were driving recklessly to meet the goal. The pizza company did not agree that the ads were the cause of several serious injury accidents, but pulled the slogan anyway. What does this have to do with Valet? Tell your employees to hurry when returning cars and they likely will, even if it puts property at risk.

Employee Theft

Internal theft is a temptation for Valet employees. Guests will make claims alleging theft, damage, and abuse of their vehicles, and more often than not, it is a false claim. All of these claims need to be investigated. Valet is a difficult area to prevent internal crime because of the mobility of the attendants. Just like Housekeeping, it is unusual for a Valet attendant to engage in minor theft from a vehicle. It does not make sense for them to risk their job for the change in an ashtray or some CDs. If you do have an attendant stealing, you will know it because of the pattern of thefts in that area. See Chapter 11 for more information on investigating internal theft. Random patrol and some camera coverage will prevent most of what the previously mentioned controls will not.

Guest Accidents and Injuries

Combining moving vehicles with pedestrians is likely to result in accidents. You have a responsibility to prevent accidents as best you can. Having guests walk across the concourse should be avoided, but if it cannot, you will need to take some extra steps. The minimum might be a painted crosswalk and speed bumps. At most, you might consider a "crossing guard." This could be a security officer, bell person, doorman, or taxi attendant. Remember that guests coming in are tired and anxious for relaxation and guests going out are preoccupied with their drive and all of their belongings. Either way, they are not as cautious as a regular pedestrian, so take extra care in protecting your guests.

Vehicle Damage

It is common for guests to claim damage to their vehicle after retrieving it from Valet. Like theft, it is not likely that a Valet attendant will damage a vehicle while it is in his possession. There are some measures you should implement, or at least consider, for your Valet. First, make sure attendants inspect the car before taking possession of it from the guest. Once they get good at it, this will be a fast and simple habit. Note damage on the rear of the ticket. Second, encourage employees to admit when they damage a car. Terminate them if they do not. Third, some hotels install camera systems that inspect the vehicle as it leaves the Valet concourse. These are nice if you can justify the expense. If you are having so many damage claims to make this a worthwhile investment, you might consider some other options like driver training, hiring experienced drivers, reconfiguring the parking area and route, and discipline for damage.

CONVENTIONS

Convention centers in most hotels consist of meeting and exhibition space and kitchen. These areas need to be patrolled after hours to make sure they are secure and employees or guests are not intruding into closed areas. During hours of use, Security will depend on what clientele are being catered to in those spaces.

Collaborate with the Convention or Catering staff to see that you are consulted on events that will be relevant to Security. You need to know well in advance of the following meeting room uses:

- Celebrity, political, or VIP attendees or exhibitors
- Groups of a controversial nature: political, activist, racial, religious, or ethnic groups
- Large concerts, speeches, or any function with more than 300 people attending
- Any party or event involving more minors than adults (quinceaneras, debutante balls, etc.)

Plan at least a 60-day notice so that security for the event can be planned and agreed upon. Smaller events may not need Security, but you will want to know if they may present a problem with protesters, media, or fans.

Risk Assessment

Law enforcement may be a big help in doing a Risk Assessment on certain groups and may already be aware of an event you have scheduled. Use their resources and advice for creating a security posture for these events. In the absence of assistance from the police, you can do your own Risk Assessment by contacting the client (event planner) and inquiring as to what types of problems he expects or has had in the past. You also can do an Internet search of events and the group to see what the talk is. Finally, contact other venues who have hosted the particular group. They will usually be very forthcoming and this satisfies the foreseeability that we discussed in Chapter 1.

Security Plan

Just like the hotel Security Plan, the individual Risk Assessment will determine the security deployment for each event. You may be able to set up standard staffing levels for some event types so your convention managers can work this out with the client in advance. For example, rap concerts and teenage birthday parties may require guest searches and bag checks at the door. Exhibitions may require an officer at each entrance and exit. You can also establish staffing proportions such as 1 officer for every 100 attendees. (Search stations are discussed in this chapter under Security Measures.)

It is a good idea to require the same security posture for each type of event. Avoid allegations of discrimination if you require searches for black rap groups and not for white country bands.

Special Event Permits

Your Convention Manager will generally take care of special permits for certain events and these vary by jurisdiction. Your involvement may be required for the fire inspection, if there is one. The event space has already passed code inspections, so if everything is kept the same, there is little to worry about for a special inspection. However, some events will want to block certain exits, extend above acceptable clearance levels, exceed occupancy levels, etc. There may be requirements for flame retardant wall coverings, vehicles being parked in an occupied space, and so forth. This can be a complicated set of rules, so it is best to establish a relationship with your local fire inspector so you know your expectations in advance. Allow enough time to make changes to layouts between the inspection and the event.

Outdoor Events

Expanding our available resources by hosting events outdoors is a testament to the flexibility and creativity of your sales and catering staff. Support these events as we discussed in the last chapter, but be aware of some special considerations.

Weather is a threat as we talked about in Chapter 1. If you have an outdoor event, make sure you are aware of seasonal weather patterns for your area as well as monitoring weather systems as the event gets closer. Work out an arrangement with your event planner as to who will have the authority and ability to cancel or change the event at the last minute if weather dictates. Make sure your temporary structures (tents, stages, lighting, signs, etc.) are constructed with weather (wind, mostly) in mind.

> At the Indiana State fair in 2011, an outdoor stage took a 60-mph wind gust and blew over. Five people were killed by the gust, which was unforeseen and described as a "fluke." The organizers had been in contact with the National Weather Service, but there was no indication of heavy winds.
>
> When we build permanent structures, we plan for every possible type of weather or disaster. Temporary structures are generally not suited to withstand extreme weather. Make sure your Risk Assessment and incident action plan for your outdoor event considers these extreme events.

Access control is another issue that is more difficult outside. You do not have your normal walls, gates, cameras, and other "levels" in place. Your security plan for the event should tell you whether you might want to install temporary cameras, gates, turnstiles, etc. These are more common than you think, and just about anything can be rented these days.

Remember staffing for outdoor events. Do not expect to "cover" an outdoor event with existing staff. This is going to leave another area weak. Use overtime or hire an outside source to make sure you have adequate personnel to protect your assets and counter threats.

PARKING

Parking is a huge responsibility that is generally given to the Security Department. Besides being responsible for protecting the assets of the lot or garage, you may be responsible for other business related to parking such as Booth Staffing, Maintenance, and Cleanliness. Each of those functions relate directly to Safety and Security, so we will discuss them and more in the following sections.

Cleanliness

An area that appears well kept, clean, and often traveled is less likely to experience crime. We have all seen how an abandoned building maintains its appearance until that first window is broken or wall is vandalized with spray paint. The same is true for parking lots. Keep your garage or parking lot free from trash, road sand, and debris. Ask your environmental services crew to assign someone to this area full time to pick up, sweep, and empty trashcans. Guests who stop at your hotel on a long road trip will use your garage to dump their trash and empty coolers. Have sufficient trash receptacles for this purpose and keep an eye out for trash dumps throughout the parking area.

Graffiti should be reported and expunged immediately. One tag is all it takes for graffiti to multiply. This makes guests feel uncomfortable anyway. In an established gang area, a tag may indicate "ownership" of turf and send the green light to local car burglars and vandals that your lot is wide open.

Abandoned vehicles should be addressed before they become obvious to others. Keep a long-term parking log for guests and employees who leave their cars parked while they take vacations or look for a spare tire. You can mark cars that are parked over two weeks and then tow them after another week.

In 1982, James Wilson and George Kelling wrote the Broken Windows Theory. This theory asserts that one broken window in an abandoned building soon attracts more vandalism and ultimately squatters, arson, and blight. The theory also applies to abandoned cars in parking lots and litter on sidewalks. New York Mayor Rudy Giuliani made the theory famous and proved it right when he applied the theory to the New York subway system. Targeting minor crimes and visible nuisances lowered the major crime rate for 10 years in that city.

This theory can be applied to your parking garage. Abandoned cars, litter, graffiti, and other minor vandalism, if immediately resolved, will keep other crimes at a minimum.

Lighting

There are minimum industry lighting standards for parking lots and garages. I suggest you exceed those until your garage or lot feels safe and comfortable. Your facilities manager will want to use cost-efficient light bulbs that turn the garage yellow or fluorescent white. Get involved in this process and make sure it stays bright and pleasant. Trash sweepers and Security personnel should be aware of lights that are out and get them replaced immediately. This goes back to the Broken Windows Theory.

Access Control

Even if you have free parking, access control to your parking area allows you to limit and track parking usage. It also allows you "the greeter" effect for potential troublemakers. If the garage has free ingress and egress, a burglar will feel much more comfortable entering to case cars. If he has to stop and take a ticket or be greeted by an employee, he is less likely to chance being remembered.

License plate recognition has become advanced, yet inexpensive, and can be a great security and marketing tool. Cameras photograph vehicle license plates as cars enter (being slowed by taking a ticket). The software of the system reads the license plate characters and compares them to a database. You may be able to use a police database and catch stolen or wanted vehicles. Alternatively, you can use your own database, which includes authorized vehicles, employees, and previous parking violators or unwanted guests. Your Marketing department can use the system to know when a VIP guest arrives and meet him in the lobby with his room key or a bouquet of flowers. Most importantly, a record of each plate coming in and out gives you evidence to be used in catching bad guys in their car or at least a time frame of when a car was stolen.

Speaking of stolen cars, having a booth attendant checking tickets as cars leave drastically reduces the chance of cars being stolen.

Security Patrol

Patrol type usually depends on the size of the parking area. Whatever patrol type you use—bikes, walking, vehicle, or perch—make sure they can cover the entire facility every hour or as your requirements dictate.

I recommend bicycle patrol for its speed, mobility, and stealth. Bicycles are relatively inexpensive, can get around almost anywhere quickly, and are a motivator for the more eager security officers. Bicycle officers must be properly trained and equipped (see Chapter 6). The Segway and other scooters might be used instead of bikes, but not as well.

Motorized security vehicles are expensive to operate and insure, but provide high visibility. This visibility is a deterrent, but also makes clear where security is not. Some hotels use a vehicle because this post tends to do double duty running errands. For inclement weather, it may be vital.

Walking patrol is the easiest to staff and maintain. Like the bike officers, make sure your officers outside are properly dressed for weather and visibility. They need to challenge suspicious persons and greet guests to provide that deterrence created by interaction.

Very few noncovered parking lots use a perch or elevated viewing platform, but they may be preferred in some areas. If you have one, staff it at all times. The false sense of security provided by having an empty perch could get you into trouble and the bad guys will figure out soon enough that it is empty.

Parking Enforcement

Enforcing parking accomplishes several objectives for your department and the hotel. The most important reason is the least obvious. Having officers looking for violators encourages them to patrol and keep their eyes open. (You have seen the rovers walking around in a daze or staring at the ground.) Enforcement also keeps the right spaces available for the right cars. You do not want employees parking in the premium guest spaces. You can use citations to discipline these employees or the annoying neighbors who use your lot without permission. Abandoned cars become more apparent when you enforce parking.

If you want to have teeth in this enforcement program, you have three options. First is the discipline, mentioned previously, that comes from an employee receiving a citation. Second, you can have a third party tow the vehicle. This gets the vehicle out of your lot, and costs the owner a lot of money to get his car back. The third option is a boot or immobilizer. This contraption secures one wheel so the car cannot move. It gives you a chance to confront the driver and explain the parking policies. You can use this opportunity to charge him a fee (which goes to your revenue instead of the tow company) and enter him into your database. This option is preferred because when you make a mistake—and you will make a mistake and boot a guest's car—it is easier to resolve than getting their car out of a tow yard.

CASINO SECURITY

Since the proliferation of gaming outside of Nevada in the 1980s, casinos are now in almost every state in the union and many other countries as well. Many of those casinos provide lodging as an amenity, so it is common to find a hotel attached to a casino. In fact, when casinos first started building large hotels in the 1970s, the hotel served two purposes. One was to get the casino patron to stay longer and spend more money. The other was to provide an amenity that the casino could give away to its patrons as a reward for losing their money. Of course, it also added some family aspect to a casino vacation where the entire family could stay and enjoy themselves while one or more parents participated in the gaming action.

Las Vegas, which has always lead the way in gaming innovation and trends, built huge megaresorts in the late 1980s with the Excalibur, Mirage, and later, the MGM Grand. Each had more rooms than any other hotel in the world at the time they were opened. This competition ran off and on for a couple of decades and when the size of a hotel maxed out at about 5,000 rooms, they started building minicities of several brands on one resort property. While the casino is still a large part of these destinations, it no longer provides the majority of the revenue. Retail, entertainment, hotel rooms, and even condominiums now contribute in a major way to the bottom line. In fact, even though big players can still get their free suite, most regular gamblers have to divide their gaming expenses into lodging, food, shopping, and entertainment.

Casino security has evolved and changed just as much as the buildings in which they work. Security was originally hired in a casino to protect the money. The antics of casino security officers are legendary and depicted in movies as hired muscle that operated as the right hand of management to exact justice on those who would dare try to cheat the owners out of their money. These stories are a bit exaggerated, but only a bit.

In the 1970s as organized crime was pushed out by large corporations, the Nevada Gaming Commission stepped up its own enforcement of the casinos. Background checks became more stringent and the "good ol' boy" system all but disappeared. Regulations within the casino operation increased exponentially to prevent internal theft, which was allegedly committed mostly by management. Simple controls and dual and triple verification, accounting, and auditing procedures were enacted and enforced. This changed security's role from private thugs to protectors of assets.

Casino Controls

Casinos use three independent methods of protecting their assets. Even though they are independent, the three processes work in relation to create the most secure system possible. The first concept is Verification. Whenever money changes hands in a casino, a paper trail is created. Often, this paper trail is in the form of a receipt or slip that has to be verified. Security is often the second or third verifier of these transactions. If money is exchanged between party A and party B, a third, uninvolved person needs to verify it, so Security is used. This is not so much because of their job function, but because they are usually the only ones around who are independent of the money departments.

For example, when casino chips are taken to a blackjack table to replenish it, a fill slip is created. The pit supervisor calls the cage and asks for certain denominations and amounts of chips to fill a bank on a table. The cashier creates a slip (just like a waiter in a restaurant). The cashier provides the chips with the slip to a security officer, who verifies the amounts match and takes two of the three copies of the slip to the table, leaving one copy of the slip with the cashier. At the table, the security officer delivers the chips and the dealer and pit supervisor sign as verifiers of the transaction. One copy of the slip is left at the table with the money, and the third copy goes back to the cage to be married with the original. Note that at every step of the process—every time money changed hands—there was a piece of paper and a signature. The cashier could have easily taken the money to the pit or the pit supervisor could have easily picked up her own chips, but the Security officer provides a third party to verify the money at each step so there is always two different people and no collusion. This is one of the most common and most visible duties of a casino Security officer. These types of transactions can vary and some properties have made them all electronic. Noncasino Security Departments can learn from these controls.

The second protection method in a casino is Surveillance. These professional observers watch employees and guests to identify theft, cheating, and fraud. They are mandated in most states to watch and record certain transactions and games. There are still some old surveillance guys around who actually crawled in the rafters of the casino, above the tables, to watch the players cheat. These same veterans have lived long enough to see great innovations in the size, range, and ability of cameras that allow them to watch from an air-conditioned office. As electronics have made the surveillance officer's job easier, it has also benefited the thief. Dozens of different methods of cheating have been tried and have succeeded over the years to gain an advantage in games of chance.

In our example of the pit fill, Surveillance watches the transaction at each step. When the chips are handed over to the Security officer, they are passed by a camera where the chips are photographed and counted and compared to the amounts on the slip. At the table, when the chips are again handed over to the dealer, Surveillance again photographs the chips and verifies the amounts. Even though the Security officer had possession of the chips alone during transport, they are verified at each end, narrowing the focus to him or her if any chips come up missing in the process.

One special place that Surveillance watches is called the count room. This is where all of the unverified money is taken each day to be counted. The cage is different; that is where money is exchanged, not verified. The cage maintains a balance of a fixed amount of money, never having more money than it is assigned until it receives a deposit from the count room. It never has less until it makes its own deposit to the company bank account. The count room does not have all of the controls and verifiers previously mentioned because it is receiving "raw" money from certain games and revenue centers. For this reason, there are multiple layers of security and numerous controls on this room. Surveillance is one of those controls and is responsible for making sure the other controls are followed.

In a casino, Surveillance performs many of the special audits and internal protection functions discussed in this chapter and Chapter 11. There are some great books dedicated entirely to casino security. If you want to learn more, search for Alan Zajic, CPP; Derk Boss; and Gary Powell.

The third protection method in a casino is one that is discussed in Chapter 11—Internal Audit or Accounting. This department, independent of all others and headed by the aptly named Controller, is the final stage of all transactions. Auditors audit the transactions and make sure that everything balances, that no money is missing, and that all regulations and policies were followed through the other steps. This creates the final leg in the "checks and balances" of a casino operation. In that original example of a pit fill, an auditor would verify all three stages of that transaction the next day. The first and second copies of the fill slip come from the cage; the third copy comes from the count room where it was retrieved from the drop box on the table; and a fourth copy is the hidden or electronic copy contained in the cage records of money sent out. These are compared with logs of money coming in at the pit. The auditor also verifies all proper signatures on the slip, makes sure there are no sequentially numbered slips missing, and that fills requested match fills processed. There are several places, or a paper trail, to find exactly when an amount was changed or a verifier missed.

Regulation Hierarchy

In Nevada casinos, and many other jurisdictions, the gaming authority will establish basic guidelines for certain operations. These are generally called regulations and they provide very broad mandates, such as: surveillance systems shall be "in accordance with the casino surveillance standards." Note that this does not really say anything except that there is some other standard you have to follow. That standard (in Nevada) says, "Access to a surveillance room must be . . . as set forth in its written surveillance system plan" (among other things). This puts a slightly tighter level of restriction on the casino, but it also transfers the remainder of the control back to the private entity. The government in this second level of control is saying, "You decide how you are going to control access, and then follow your own rules." Gaming Control will then audit you and enforce your own regulations against you. These are called internal controls. The next level is simply called house policy. For example, the Surveillance room may have a sign-in log or require an ID badge for entry. That is not required by a government agency, but it is your own policy for following the higher level of control. Then, to finish our example of these cascading regulations, the Surveillance department policy for entry to its room might be that officers only allow entry after verifying proper ID and with authorization from the room supervisor.

For better understanding, look at our own country's system of laws. At the top, we have the Constitution, which provides a broad framework to follow. The next level is federal laws, which give restrictions that are more detailed, but must adhere to the minimum set in the Constitution. The next level (generally) is the laws of each state. The state can have a law that is more restrictive than a federal law, but not less, so they are usually just more specific. Then we have local ordinances and even private property policies.

I explain gaming laws in this manner to illustrate that most rules that we follow in a casino are not really laws at all. They are often house policies put in place to make sure we follow those broad laws and regulations. This is important when enforcing and following rules. It is also helpful to know that because most of the procedures that officers follow are created by the casino, they can be changed by the casino. If you are doing a pit drop at 2 a.m. every day, which also happens to be the closing time for all the nightclubs in your area, you might want to change one of those times.

Casino Patrol

Besides the previous examples, Security provides many more administrative and regulatory functions in a casino. This includes drops (removing money from a device), escorts, transfers, and key issuance. Security also patrols as outlined in this chapter. In addition to normal protective patrol, they also are responsible for keeping minors off the gaming floor, addressing those suspected of fraudulent acts (e.g., taking money from a machine without placing a wager), and enforcing alcoholic beverage laws.

Some jurisdictions do not supply free drinks or allow smoking as they do in Nevada, so alcohol is a major factor in most security-related issues in casinos there. Security officers need to be specially trained in recognizing intoxication as well as managing those who have had too much. Even though Nevada's dram shop laws (more detail is in Nightclubs and Bars in this chapter) place responsibility on the person doing the drinking, casino Security officers are very aware of their moral responsibility in handling intoxicated persons. We no longer see officers throwing drunken patrons out the back doors into the alley. Sensitivity and responsibility have prevailed and now officers will go to great lengths to protect an intoxicated person. This may include taxi service, phoning a friend, all the way up to providing a room (for good players). This is good business more than a matter of legality.

Casino security officers need to be specially trained in cheating laws in their jurisdiction. This brings us to the difference in Surveillance and Security. Many people confuse and even merge these two casino functions—probably based on movies and television.

160

Like everything else, properties vary, but the differences are fundamental and very clear. Surveillance reports directly to the Controller or General Manager. They are an oversight department like Accounting and have to be separate in the chain of command from Security. Surveillance is the "eye in the sky," primarily watching anything that has to do with gaming, money, or compliance. I say "primarily" because more and more, Surveillance departments are using "dataveillance" to watch their assets. They have the unique ability to take a transaction from an exception report in the accounting system and actually observe it live or recorded to see what really happened. A good Surveillance department uses any tool that it can get to catch internal and external theft and fraud.

Security in a casino is the more visible representation of enforcement and prevention. Security physically patrols and responds to incidents of all types. In fact, if Surveillance sees a crime in progress, they will generally call in Security to make the arrest or detention. Security also may monitor certain cameras, but usually they are related to guest and employee safety, such as the common areas, access points, garage, perimeters, and stairs. Some jurisdictions— not Nevada—have a gaming agent who is actually employed on property to ensure compliance and enforce gaming laws. So, in these cases, Security may have nothing to do with a gaming crime because Surveillance will work directly with the agent in-house.

Detention

Also in Nevada, and in some other states and tribal areas, gaming laws allow for "detention" rather than arrest. For example, if a Security officer has reason to believe a person committed a gaming crime, he may detain that person to notify a gaming agent. Notice the difference is that they do not have to know a crime occurred or even witness it. This protects the casino from liability and allows the gaming agents to perform an investigation if they merely suspect a criminal cheat. The example in the textbox below shows the abuse of this enforcement tool.

> In 2010, a guest at a large Las Vegas casino was suspected of cheating at a table game. Security followed the man to his hotel room, detained him, transported him to a holding room, searched him, and took $500 in gaming chips that the casino would have won if the bet had been completed. Security then "trespassed" the man and evicted him from the hotel, never notifying a police officer.
>
> Although most gambling jurisdictions have special laws designed to assist in the investigation of cheating, there are no laws that can trump a person's constitutional rights. This "arrest" violated federal law, state law, gaming law, and even the casino's own policies. As usual, the $500 return on this situation will not even come close to the likely settlement that will be made.

Deployment

Deployment of security officers depends entirely on the size of the casino and what other facilities it has, such as hotels, restaurants, shopping, and parking. In the old days, the priority was on the money and all you saw was an officer stationed near the cashier cage and the rest of the officers moving money about the floor. As we have evolved, we realized that money is an asset secondary to our guests' safety. Now most casinos have officers patrolling the floor, perimeter, and other areas watching for troublemakers and preventing problems.

If you have a casino on your hotel property (or a hotel on your casino property), you likely have a done a Risk Assessment and made a Security Plan as described in Chapters 1 and 2. You also know that the money in the cashier cage is insured and worth far less than a rape or a physical assault in your garage. Besides, your cage robbery procedures probably instruct cashiers to give robbers whatever they ask for to protect employees and bystanders. However, there is at least one simple thing you can do to increase your patrol coverage or reduce your workforce. That savings comes in the form of all of the regulatory functions that you provide. This requires some collaboration with other departments. See if you can schedule all of your drops and other duties in a sequential format. For example, instead of starting the pit drop and the validator drop, try to change the start time of the pit drop to be first, then the validators immediately after. Most casinos used to schedule four officers (or more) at that one hour of the shift just to complete those tasks. Only two are needed if scheduled sequentially. I once knew of a very large casino that scheduled 12 officers between 2 a.m. and 4 a.m. just for drops. The controller wanted everything in the casino dropped simultaneously to make the paperwork look cleaner. Someone finally convinced this controller that the cost of security for this daily event far exceeded whatever convenience it was for the accountants.

Innovation

Casinos invest more than the average business in surveillance and detection equipment, hire and train teams of officers to staff surveillance rooms, and have unusual situations and crimes. Therefore, the casino industry has given the rest of us many innovations and methods that we might have never encountered.

For decades, Security Departments placed cameras in a manner that allowed us to get a great view of the top of customers' heads. We have since learned that we can get better images of faces from cameras mounted at a farther angle on the ceiling or even mounting them on the wall and in doorsills. Casinos are also very good at using what are called "choke points" and high traffic areas to get identifiable shots of perpetrators. An overhead camera can get a view of a certain activity and then a camera placed in a high traffic area can be used to identify the person. Despite what you see on television, facial recognition has not been refined to a practical application, but casinos are getting very close. I suspect they will be the first to master this emerging technology.

Casino surveillance officers have perfected the science of video patrol and investigations. These experts have developed techniques that maximize the power of video. Where we used to use video to passively monitor a particular area, casinos have taught us to identify suspicious behavior, zoom in on it, and use multiple angles to determine criminal behavior or undesirable activity. There is more information on video patrol in Chapter 9.

Casino accounting departments regularly use video to audit gaming. They may use it to recall a Keno game or verify a large jackpot. In casinos, it is very common for a department head to have a video feed right to her office to monitor her employees and customers.

Casinos have also taken interproperty communication to levels that are more effective. Besides just having meetings where suspect and criminal information is shared, they have gotten very good at transmitting this data in real time to their neighbors. Video links, Internet streaming, and email are just a few of the ways that casinos can send images up and down the "strip" before the bad guy even gets to his next destination.

There is no patent or ownership of these ideas and techniques. Take advantage of this experience and utilize these concepts wherever you can find them useful in your operation.

NIGHTCLUBS AND BARS

Most hotels offer some sort of adult entertainment in the form of a bar that serves alcoholic beverages. Many hotels have enhanced the simple bar into one or more nightclubs. Of course, there are also stand-alone nightclubs and bars. All of these business models are addressed in this section.

Need for Security

Before we get into the protection of these types of assets, we need to determine which ones actually need security. This was addressed in Chapter 1. As a simple review, for any location, such as a bar or nightclub, you will need to assess the threats and probabilities associated with those threats and determine if the location is in need of physical security. Some locations may need only the very basic layers of security and no human security presence. Still others, because of their large size, location, and type of clientele, will need a sizable security force.

Human Security

If your Risk Assessment has determined that your club or bar needs security officers, the worst thing you can do is compromise on the staffing and training. Problems occur when management hires a maître d' or other operational employee and assigns him or her to double as a "bouncer" or security officer.

Security officers (door host, if you prefer) require training and cannot be expected to perform both jobs efficiently if they are tasked with something else besides protection of assets. For this reason, many clubs replace the traditional door host/hostess with a fully trained Security officer. Let's look at some of the roles and duties associated with Security in a bar or nightclub.

Door Host

This may be the most important job function in the business. This officer has several duties that affect the entire demeanor of the crowd and the success of the business.

ID checks—Every person entering a crowded club needs to be identified. The primary reason is to verify legal age. Some training and tools need to be provided to the door host so he or she can adequately scrutinize identification. Jurisdictions across the country have rings of ID forgers that cater to college students. Make sure your hosts are familiar with real and fake IDs. Create a policy about alternate identification that will be accepted. The International Driver's License is a popular fake ID for minors. These can be purchased from the Internet and there is no such legitimate thing. The host should investigate further why the person does not have a local ID. Several devices available verify ID. They are not foolproof, but they read the magnetic or barcode strip on the license and display the current age and name on the device so the host can verify that against the front of the document. The extra benefit of these machines is that they keep a record of every person entering the establishment in case there is some criminal investigation later. If you are clever, the output of this device can be superimposed onto the video of the door. Then you will have a face and identity of each person who walks in. That would be very useful if there is a fight or worse. The Marketing Department may also want to get their hands on this database of names and addresses.

So what's the big deal with fake IDs and minors drinking? Besides the ethical and moral reasons of enforcing the minimum drinking age, there are some legal ones. Many jurisdictions conduct "stings" to make sure you are following this law. The bartender generally gets a big fine, but your liquor license is in jeopardy as well. This is multiplied by the several agencies that can enforce these laws. The state or county alcohol board, the city code compliance, city police, county sheriffs, and state police can operate these stings and write you a citation. In a casino, the gaming agency gets involved as well.

Consider running your own stings on your bartenders to find out which ones ignore the policy of checking ID. You can do this with servers and door hosts as well. This will show those enforcement agencies that you are trying to comply with the law and do not tolerate illegal activity from your employees. Check with your local police before you start confiscating IDs.

Occupancy count—It is the door host's responsibility to maintain a headcount of total occupancy. There is already a limit established by the fire department, but you should have a limit of your own (less than the fire department's) that you feel can be controlled with the staff you have. You can use a mechanical clicker, the ID machine described previously, or an electronic counter. Of course, you need to count those leaving as well to have an accurate count. Keep this count on a log with entries at least hourly. This document will be used if the fire marshal comes for an inspection, and is required by some licensees.

Behavioral assessment—The door host needs to be trained in behavioral recognition. She should have the ability to scrutinize customers or refuse admittance to those who act suspiciously or meet certain criteria. The door host also enforces the dress code. This is the best way to prevent trouble. Dress codes are discussed later in this section.

Search—If your business searches customers, the search is performed at the entrance. Searches are for weapons, controlled substances, and outside food and liquor. This also requires training and discretion. Searches are also discussed later.

Queue lines—A successful club will have a waiting line for entry. This line is a good opportunity to assess the behavior of potential customers. Those who are provoking fights, already drunk, or creating a disturbance should simply be refused entry. Whatever minor infractions that occur in line will just get worse inside, so take advantage of this chance. Warnings are usually a waste of time because the line is where people are the least intoxicated and know they are being watched. Prevent problems by refusing entry to these persons. Make sure the line is orderly and not blocking public sidewalks or creating a disturbance that would bring negative attention from the police or neighbors.

VIP entry—Door hosts traditionally make a huge income accepting tips for special favors (like avoiding the queue line). They also will allow entry for their friends, friends of the DJ or band, and "promoters" who bring in business. This is a huge problem for some clubs, so whatever your policy on tips and special entry, make sure management closely and strictly enforces it. It is too easy for a door host to acquire a little too much power and control over your business.

Controlling the exit—It is so tempting for a club or bar to think of an exiting patron as just another empty bar stool. Dram shop laws protect bars from liability for a person after he leaves, but you will be sued if your patron walks out in front of a bus, so take steps to lessen that chance. Someone walking out who is visibly intoxicated should have a designated driver with him. It is good business to see that these persons are not driving and get into a taxi or a friend's car. Consider a lone woman being escorted out by a couple of men. Is this a potential rape scenario? The door host should be able to get some affirmation from the woman that she is leaving with friends and make a reasonable effort to intervene. A brief scrutiny of the men by Security is reasonable enough to dissuade most assailants. If in doubt, the police should be called. This is not an arrest or detention scenario, so be sure of what you can legally do.

Dram shop is a legal term for a bar that serves alcoholic beverages. Dram shop laws vary from state to state as do the court cases involving liability with serving alcohol. There have been many verdicts on both sides—and everywhere in between—deciding for and against bar owners and bartenders on the subject of over-serving patrons. Regardless of the verdicts, which are too numerous and varied to mention here, one thing is clear: Owners and employees have an obligation to be responsible in their serving of alcohol. Everything works against common sense in these incidents. The owner is motivated by profit from sales, the bartender is motivated by tips from the patrons, and the patrons are motivated by wanting to drink until they are intoxicated. Management needs to take the high road here and continually monitor bar activity to prevent over-pouring and having guests drive drunk. This responsibility can extend outside the bar or lounge to Security, Valet, and other departments that interact with intoxicated guests.

Remember how critical the door host position is. Put your best officer there and make sure he or she gets sufficient breaks. Keep a close eye on the power this position wields. Rotating positions in a nightclub is a good way to avoid corruption at that post and to keep your hosts friendly and fresh.

Floor Patrol

Nightclubs can be fraught with criminal activity, drugs, sex, organized crime, and anything else you can imagine. The notion that these people have paid a cover charge or passed through security, thereby exempting them from responsible behavior, is dangerous to the business. Therefore, patrol of all areas of the club is necessary.

- Dance floor—One or more officers should be stationed at the dance floor to watch for drug exchanges, sexual activity, fights, and intoxicated persons who could cause accidents.
- Cabanas or private booths—These are dangerous and are not recommended. The only reason anyone in a club would want his or her activity to be hidden is because that activity is not allowed. If you want to allow sex or drug use in these areas, that is up to you, but the consequences of rape allegations or other violent behavior are serious. Instead, make the booths semiprivate without a curtain or door. Make regular checks of these areas to ensure everyone has their clothes on and there is not inappropriate or illegal activity.
- Restrooms—Restrooms are another popular place for drug activity and sex. In this atmosphere, men and women tend to lose inhibitions about which restroom they use. It is very common to see males and females using either gender's facilities, especially for having sex. (The problem here is not the sex, but the allegations of rape that can come afterward.) Drug use and fights are prevalent in restrooms as well, partially because there are no cameras. The best security for a restroom is to have an attendant who will deter almost all of these situations, but can summon security if they still occur. Just like in the rest of the hotel, public facilities need to be checked regularly; more often in a busy club or bar. Document these checks and use cleaning and maintenance personnel to multiply your checks. Make sure they are trained on what to look for and what to report. If there are no female security officers, assign another female employee to check the female-only area and report. (See "Restrooms" as a separate section in this chapter for more information).
- Back of the house—This area includes the employee-only areas, but may also include emergency exits and hallways or offices and store rooms. Regular patrol is required in these areas to ensure persons are not loitering. Hidden areas, as explained previously, are common places for people to step out of the public eye to take care of business. This is also a common way for employees to interact wrongfully with customers. Do not allow anyone to congregate out of view of security even if he or she is just trying to get air or is claustrophobic. These people can leave the facility entirely if they do not like the atmosphere. All exits should be monitored. Ideally, the exit is next to the entrance where it can be monitored by the door hosts. If not, you will have to assign someone to watch exits for re-entry, theft, and inappropriate behavior. Of course you have to have emergency exits, but make sure they are alarmed and that each alarm is checked and reset swiftly.

Management does have some responsibility when their patrons engage in mutual combat. There are two main considerations when these cases go to court. Foreseeability is first. Liability on management may come into play if they should have reasonably known that violence was going to occur. Was there an argument or some other disturbance? Were threats made? These factors give management a warning that something may happen, so they should be acted upon in their early stages. The second consideration when a fight occurs is the innocent bystanders. Two people engaged in mutual combat may be on their own, but on a dance floor where others can get hurt is a different story. Security has a duty to protect the other dancers in their establishment so that they are not inadvertently injured. In 2008, a knife fight occurred in a Connecticut nightclub. Two uninvolved patrons were stabbed and they sued the nightclub for negligence. The court sided with the plaintiffs, saying that the nightclub was negligent in monitoring the property.

Alcohol Service

Alcohol is the main attraction at any bar or nightclub. The band or DJ is secondary. Without alcohol, your club would not survive. Be careful not to take the responsibility of serving alcohol for granted. It is a privilege, as your jurisdictional authorities may remind you with inspections, regulations, and fines. Keep your eye on the following issues to keep your venue "alcohol-safe."

Training—Everyone who serves or deals with alcohol in any way should be trained in responsible alcohol service. This training includes recognizing intoxication levels, proper cut-off procedures, ID recognition, and how to deal with intoxicated persons.

Over-pouring—Bartenders and drink servers can make huge tip money that can affect their judgment. Make sure your policy on serving to patrons and potentially intoxicated patrons is enforced by Security and management. If they know that their job is in jeopardy, they are more likely to follow those policies.

Minors—A minor being allowed entry and then served alcohol is likely your greatest liability. Strong policies, such as checking every ID, is recommended. This takes the heat off the bartender and server who are motivated by tips. If you come across a minor who is intoxicated, make sure you turn him or her over to a responsible adult or the police. Putting him or her back on the street just increases your exposure. Document these situations very carefully to show you acted reasonably and responsibly.

Intoxicated persons—Everyone in a bar or nightclub has some level of intoxication. The club should have a liberal designated driver policy. Providing free coffee and soda to designated drivers is cheap insurance. Beyond that, your staff needs to be aware when guests have reached their limit. Some behavioral recognition skills come into play and are taught in awareness classes. Absent that training, reasonable judgment needs to prevail. Someone who cannot clearly speak, walk, or make simple decisions is past his or her limit.

While the guest is still inside, the first step is to cut him off. This needs to be done gently and with tact. Rather than yelling to someone, "You're cut off," have a manager or Security do it. Then explain to the person that you have strict policies about over-serving and he needs to prove he can handle another drink before he gets one. He does not have to leave. He can have something besides alcohol to drink, or he can walk around, go to the restroom, whatever. This gives you the opportunity to evaluate further his motor skills and judgment. Few people will accept this alternative unless they think you will forget about them and serve them again later.

When it is time for an intoxicated person to leave, the worst thing to do is to dump her in the hotel lobby or out on the sidewalk. First, find a friend who can take responsibility for her. Second, get her a taxi. If someone absolutely refuses either, notify the police as you stall, get their license plate number, etc. (A billing arrangement with a taxi service is cheaper than a lawsuit from a drunk driver victim.) In a hotel, every employee has an obligation to monitor guests leaving a bar or nightclub and heading home. If someone is exhibiting signs of being intoxicated, the employee should report that person to security. The final check is at Valet. Valet attendants need to do a brief assessment to determine if someone is visibly too drunk to drive. The attendant should call Security if there is any doubt. Anyone who gets away and drives away drunk should be reported to the police.

It is common for contract security officers to take persons with whom they have problems in a nightclub and eject them into the public area of the hotel. That does not solve the problem for the hotel and is shortsighted. If they are not wanted in the nightclub, they certainly are not wanted in the rest of the property. Work out an arrangement with Security in the nightclub to either hand off the undesirable to hotel Security or walk them all the way off property.

Dress Code

A strong dress code is a good way to limit trouble. Make sure the dress code does not target a certain protected class, such as race, gender, or age. It needs to be unambiguous so there is little discretion by Security. Saggy pants and baseball caps are often listed as being prohibited on a dress code. If you exclude those, remember that the women whose thongs are visible or are wearing a hat would also have to be excluded. Instead of excluding "Raiders" jackets, just exclude sports clothing or heavy jackets. Get ideas from other clubs and even a high school.

In and Out Privileges

Guests have many reasons for wanting to leave a club and come back. One is that they are simply hopping around until they find the best crowd. Second is they are leaving to use drugs, have sex, or buy cheaper alcohol. None of these reasons is good for business, so it is best to restrict it. Those who leave can go to the back of the line and pay the cover again. If your establishment does not allow smoking, you should probably have a smoking area that is separate and allows re-entry. A cordoned area near the exit is good because the hosts can watch it and control re-entry.

Does management have any responsibility for the safety of guests after they exit the building? In 1998, a nightclub in Washington, D.C. had its patrons exit through a door into an alley at closing. The door locked from the outside, preventing re-entry. Seventeen security officers were stationed inside the club and none outside. One customer was attacked in the alley and suffered permanent brain damage before Security realized there was a disturbance and broke up the fight.

This case went through several appeals and the original verdict of $4 million dollars was affirmed for the victim. The court determined that the nightclub violated a national "standard of security" that provided for security to be posted outside nightclubs at closing.

Wristbands and Stamps

Many facilities use some sort of mark to let staff know that the person's ID was checked and sometimes for re-entry privileges. A device has not been invented that cannot be altered or duplicated. I have seen very creative ways of removing and reapplying wrist bands and duplicating ink stamps. (Layered security was discussed in Chapter 1). Markings are just one layer, so you need a backup. The backup is employee discretion. Inform guests or post signage that every guest is subject to re-identification at any time. Bartenders, servers, and Security should randomly check ID, as well as whenever there is doubt when serving a drink.

Gratuities

Most service employees would not work at all if it were not for tips. Good tips will attract good employees, but they also attract the bad ones. Your management team needs to decide two things regarding tips. First, will tips be shared, and by whom? Second, will Security accept tips? Either way, you will have some important enforcement issues.

Sharing, or pooling, tips is common in many service businesses. The total money taken in on a shift, or day, or week, is combined and then split evenly among the stakeholders. There are several considerations for management. If management supports the split, they may have to declare the tips as income. Will the support personnel, such as bus persons and maintenance be included? Will supervisors or managers have a stake? (The Wynn Corporation has been through several lawsuits and labor disputes over this issue.) Will Security be included in the split? One advantage of pooling is that it discourages hustling and employees competing for tips. A disadvantage is employees who pocket tips instead of putting them into the pool.

Tips that are not shared (going for your own) have their own issues. Those who work harder earn better tips, but they also tend to compete or fight over tips and turf. Employees also will accept an unreasonably large gratuity, such as for cutting in line, if they know they pocket the entire amount. Finally, if bus persons and other staff are expecting to receive a cut, they will be dependent on the generosity of each server.

As for Security accepting tips, I have seen this go very bad, so I do not recommend it. Security is supposed to be protecting the company's assets, so accepting a gratuity is likely to encourage the bending or breaking of house policies. Most commonly, tips are given to door hosts to gain free or special entry, ignore a fake ID, or to forget the dress code. Tips that are given out of courtesy might come with an expectation of getting a break later. All of these circumstances hurt the business, so tips should be avoided. Enforcement is difficult and you will not catch everyone, but when you do, discipline should be severe to deter others.

Contract Security

Many hotels will have a third-party management company run the nightclub. With that often comes a contract security force. You likely will not have much say as to the policies and procedures of this group, but you should. This needs to be written into the contract so you can require a certain level of training, staffing, and supervision.

"Bouncers" tend to think they are hired for their muscle and size and not their skills in dealing with people. If they do not answer to you, there should at least be some agreements as to how common issues are resolved. Persons who are ejected from the club should be removed from the property entirely and not just dumped in the hotel lobby. I hope that you can have an arrangement where hotel Security is called to accept the supervision of anyone who is removed from the bar.

There is no shortage of one-syllable nightclubs in Las Vegas and third parties manage most of those. In July 2009, one hotel casino was heavily fined by authorities alleging sexual assault, serving to minors, mistreating intoxicated customers, and employee misconduct. This property, which apparently turned a blind eye to the activities in its nightclub, was made an example by the Gaming Commission and had to re-evaluate the security measures and policies at its nightclub, even though it was managed by a third party.

Staffing Ratio

You may find some recommended ratios of Security officers to guests, but they are so variable that it is not worth printing them. A formula like 1 officer to 100 guests would be nice for some venues, but it entirely depends on the location of the club, the layout, type of entertainment, type of clientele, and the Risk Assessment. Remember in Chapter 1 how we calculated how many officers we would need? That assessment will be used to create a Security Plan for your club that includes camera locations, staffing, policies, and other security procedures.

A suggestion to ease this process is to look at similar clubs. Check out their security at the height of their business and during slow times. See if they seem to be handling the crowd well, or are over- or under-staffed. Use that as a guide, but do not duplicate. Your location, building type, and other factors may be different, so use it as a starting point and adjust accordingly.

Occupancy

The leading contributors to most deaths in enclosed venues like nightclubs are overcrowding and panic. Fire, smoke, pepper spray, gunshots, fights, and even power outages can cause panic, stampedes, and death. Any of these events can send everyone running for a single exit. Most people, by nature, will exit the way they entered, regardless of signs and proximity. Besides taking steps to prevent these events, officers need to be trained and ready to direct occupants to safety. This starts with awareness by all employees of the exits and how to use them. Employees should be drilled and encouraged to use emergency exits as often as possible. Security should maintain constant patrols that ensure exits, aisles, and hallways are kept clear. During an emergency, officers should automatically post at exit routes to direct people out. Someone should turn lights on and use the PA system if possible to direct guests. Nonsecurity employees, if trained properly, can supplement Security in emergencies. Emergency plans are discussed in detail in Chapter 10.

In 2003, a fire erupted during a band performance at a nightclub in Rhode Island. Most of the 492 occupants tried to escape through the door in which they entered. One hundred people died from inhalation, burns, and trampling. The fire, which was caused by pyrotechnics, quickly spread black smoke as it burned foam acoustic material. The fire did not actually kill as many victims as did the resulting panic. As you might guess, every person who owned or managed the club, every person related to the band, and even the maker of the foam were sued for hundreds of millions of dollars. Several of them were criminally prosecuted. Besides fire prevention, all employees need to be trained to direct people out of the proper exits.

Room Search

It is a good idea to have security completely search the entire club after closing. This is when paraphernalia related to drugs, sex, and other prohibited behavior will be found. Condom wrappers, condoms, and underwear indicate those areas need to be patrolled better. Syringes, baggies, pill bottles, and other related items indicate where drugs are being used. Officers, using proper personal protective equipment, should check under tables, inside seat cushions, under bathroom sinks, in stalls, and behind curtains. Use this intelligence to alter patrol frequency and awareness of security. Consider saving these items as evidence in case there is an allegation of sexual assault or a drug deal made later.

Some clubs will suspend activity at certain times during the night to do this search. This can be done during a band break, intermission, or DJ change.

Manual

Finally, the nightclub will need its own policy manual (many of those policies are described in this chapter). Including it in the department manual may not be appropriate if you have separate security officers for this venue that will have specialized training or may even be from a different employer. Use the format outlined in Chapter 4.

SECURITY MEASURES

Consider what follows as your toolbox. Each of the tools has a specific use and may be combined with other tools to create multiple layers of Security. Not every tool applies to every venue, and some may not fit into your Security Plan, your budget, or your management style. However, you may find some that you did not consider before. You may employ all of them or some of them in combinations, and possibly others of your own not described here.

Behavioral Recognition

There are many training programs available to teach your security staff how to recognize suspicious behavior. While they focus on one type of activity, such as suicide bombers, active shooters, and other violent behavior, we can use the basics of these programs to identify just about anyone who might threaten our assets. This is touched on in the Retail Policies section in this chapter and the Active Shooter section in Chapter 10, but following is a general overview of the program.

Profiling has gotten a bad name as some lawyers and others misconstrued it as discriminating based on protected classes, such as race. Discriminating based on physical characteristics is not what behavioral recognition is about. The only time we would use physical characteristics to suspect someone is if he or she matched a description of a known criminal or from a group of potential offenders. For example, if you were trying to challenge any member of a Hispanic gang from entering your facility due to a Hispanic wedding taking place, you would use "Hispanic males" as one of the identifiers of those whom you stopped. Note that I said "one identifier" because not all Hispanic males are gang members. The public learned shortly after 9/11 that not all terrorists are of Middle-Eastern descent. Not all Middle Easterners are Muslims and not all Muslims are terrorists. Therefore, we concentrate more on behavior than on appearance, but we do not exclude appearance completely.

The following steps need to be implemented outside the building whenever possible. Once a perpetrator gets in the building, it is much more difficult to get him or her out. In the case of a random shooter or bomber, all he or she wants is to be inside, so it may be too late. This applies to nightclubs, amusement parks, etc.

The first step is to define the activity we are looking to prevent. In a hospitality environment, it may be a suicide bomber, active shooter, violent employee, or other unwanted persons like gang members, drug dealers, and pedophiles. Of course, your answer is that you want no one from that list on your property. That is fine as long as your spotters know what their objective is.

Next is to observe persons approaching the property. Because we are trying to prevent so many types of behavior that are dissimilar, it is simpler to find the behavior that is out of place. After watching guests for a few hours, you build a "profile" of what a hotel guest or nightclub visitor looks like. Then you look for the ones who do not match that profile. It may be a little different from hotel to hotel, but it may include persons who arrive by bus or walk to the property; persons with no luggage; persons traveling alone; young males alone; persons not talking or texting on a phone; persons wearing different clothing, such as heavy jackets, caps, sunglasses at night; and so on. Note that this is where some people get into trouble. None of the activities from this list constitutes violent or criminal behavior. Combined with other characteristics, they may exhibit behavior worth watching: looking around at cameras and security elements, avoiding eye contact, fixed stare or gaze, and being nervous or agitated.

Step 3 is what I call the second opinion or inside layer. Ideally, the outside officer sees a person with a heavy coat, walking alone, with a fixed stare, heading toward the front doors. She radios it in to the officer watching the lobby or a dispatcher who can track the person on camera. The second officer makes the same observations and either confirms it or discounts it with new information. This officer or dispatcher makes the call to challenge the subject.

Step 4 is the challenge. In the hospitality environment, we have to balance the elements of our mission in all situations, especially this one. We want to know who this person is and what he is doing, but we also want to make our guests feel welcome and comfortable. Therefore, while we consider this a "challenge" of the subject's attention, those around us should see this as simple guest service. This is where training meets professionalism and attitude. One—and only one—officer should approach the person outside of the entrance and simply ask some service-related question. "Can I help you find something?" A regular guest will answer quite normally. "I am looking for my family" or "Yes. Where is the restroom?"

This gives the officer a chance to do some close-up analysis of the subject. Eye contact, smile, nervousness, and other facial and body language will decide whether more questions should be asked. Follow-up on the answer to the first question or ask other questions to find his intent in the building. Honest persons will provide quick, helpful answers. Persons who are lying tend to have slow, broken answers, with lots of mistakes in grammar and content. This is because they are processing the story they memorized and repeating it back. This also causes heightened arousal, which can lead to sweating, facial itches, fake yawning or chewing, and agitation. At some point, the subject either will convince you he is a legitimate guest or he is uncooperative and that is the point you ask him to leave. The bottom line here is that this is private property and if you are not a guest, we have no use for you, so have a nice day. Of course, we use courtesy and firmness to avoid offending anyone. I treat everyone as if he is the son of my boss, who will be reporting to her on my actions.

Avoid lying when approaching suspicious persons. I have seen officers tell the subject that he looks like someone in a wanted photo or someone they kicked out before. You do not need a reason for stopping and talking to a guest. If it is done in a friendly way, a legitimate guest will not have a problem with it. You can always tell the truth—tell them they looked suspicious wearing a big jacket in a warm building or they were sweating and pale so you were concerned for their health.

While traveling in a major U.S. city with my teenage son, we entered a famous office building looking for the observation platform on the top floor. As soon as we walked in the main doors, two plainclothes security officers immediately approached us from opposite sides of the lobby. One asked me if he could help me. I was dressed as a tourist, so it was obvious I was not a businessman and had entered the wrong doors. I told him I was looking for the entrance to the platform elevators and he explained I was in the tenant entrance and directed me to the proper place to go. I was not offended or embarrassed and later told my son they probably had Uzis under their jackets for the real bad guys. They were well trained in customer service, behavioral recognition, and probably combat. Security officers need to be better trained and use more discretion than "guards" who do not know better.

If we could put metal detectors and x-ray machines at our front doors, we would not have to think of clever ways to predict behavior. Unfortunately, this is not conducive to our hospitality environment. Instead, your detectors are the employees who staff the entrances of your facility. In a hotel, that would include Parking Attendants, Valet, Bell Desk, Front Desk, Landscapers, Maintenance, and Housekeeping. These employees should be exposed to a behavioral recognition class that provides the awareness needed to identify unusual or aggressive behavior and the steps of notification.

These employees should be watching out for physical and behavioral signs mentioned previously. It is also advisable to provide photos or BOLOs (Be on the Lookout) to these departments. Not only does this make them aware of known criminals in the area, but also it gets them accustomed to watching people's faces.

When employees observe suspicious behavior or see a suspected bad guy, they should have a system in place for contacting security. This can be a simple phone call, a silent alarm that activates door cameras, or even hand signals to other employees. This information, one way or another, needs to get to security or the appropriate person who will challenge the person.

Search Stations

We don't normally associate personal and bag searches with hospitality, but more and more we are seeing this type of access control at our facilities. Common applications are parties or concerts of a certain demographic and VIP events. If you pick and choose which events have their guests searched, make sure it is for good reason. For example, if you search people going into a rap concert, but not a country/western concert, it will appear discriminatory. However, if prior incidents have been associated with a certain band or singer, that gives you enough justification to search those attendees.

If you are going to set up a search station, you are taking on a substantial responsibility. The search gives guests the impression that they are safe from weapons in the event. Here are some Dos and Don'ts of searches.

Do use common sense. A woman wearing skin-tight spandex, where a weapon could be seen, does not need to be searched.

Do provide signs of what items are prohibited and for what items you are searching.

Do provide check-in for prohibited items such as lighters or pocketknives.

Do have a policy for handling contraband, such as drugs.

Do provide camera coverage and at least one witness to all searches.

Do properly train search staff on what they are looking for, what to do if they find it, maintaining a courteous attitude, and how to avoid inappropriate comments and touching.

Do not limit the search to large bags. If you are going to search, search every person and his or her belongings.

Do not use physical (touching) searches. This will cause more problems than you want. Use handheld metal detectors.

Do not empty purses, bags, or pockets. Make a visual check with gloves.

Do not put your hands into pockets or purses. This will avoid allegations of impropriety and theft.

Do not allow exceptions to searches. VIPs, special guests, small children, and little old ladies all get the same search. Discrimination or "profiling" allegations are the last thing you want.

I notice most searches at amusement parks and sporting events are for glass bottles. I suspect this is more to increase alcohol sales than safety. I have never once had my fanny pack checked when entering one of these venues.

In 2010, a man at a nightclub noticed some guests being pat-searched and wanded with a metal detector and others being allowed to enter through another door with no Security measures. During the event, the man was shot by someone who entered through the unsecured entrance. The shooting victim successfully sued the venue for negligence for not following its own admissions policies.

It is important for a Security Plan to be consistently created and implemented so that all persons are treated equally and all risks are mitigated. The second entrance in this case may have been for VIP or known guests, but as this incident proves, it was not a successful practice to treat the two sets of guests differently.

Arrests

As mentioned elsewhere in this book, arresting an offender is your very worst option, so it should be your very last resort. There are a couple of other options for dealing with criminals that are less dangerous, less expensive, and less time-consuming.

Refuse Service

The theme of this book is prevention and the easiest way to deal with problem people is to prevent them from entering your property in the first place. One of the greatest advantages of private security in private enterprise is to refuse service to persons who you deem undesirable to your business. Within your behavioral recognition layer, when someone who will potentially cause trouble is identified, he or she can simply be denied entry. This may include known troublemakers or criminals, ex-employees, or persons who are perceived as being a potential problem. This is one of our greatest tools. We do not need a reason, any evidence, or permission from anyone. We don't even need a sign. Of course, you cannot discriminate—refusing entry to blacks, women, or short persons—but you can refuse service to someone who stinks, who is smoking, or who is playing their music too loud. Remember behavior, not appearance.

Trespassing

The trespass law is one of the most useful tools in our arsenal. States differ in their elements of this crime, but most put trespassing into three parts. The first one relies on posted signs, "No Trespassing", which is not conducive to our open environment. The second part is entering a property after being warned not to enter. This is like the posted sign, except we specifically and verbally warn a certain person not to enter. When they ignore our warning, they are trespassing. This is commonly called an "86" and like the refusal of service, requires no legal reason. You can "trespass" former employees, persons who cause a disturbance, or anyone who you think might have committed a crime. Isn't this a great tool? Just like your own living room, you require no reason. However, for your own sake, you should have policies and criteria on why you 86 people so you can defend these decisions to your boss or your lawyers.

The advantage of trespassing rather than arresting is that you do not need to prove a crime, but it provides the same result. Your job to protect the assets means keeping criminals out. Excluding them from your property keeps criminals out just as well as arresting them, right? In fact, arresting someone does not exclude him or her from returning after he or she gets out of jail.

The third part of trespassing is refusing to leave. Suppose you have someone creating a disturbance. You could try to arrest him for disturbing the peace, which is very difficult to prove and requires testifying witnesses. On the other hand, you can tell him to leave and if he refuses, he is trespassing. The law generally requires one warning, along with the consequences of refusal (arrest). This is a legally stronger arrest, and does not involve other customers. Although it is not required, you should use another security witness and give more than one public warning. For example, holding a first, second, and third finger in the air tells the suspect, nearby guests, Security, and the cameras that you are being reasonable and clear in your warnings to leave.

Last Resort

Arrests cause injury, look bad to everyone, and open you up to false arrest, excessive force, and other legal issues. Less serious, but still troublesome, is the drain on work force, payroll, and lack of security in the rest of the property. Then there is the time taken by the police, jail overcrowding, and so on.

However, sometimes there is no other choice but to make an arrest. Most jurisdictions allow a private person to make a misdemeanor arrest committed in their presence and a felony arrest when reasonable cause exists. Those same laws generally require Security to turn over the arrestee to a police officer. This requires some procedures, equipment, training, and space. Here are some examples of procedures to have in place for when (not if) you make an arrest.

Procedures

When possible, a supervisor should make the decision to make the arrest.

Officers should use company "use of force" policies, approved restraint and compliance methods, and company approved or provided equipment (handcuffs).

For guest and officer safety, two officers should remove a handcuffed person from public view and take him to a dedicated holding area immediately. At least one officer should physically hold the arrestee to prevent injury from fall and to prevent escape.

Once arrest is complete, all force is suspended except that force necessary to transfer the subject to the holding area.

The holding area should be a secure room, away from the public, audio and video recorded, with a bench or chair that is secured to the floor and with a locking seat belt to prevent escape.

The holding room should be inspected before and after every incident to prevent hidden weapons and contraband.

A search is made for weapons for officer safety only. Do not search for drugs, stolen property, or identification. The police will do that.

Remember that the room is recorded, so keep unofficial antics and dialog to a minimum.

Do not allow eating, smoking, or phone calls by the arrestee. The police are responsible for this and will decide what is necessary. Do not allow a restroom break unless the police are extremely long in arriving. Have a procedure in place for this in case you need it.

Have procedures developed for releasing a subject: one for releasing after a bad arrest and one for releasing if the police are not there within a certain time. Discuss this with your counsel. In my opinion, if you make a bad arrest, you are going to be sued, so you should at least be reasonable and release the subject immediately. The old line of thinking was to hold the subject until police arrived and hope for a miracle. If you release the subject and apologize for the inconvenience, you at least appear on video to be reasonable and not trying to do harm intentionally. The lawsuit is going to include false imprisonment and five minutes is certainly better than one hour.

If you are releasing a subject because the police cannot respond (a citywide emergency for example), make that call to the police in the room where it is being recorded. Tell the subject on video why you are releasing him or her, that you will still make a report to the police, and he or she may still be subject to arrest later.

In conclusion, make arrests a last resort. If you are going to deprive someone of his or her liberty, make sure it is lawful and that you can prove it. Be sure to document every step of the arrest and record and save as much video as possible to protect your lawful actions.

Video Patrol

Video patrol is a technique perfected by casino surveillance experts. Casinos and other venues that use cameras to prevent loss, such as retail outlets, are quite good at using cameras to observe, record, and apprehend criminals of all types. The basics included below are a good foundation for your own officers to enhance their skills and increase your effectiveness with camera systems.

Patrol Routes

Just like human patrols, surveillance officers use patrol routes for cameras as well. Routes are areas visible to cameras that can be "patrolled" electronically. Establish these patrol routes based on prior incidents, criticality of loss, and your risk assessment. Camera patrols should be documented and the documents reviewed to ensure no area is being overlooked or neglected. Routes also keep your officers focused and productive, rather than engaged in inefficient, aimless camera patrolling.

Patrol Techniques

See Chapter 9 for monitor positioning. During routine patrol, officers should observe the following:

Guest behavior—This is more recognition. Do they look like guests? Are they acting like guests? Is there any suspicious behavior or suspicious items in their possession?

Employee behavior—Are they in their proper area? Engaged in normal work duties? Acting suspicious? Carrying anything suspicious or out of place? Is Security doing its job?

Property—Are doors closed and secure? Proper lighting? Any visible safety hazards? Anything that just does not look right?

JDLR (Just doesn't look right)—I don't know who coined this phrase, but it fits here perfectly. As your officer is video patrolling, she or he may see something that JDLR. This is where the camera has the advantage: Keep watching the activity until it looks right. Otherwise, it may be something that requires attention and officers are sent.

Camera Positions

Once a suspicious or important activity is identified that will require video coverage, such as a fight or theft in progress, the surveillance officer will manually place cameras. First is the suspect shot. The camera that has been following the suspect should remain on the suspect to get facial images and detail of the actual crime. Second is an overview shot. This angle shows the suspect in relation to his location (e.g., overview of the store, the lobby, or the dance floor). Third is also an overview, but at a slightly closer and opposing angle. This view will show the suspect's and accomplice's faces, hands, and contact with responding officers.

Smaller Operations

We discussed the need and use for cameras and alarm systems in several other locations in this book. Cameras, if watched live, can add more sets of eyes to the behavioral recognition process. Panic alarms can provide notification as described previously. In a large hotel with a security force and a video monitoring room, the advantage is obvious. A smaller hotel that may have a front desk associate and a night auditor also can make use of these types of alarms as signaling devices. When a suspicious person enters the building, the first employee could activate a button that simply notifies the other employee in the back that something is happening. Similarly, in a small operation, a door entry alert will let everyone know that someone has walked in so that he or she can be monitored.

9

Systems and Equipment

The only thing constant in life is change.

François de la Rochefoucauld, author

Innovation is moving at an incredible rate and our industry is right in there reaping the benefits and pondering the questions plaguing so many industry managers. It seems as though as soon as you get the money to install a new gadget or system, it is redesigned the next year. We cannot always keep up fiscally and it may not be necessary. Some systems are absolute requirements while others are just more convenient. Be careful not to get so far behind the technology curve that you are not providing adequate security. The many systems used in the hospitality industry are not necessarily electronic in nature, but I have tried to spend some time and space here with at least a general overview so you will know what to look for in your systems.

FIRE ALARMS

Fire alarms are generally designed, installed, and maintained by an outside vendor or possibly another department, such as Facilities or Engineering. Some properties prefer to have the Security Director (Safety) responsible for the operation of this important system. No matter what your involvement in the fire system is, your department will definitely be involved when it activates, so some knowledge of how it works is required.

The basic fire system has two main objectives: notification and suppression. In other words, it should alert occupants and the fire department and put out the fire. The notification part of the system consists of automatic detectors, manual switches, the control panel, communications interface, and alert devices. The suppression system consists of detectors, water pumps, standpipes, chemical supplies, and sprinklers or chemical emitters. Remember, this is a general overview and your system may contain many more-complicated devices.

Automatic Detectors

The most common visual detector is the smoke or ion detector. This device is often mounted on the ceiling and looks and acts like the smoke detector in your home. It detects smoke with a photoelectric beam just like the one used in a store to alert the clerk of an entering customer. When smoke crosses the beam, a switch is activated. These are commonly tampered with by hotel guests who smoke in their rooms and can be activated in rare cases by an extremely steamy shower.

The ion detector is a bit more complicated to explain, but is also much cheaper and therefore more common. An ion detector uses an extremely small amount of radioactive material to ionize particles that enter a chamber. Smoke particles have a different value than regular oxygen particles do, so they are detected and the switch is activated. Ion detectors are considered better detectors because a fire with high flame has less smoke and sometimes it is not as quickly detected by photoelectric detectors.

Where steam or smoke may be normal, such as bathrooms and kitchens, heat sensors may be used. These simply activate the switch when the temperature in a room reaches a preset threshold.

Carbon monoxide detectors are less common in business applications, but may be used to detect the dangerous invisible gas emitted by gas engines and fires.

Suppression sprinklers, which are addressed later, also act as detectors and do not need any electricity to operate. A fire sprinkler is a valve attached to a water pipe in the ceiling. The valve is held closed by a mechanical detector that is either soft metal or liquid in a vial. The metal or the vial holds the valve closed. When fire in the room heats the metal to its melting point, or the liquid to its boiling point, it breaks and allows the valve to spring open. Water flows from the pipe and extinguishes the fire. There is also a water flow switch somewhere within the pipe. This switch is usually a small flap, like a pendulum, that moves to the side when water starts flowing through the pipe. Water will only flow if a pipe breaks or a sprinkler has been opened. Sprinklers in hotel rooms may be accidentally tampered with if guests use them to hang their clothes on or otherwise tamper with them. Other causes might be a sprinkler being broken off or freezing and breaking. Water flow alarms, because they are mechanical, are generally not false. It means water is flowing somewhere for some reason and that means trouble.

Manual Switches

A manual switch is most commonly seen at a pull station. A handle or button activates the fire alarm when someone engages it. These may be required by some codes and ordinances and they are very useful for evacuating buildings for reasons other than fires. Kitchen hood suppression systems may employ manual switches as well.

Control Panel

The control panel is really the user interface for the brains of the system. It ties all of the external components together, makes the "decisions" for the system, communicates to other components and the alarm company, and annunciates the activity of the alarm.

When a detector, pull station, or other device is activated, it sends a signal to the control panel. The panel carries out several actions depending on its programming. It will annunciate the alarm (provide some sort of readable signal like a light or buzzer) that tells the type and location of alarm (e.g., "third floor water flow"). It also will activate communication to an alarm company, usually via phone lines, and maybe to other locations throughout the complex (e.g., PBX, Security, and Front Desk). The control panel also activates signals, such as sirens and strobe lights, to warn guests of the alarm. Many larger, more modern systems also have an automatic evacuation message. The brains of the alarm system also make more advanced decisions, such as closing and opening certain air vents, activating automatic door closures, and switching elevators to fire mode.

Many large hotels have a Fire Command Center. Fire Command is a room located in a place convenient to responding fire personnel and away from the mayhem of a fire alarm. This room houses all of the brains and ancillary equipment used for the alarm. Communications panels, public address systems, HVAC (heat, ventilation, and air-conditioning) control panels, and other associated systems are maintained in this room. It is advisable (and often required) that this room is accessible by a "Knox box" or a key to the room held in a locked box that every fire truck has. Fire Command also should be a central meeting point for fire chiefs, security, and facility supervisors, and should contain the following equipment: master keys for offices, guest rooms, and elevators; megaphones, safety vests, flashlights, and other evacuation equipment; architectural plans for the building including structural, electrical, alarm wiring, plumbing, and HVAC; evacuation plans and instructions; a phone and important phone numbers (see Chapter 10, Emergency Planning for more details).

Depending on the size of the hotel, enunciator panels may be located in strategic areas within the complex. A smaller building that does not have a Fire Command Center generally has this panel near the main entrance. If there is a security control room, a panel may be installed there. This expedites the deployment of staff to the location of the alarm without first going to Fire Command. Buildings without such a security room may have a panel at a main reception area, front desk, PBX room, or maintenance control room.

Alert Devices

There are several ways the alarm system tells us there is a fire. That is, after all, the reason for having a fire alarm—to have us evacuate. This used to be accomplished with bells. Now we use bells, sirens, horns, and even lights. Because of excessive noise in some applications and because some people have hearing loss or difficulty, strobe lights are required as well as audible signals. We also now use voice messages to remind people that when an alarm activates, it is better to leave the building. There also may be an "all clear" message when the alarm has been verified to be false.

Suppression

The second objective of a fire system is suppression. Automatic and manual suppression systems are routine and required in most hotels.

Water Sprinklers

Water sprinklers, as mentioned previously, serve the dual role of detection and suppression. Each sprinkler head is connected to the same water supply, but acts independently because it is mechanical. The head is a valve that is held closed by a material that is sensitive to heat. When the heat from a fire rises to that temperature, the material melts (metal) or boils (liquid in glass) and breaks. The valve opens and water flows under high pressure and disperses just like a lawn sprinkler to extinguish the fire. Once open, this water flow does not stop until the entire supply is turned off. In a freezing environment like a parking garage, the water pipes may be filled with pressurized air. When one of these heads breaks, airflow is followed by the water in the pipes from underground or inside the building.

Occasionally, a water-filled sprinkler head may become exposed to freezing temperatures if the weather becomes unexpectedly cold. Just like in a house with exposed plumbing, the head may break as the freezing water expands, and when the temperature warms, the ice melts and water will flow from the broken head. This can be an unexpected mess, avoided by keeping those water pipes above 32°.

Chemical Suppression

There are two types of chemical suppression used in most hotels: those that smother the fire (eliminate the oxygen), and those that alter the chemical reaction of the fire. These systems may be wet foam, dry powder, or gas. They are usually manually controlled, but may be connected to automatic sensors. Although Halon is rarely used anymore, there may be areas in your hotel that use a similar chemical that removes oxygen from a room and is dangerous to humans. Some older systems are under such pressure they can blow out windows, so they are dangerous as well. Be sure your emergency procedures consider these systems to ensure that everyone is safe in the event they are employed.

Standpipes

Standpipes are simply pipes that carry water vertically within a building so that fire fighters can have a water supply on each floor. A wet standpipe is tied into the pressurized internal water system and is ready to supply water when a firefighter connects a hose to it. A dry standpipe is an empty pipe that goes into the building from the outside. The fire department plugs into these at the street level and supplies water to the firefighters on the floor. Dry standpipes have to be used in outside applications and where there is not enough building water pressure.

PANIC ALARMS

Panic alarms are manually activated alarms used to provide an extra layer of security in certain areas of the property. We commonly associate panic alarms with bank robberies and similar events. In the case of a bank or jewelry store, it may be connected to a dialer that communicates a silent alarm to a monitoring station where the police are dispatched. This is the scenario advisable for smaller hotels where there is nobody to monitor the activation of the alarm. (Contrary to popular belief, most police departments will not allow these alarms to communicate directly with them.) In larger organizations that have a full-time security force, it may be more efficient to have a panic alarm that communicates directly to the Security Department.

Installation

If the infrastructure and size of the property can handle it, panic alarms are best combined with a closed-circuit television (CCTV) system. For example, when a frontdesk clerk is robbed and presses the panic button, cameras automatically engage on the location of that button, bring that view up on a Security monitor, and begin recording that view. Without much more work, other layers can be added as well.

Before installing this type of system, determine what types of threats are to be prevented. Silent panic alarms that will be monitored by an outside company resulting in a police response should be used for robbery and assault only. The idea of a panic button is that it is hidden and used without the assailant's knowledge. Fire panic buttons should be used only for fires, not for medical or other emergencies. Consider the response expected before installing these buttons and training the users on their operation.

Your local police department will not take kindly to continual "false" alarms where they responded to a robbery alarm to find a group of unruly teenagers or a guest with stomach pains.

When a night clerk at a nationally known motel chain was assaulted while on the job, the panic button at her desk did not work. The alarm company knew that the alarm had been broken for four months. The woman, who ultimately escaped the attacker, settled out of court for $2.5 million. Security equipment that does not work is not only useless, but also provides a false sense of security. Regular inspections will not only ensure that the equipment is working, but also will provide a good defense against lawsuits like this.

Silent alarm switches should be hidden in a place where they are easy enough to access, but not where they will be activated accidentally. The switch can be the best accident avoidance just by its design. Some require a two-finger pinch or a hole where the finger has to be inserted. These cannot be depressed with a knee bump if under a desk. Another idea for a cash drawer is a bait clip or "mousetrap" switch. The two leads on this type of switch are separated by money within the till. When the money is pulled during a robbery, the two leads touch and cause the alarm. There are also foot switches, pull cords, and just about anything that can be a switch. If the purpose of the alarm is a medical emergency or something where its activation will not jeopardize the safety of the user, it can be mounted on a wall, desk, or just about anywhere. The more visible this type of switch is the better.

Associated Equipment

Camera operation during an alarm is also dependent on what will be the reason for the alarm switched to be pressed. Several cameras may be needed to cover the area where the alarm is tripped, the egress points of the area, and an overview. In the old days, the cameras in a bank were film recorders so they would not even record at all until the switch or bait money was pulled. Then every camera in the bank would begin recording. Now, with digital recording and cheaper cameras, we can use the same concept, but instead of starting the recording, the switch might cause movable (PTZ: pan, tilt, and zoom) cameras to turn and zoom into those certain areas. For example, suppose you have four cameras covering overview shots of your main lobby. When a panic button is depressed, one camera zooms in on the main doors, another on the elevators, and one on each side of the front desk to get opposing shots of the incident.

Camera "salvos" like these are dependent on your camera types and their interface with your alarms. If you have someone monitoring video all the time, this modified view of the emergency can assist deployment of security staff or even allow someone to phone the police with an update of the situation. Some companies use the panic button to activate other hardware besides cameras. You can connect lights that alert other persons, lock or unlock certain doors, activate safety shields, and so forth. The possibilities are endless.

Operation

Training on the use of these panic buttons is critical. As mentioned before, the police tend to assume silent alarms are robberies in progress. If your employee uses it for someone with a counterfeit bill or a bad check, the police are going to scold you for crying wolf and may even levy fines. The opposite is also true. If an employee hits the medical emergency button for a man with a gun, medical personnel and unarmed security may come running into an unsafe situation. I suggest testing these alarms on a monthly basis. Make sure it communicates properly (after telling the communications center first) and that cameras and other equipment tied to the alarm work properly. Use this testing as an opportunity to reinforce training. Have the users push the button so they know how to do it and ask them under what conditions they would press it. One minute of training could save lives.

INTRUSION ALARMS

Intrusion (or burglar) alarms are very different from robbery or panic alarms. The main difference is that a burglar alarm is automatic, being activated by the actions of an intruder. The panic alarm is activated by an employee or victim of a robbery. Intrusion alarms use several different types of switches or sensors to activate the alarm. Then that activation is sent to a communications center for police dispatch or to the in-house monitoring area. In some cases, burglar alarms are "local," which means they do not communicate at all and just activate a bell, light, or even a camera.

You may think we do not need burglar alarms because hotels never close. However, there may be some areas that need to be secured even when the facility is open, such as store rooms, and some areas that are restricted at night, such as offices or kitchen areas. So, consider these methods of using alarms to keep your hotel secure and possibly reduce the amount of Security staff.

The first component of a burglar, or intrusion, alarm is the switch. The most common switch is the magnet switch or contact switch used on doors or windows. It is simple: bad guy opens the door or breaks the window and circuit is broken causing the alarm. Next most popular is a motion detector. These can be infrared, photoelectric, or any of several more complicated technologies. These very versatile devices can be used easily to detect persons in a kitchen or convention area. Your Facilities Department may already use these types of devices to monitor climate, boiler pressure, and other comfort and critical systems.

Main Processor

As with a fire alarm, we need a brain to gather information from these systems and decide what to do with the signals. It may communicate to a dialer that notifies the alarm company for police dispatch or your monitoring facility on property. It also may activate a bell, siren, light, camera, or other alerting device. Even cell phones can be the receiver of an alarm.

Most digital camera systems also conduct motion sensing and intrusion functions. These are discussed in the CCTV section of this chapter.

Monitoring

The final component of an intrusion system is the monitoring station. If it is a security facility, then it will be tied in with the design of the control center with procedures for responding to such alarms. A smaller hotel may utilize the frontdesk clerks, who are usually the only people awake all night. They can have a panel that tells them when someone is entering the closed pool, the closed meeting rooms, or breaking into the arcade games. Once again, the possibilities are endless and a little creativity will eliminate some of the need for human patrol during certain hours.

OTHER MONITORING SYSTEMS

Security is often tasked with monitoring many other systems besides Fire and Intrusion. Either this is because of their relevance to Safety or because Security is the department best equipped with a monitoring facility.

Some systems requiring monitoring in a hotel are elevators, escalators, water boilers, generators, valves, HVAC systems, and pool equipment. Many of these systems used to require a human to babysit them and ensure that the machinery did not malfunction, overheat, or cause some sort of safety hazard. Technology has allowed us to watch these components of our hotel remotely and thereby with fewer humans. For example, many hotels still in existence today require an engineer to watch water boilers to ensure that they do not leak or overheat, resulting in an explosion. Modern boilers are built a little safer and with sensors that can be monitored remotely. It is a much more efficient use of time and resources to allow one person, whether it is a security officer or engineer, to monitor all of the systems from one control room. If you have such a control room for video monitoring, dispatching, or alarm monitoring, consider using cameras or sensors to watch some of these important nonsecurity functions.

ACCESS CONTROL

Access control is one of the main functions of Security Departments everywhere. This goes to the very infancy of our industry where asset protection was best accomplished by controlling access. Access control includes locks on doors, remote switches that open locks, officers watching doors, and electronic access systems.

Most hotels now employ some sort of access control system on their guest rooms. Still, more facilities fortify their security with access control to their restricted areas, elevators, and offices. The concept of electronically controlled access requires a reader, an authorization, a mechanism, and, of course, a procedure.

Reader

There are many types of readers and technology is constantly finding ways to make them stronger and more convenient. The reader in its most primitive form is the tumbler or pins within a lock. A key is inserted and the pins are arranged by the key into a unique configuration that allows the cylinder to rotate. The weakest part of this system became the key, which is easily duplicated, lost, or broken.

The next basic reader was a magnetic strip. This method works just like a credit card reader. A card with a strip is inserted into a slot and a magnetic head reads the code from the strip and activates a solenoid or a motor to open the lock. This system still prevalent in hotels has a few faults. The magnetic strip can become worn or demagnetized, the codes can easily be read and duplicated, and the card can break or get lost. Few systems use a bar code in the exact same way as the magnetic strip. These are very easy to duplicate.

Radio frequency (RF) chips are a bit newer than magnetic cards and slightly more secure. An RFID tag is embedded into a card or other object. The lock produces a radio signal that bounces off the RFID tag and receives its data or code. The code is the key that opens the lock. RF locks are a little more expensive, but also more difficult to hack. However, technology is advancing very rapidly that can read these tags from a short distance and obtain their coded information for duplication.

A technology that is really exploding turns the human body into a key. Biometrics allows the reader to read unique features of our anatomy as a key to open a lock. Patterns in the human eye, fingerprints, voice, and now vascular systems are some of the ways we use humans to open doors. This technology is becoming more prevalent and less expensive and is, thus far, almost impossible to circumvent.

Authorization

The second part of the lock is the portion that allows the lock to be opened. In a pin and tumbler lock, it would be the pins. The key puts the tumblers into a certain position and the pins have to align and allow the cylinder to be turned.

In a magnetic or barcode reader, the authorization is in one of two forms. A stand-alone lock, such as older hotel locks, may have a list of authorized codes that allows entry. The guest key code might be 1234, the housekeeper code might be 2234, and the manager master code might be 9234. Each code will work because it is on the list in the memory of the lock. The different codes allow for different levels of access and for identification of which key was used.

In an integrated system, such as one that uses a computer to control several locks in a building, the reader transmits the code to the computer for verification. The computer has a database of authorized persons and the corresponding code allows the door to be opened.

RF keys work in a similar manner. The lock reads the code from the tag and compares it with its internal memory or through a wired system that reads a database.

In biometrics, the reader turns the anatomical pattern into a numerical value called an algorithm. The algorithm converts to a simple integer and compares with a database just as above.

Mechanism

Mechanisms that open locks have little to do with the reader. Thus, a magnetic reader may be used with a motorized lock and a biometric reader may be used with a solenoid lock and vice versa.

In a motorized lock, once the reader authorizes entry, a switch or relay is opened allowing electrical current to flow to a motor, which turns a gear, which slides the latch open. This motor also has to close the latch after entry.

A solenoid lock allows current to flow to a solenoid (kind of an electric spring), which moves a pin or bolt that allows the latch to be turned manually. (A solenoid is the device on a pinball machine that kicks the ball back into the field when struck.)

Motors and solenoids are sometimes used in combination in various types of locks.

As you have probably experienced, these components of a lock do not have to be inside the lock. The reader may be mounted on a wall, the computer may be in a closet, and the mechanism embedded in the doorframe.

Remember that a lock is just one layer of security and should not be expected to be impenetrable. Each type of lock can be defeated electronically or mechanically with simple tools and skills.

KEY CONTROL

One of the responsibilities of the Security Director is key control. Whether you have electronic access control, metal keys, or a combination of both, the accountability for these systems is paramount. We will go over the basic and various components of the two systems and the proper accountability methods that you can customize for your property.

Access Levels

Key systems consist of a hierarchy of access levels that are generally classified as individual, group or submaster, master, and grand master. The hotel may have different names for these levels like room, floor, section, zone, and master or emergency. Do not worry if you are missing a level or have some extra levels. That is not important right now.

Access to a particular level or group of locks is based on job necessity. A maid, who is cleaning rooms on one floor, does not need a key that fits every room in the building. Just like the Marketing Director does not need a key to the accounting office. Therefore, we issue keys and group locks by user instead of by location. Most electronic systems will allow you to program a key to fit just those rooms you need. Older systems group the rooms and keys by floor. Key locks for your offices are by department.

The grouping of keys needs to be in some order before the master keying of a property can be done. Not as important for magnetic locks is the tumbler configuration in a key lock. Your locksmith can explain this better than I can, but pins of different lengths are aligned to allow a cylinder to turn when a key is inserted. To allow a submaster and a grand master to work on this lock, another level of pins is utilized within the cylinder. Therefore, to configure the pins for the unique key, the locksmith will need to know which group or submaster is going to also be used for this lock.

In a hotel, we generally group locks by department. All the administrative offices may be one group, the maintenance storage rooms another group, and perimeter doors another. When the locksmith is keying each of those locks, he or she will also configure the pins for the group master and, of course, the grand master.

Group masters or submasters are those keys that fit more than one lock in a group. Management sometimes is carried away with this system and gives everyone in a department a group master so they will not have to carry so many keys. If the convention sales coordinator needs a key to his office and a key to the supply storage room, give him those two keys. Giving him a key to the entire sales group is a waste and gives him access to areas he does not need. What is the big deal with this if we trust him? Plenty. If he loses his group master, you will have to rekey locks on every door in the group and reissue keys to everyone in that group. Moreover, if something comes up missing from one of those offices or storerooms, now you have more suspects to consider.

The only one who needs a group master is the one who needs access to every door in that group. That is not necessarily the boss, although he or she will want one. Perhaps it is the secretary or the person responsible for inventory. It is very important that keys be issued and accounted for by one person or department, such as Security. There should be a process in hiring, firing, and transfers that ensures only current employees have access to their specific areas. What tends to happen is, employees come and go and they may forget to turn in their keys, or only turn in some of them because they put their office key with their house key and they forget about it. When that loss occurs, you don't know who the suspects are because there are unknown keys in circulation. Worse, a termed employee turns violent and now we don't know who has access to the new boss's office. If we have an accounting of who has which keys at any given time, the necessity and expense of changing locks becomes moot.

Grand Masters

Grand master keys—those that fit every lock in the building—are usually not taken as seriously as they should be. Everyone wants one as a matter of prestige. The General Manager wants one, the CFO wants one; in fact, most department heads will justify their need for one in case they are working late in the office or showing clients and vendors around. This is a huge liability and you need to put your foot down on this one. None of these people needs a key to every single door in the property. Maybe a submaster will do. Explain to them the cost of rekeying every lock when they lose theirs. Explain to them that they will have to be investigated like everyone else who has a key when property comes up missing. Tell them they will have to justify their whereabouts if a witness reports two people having sex in a linen closet after business hours.

Grand master keys should be limited to those that need emergency access to every part of the building at all hours. Ideally, it is checked out as needed and never leaves the property. There needs to be one or more available for fire department and SWAT team personnel and that is about it. If someone needs to get into the controller's office because he is away on vacation, then he or she can call Security.

If you are fortunate enough to key or rekey your building from scratch, keep these considerations in mind. Do some research on quality locks. Endurance of the parts is more important than the unique key configurations. If you are replacing hundreds or thousands of locks, go with a company that will provide a unique key profile (one that is hard to find at the local hardware store). Remember that a lock will not keep out criminals. Locks are a deterrent to unauthorized entry, so they really just keep people honest. If you are trying to secure a room against entry, you need multiple layers such as cameras, alarms, and other locks. Establish a numbering and filing system for keys and their users. This system should be based on the grouping we discussed previously. Finally, make sure strong and thorough policies are in place to protect the integrity of your lock system: duplication of keys, reporting lost keys, turning in keys upon termination, unauthorized use and trading of keys, etc.

CCTV

Closed circuit television is really an outdated term, but it is technically an accurate way to describe video systems. Video systems have changed dramatically over the past 20 years, with the most drastic innovation being digital. The main components of a video system are the camera (input), a switch (control), a recording medium (output), and a monitor (output).

Cameras

Even if we have not been intimately involved in their operation, we have all seen how cameras have progressed over the years. Of course, like everything else, they are smaller, but they also have improved in color, clarity or resolution, and image type (digital versus analog).

Analog cameras are still very much in use, but they are slowly being phased out. Analog cameras are the ones you have in your facility if it is more than five years old. Without getting too deep into the technical stuff, analog is the format delivered through the modulation and amplitude of linear frequencies. The bandwidth used to deliver the image does not change, so storage and resolution do not really change.

For analog cameras to record their image onto a digital recorder, such as a DVR, their signal needs to be converted to a digital format. This is often through an external piece of hardware installed somewhere between the camera and the DVR or in the DVR itself.

Digital cameras convert images to data instead of frequency and amplitude. Therefore, the image does not degrade through copying or transmission. Either it makes it or it does not. Analog television that has interference gets shadows, wavy lines, and distorted images. Digital television has the same clarity regardless of the interference. The interrupted pixels are just taken out, resulting in a blocky image.

Camera installation depends on the application and the purpose of the camera. Fixed cameras—those that do not remotely move or adjust—are used to watch a single two-dimensional rectangle image. If everything that needs to be viewed is within that rectangle, then a fixed camera is the way to go. Different lenses and add-ons can be used for wide angle, telephoto, and low light conditions. Remotely operated or automatically moving cameras, called PTZ have motors in them that move the camera side to side, up and down, and in and out. Side to side is actually a rotating function, turning the base of the camera any place within a complete circle. Tilt refers to pivoting the camera on its base and zoom is controlled by the lens motor like a consumer camera. The focus and iris generally have a motor to keep objects in focus and the light balanced as the camera moves. These moving cameras cost about 10 times that of a fixed camera, so you need to justify their installation.

A PTZ camera really has more than a 360-degree field of view. Think of a camera mounted on a ceiling. It can rotate 360 degrees around in a circle. It also can tilt from the horizontal view of the ceiling all the way down to a vertical view of the floor. This is 90 degrees of tilt, but because the camera can rotate around, the camera sees 90 degrees back up the opposite side. In other words, if the camera were mounted inside of a globe, it could see the entire southern hemisphere of that globe.

PTZ cameras are used in two applications. First, they can be programmed to automatically "patrol" any area within their 360- × 180-degree field of view. Whereas they used to just "pan" from side to side, now we can build a "macro" that rotates, tilts, and zooms the camera all over the field of view. This is common in a large area like a parking lot where the camera patrols the outer perimeter, then angles down to each lane of the lot as it tours the entire area.

In reality, these cameras, depending on how long their tour is, will miss many of the important incidents you are trying to capture. While the camera is looking at one side of the lot, the crime could be occurring on the opposite side. However, the deterrent is there, and if the camera is concealed in a dark housing, the bad guys will not know where it is looking. The automatic camera also provides some other investigative tools, such as "time-framing." If you are looking to see when an incident happened, such as a broken window, you can narrow it down to the time of the camera tour by reviewing the video.

The second application for a PTZ camera is where monitoring takes place live. Casinos regularly use PTZ cameras to view the action on table games or to follow subjects around their property.

A third type of camera is fixed but also allows for the features of a PTZ. These cameras are referred to by many names, brands, and technologies, and produce a 360-degree image all at once. Imagine your favorite Internet map site. You can go to street level and look at a view of your neighborhood in a 360-degree circle. This is done by a car driving on your street with four (usually) cameras that have a 90-degree field of vision. The cameras are in time sync and software within "stitches" the four images together so it seems like it is one image. Another method of doing this is a special lens that is like a "fisheye," but produces

Most nonsecurity managers will turn to cameras to solve their crime problems. Meat is missing from the freezer—put up a camera. Employees are having sex in a closet—install a camera. Graffiti is found in the parking lot—buy another camera. It is important to remind these managers that a camera is not the answer. You will not catch a crime in progress with a camera unless you have the workforce to monitor it live. Even if you get a video image of the suspect, you may not be able to identify him or her. Even if you identify the suspect, you would have to get police to file charges and go after him or her. After all that, recovering the loss is unlikely.

Cameras are a good deterrent because most criminals are hesitant to commit a crime on video. Some companies take this to the extreme of installing dummy cameras that do not work. Most lawyers will advise you against this as it provides a false sense of security if someone is being assaulted and is relying on these cameras to catch the act in progress.

the same hemispherical image with one camera. So, when monitoring the same parking lot, instead of moving the camera, you just increase the magnification of the area of the lot you want to see. This is like a virtual PTZ because the entire range of the camera is available for view; you are just moving your view of that image. These cameras eliminate the missed images from the auto pan camera and they are coming down in price because they do not need the motors used in a PTZ.

Camera Mounting

The standard practice for mounting cameras has generally been on the ceiling or high up on a wall. This prevents tampering, blocking, and generally provides a good overview of the area. In some situations, this may not be the best practice. If the purpose of the camera is for facial recognition or to get a good view of a subject's face, being high up is now one of the worst locations. Most bad guys tend to look down so people will not see their faces and they wear hoods and caps that mask them from high cameras. License plates on cars also are not read very well from a high angle. These need to be viewed from plate level. The good news is that cameras are now smaller, easier to conceal or put out of the way, and can be made to be tamper resistant. Many teller windows in banks and retail now have cameras affixed to the counter. The camera gets a facial view of the customer. Even if he does not want his face seen, by the time he notices the camera and blocks it, we already have his image. You also can mount a camera in a tamper-resistant bubble right at eye level near a doorway or at an intersection in a crowded lobby. By the time most people see it, it is too late to avoid it. Even if they do know it is there, it is a great deterrent, like the greeter at a retail store. Cameras can provide a very good image from a very small hole, so cameras can be mounted in walls, cabinets, fixtures, door frames, and just about anywhere else.

Covert cameras can be very revealing, but can get you into trouble if used in the wrong setting or for the wrong purpose. Generally, you should not put a camera in a place where someone has an expectation of privacy. Bathrooms, locker rooms, and guest rooms are big no-nos. Even offices may be trouble if they are considered private. Audio recording laws vary by state, but generally do not permit recording unless notice is given. Check with your lawyer for these applications.

The bottom line on mounting cameras: Decide what it is you are trying to view, the best angle from which to view it, and then figure a way to get the camera to mount in that place.

The Switch

There are many different names and configurations for the hardware that controls the cameras and routes their signals to recorders and monitors. Commonly referred to as a switch, this device or set of devices acts like a phone switchboard and takes the input of the camera signal, marries it with the remote controls for the camera, and assigns the signals to the outputs: the recorders and the monitors.

The switch allows you to have more than one remote controller within the system. The security control room will have one, but the hotel manager may want one of his own. This is not difficult to install, but you must ensure that the security controller can override the others in the event of an emergency or important investigation.

Many newer systems have a "virtual" switch. In this situation, all the cameras go into the computer and the software assigns them to various monitors and recorders and provides remote controls.

Monitors

Video monitors in analog systems are installed parallel to the recorders. The video signal comes from the switch and is split between the monitor and the recorder. The monitor is viewing exactly what the recorder is recording. In a digital system or one with a virtual switch, the monitor is viewing whatever the software sends to it. So, while the recorder is recording live, real-time images, the monitor can be used to watch other cameras, playback of recorded material, or enhanced and multiple images created by the software.

In older configurations, we would use one monitor to watch one camera view, or split views of two or more cameras. The cameras assigned to the monitors could be changed, but that created confusion when reviewing playback. With a software system, any configuration of views can be displayed and changed without affecting recording or playback.

Therefore, configuration of monitors (what we want to watch live) is dependent on who is watching, what is being watched, and what the purpose of watching it is. We need to know who is watching it because a hotel manager is looking at his employees goofing off, if there are long lines in his lobby or valet, and other business-related functions. The chief engineer wants to see that his equipment is running properly and nobody is tampering with it. These are self-explanatory configurations and their monitor setup will not affect the security of the building.

The security monitor setup is much more important. Before we look at the physical setup, we need to tend to the human aspect of watching video. Most studies have shown that a person cannot effectively watch more than about 10 monitors. Even at 10, there is fatigue that occurs after some time and is dependent on other duties, such as dispatching and logging of activity. It also depends on what is being watched. A person trying to watch 10 images with a lot of activity will not see everything he should. If he is just watching 10 doors to see if someone enters them, then that would be easier. To have the most effective video monitoring station, set it up something like the following:

Create a video wall of monitors on a vertical surface in front of the operator. Three-sided viewing stations or curved walls cause blind spots and fatigue from the officer moving his head around. This wall will use peripheral as well as direct eyesight. The distance of the wall from the operator depends on the width of the wall. If the wall is wide, it needs to be farther back or vice versa. Keep the distances short enough so the operator will hardly move his head, but just move his eyes from one side to the other.

Those images that have less activity are placed near the outer edges of the wall. They can be of a smaller size because we are not looking for detail, just movement: a back door of the hotel, the company safe, the receiving dock at night. Near the center of the field of view (eye level) should be the larger monitors showing important areas of activity: the main lobby, the pool, nightclub, retail center. At desktop level, right in front of the operator, are two or three working monitors. These cameras may show alarm views, and will be used for patrol. These also can be used to bring up images seen on the smaller monitors that require an extra look. (This was discussed in Chapter 8.)

Recorders

Once again, back in the old days, we used videocassette recorders. We started with one recorder recording one camera, and many older buildings still employ this type of system. In the late 1980s, we advanced to multiple recordings of cameras onto one tape. These multi-recorders took an input of (up to) 16 cameras, recorded a frame from each of them every second, and recorded it on the tape. Using the same machine to play back the images, we saw one frame of video per second. This created a choppy image (TV is about 30 frames per second) and was useless for watching currency transactions, but acceptable for watching closed areas for activity. The advantage was using one video cassette instead of 16. Digital video recorders (DVRs) came on the scene in the late 1990s and made this process much better. The frame rate on a DVR can be adjusted from 1 to 30 so the clarity of the image is improved. Also improving the image is digital recording instead of analog. Because each pixel from the camera is duplicated onto the recorder as data, there is little or no loss of clarity. Finally, compression has allowed us to save storage space on the DVR with less loss of picture.

If you are like me, you care less about how the DVR does its job and more about *if* it does it. Here are the basics you need to know when selecting a DVR configuration.

Frame rate is from 1 (choppy) to 30 (smooth). Thirty frames per second is better, of course, but uses way more storage space. And, it is really not needed. A view of a door or gate can be at a lower frame rate because the movement is less important. A camera view of a poker game requires a higher frame rate to see the cards, the action of the deal, and the money exchanging hands.

Number of ports only matters in the event of a failure. If you lose the DVR or the hard drive crashes, you lose all of those camera feeds. There are different types of backups or even redundant systems that should be employed in case a unit fails or even becomes full.

Storage space is now relatively small and inexpensive. The problem is that as we get storage space more compact, we also get better camera resolution, which uses more storage space. You just need to watch as you increase resolution that you have your storage limits increased proportionately. Over 30 days is probably not necessary and most hotels find that 7 to 10 days of storage is acceptable. Remember that panning cameras and those with more motion use much more storage than fixed cameras with no activity. This is not due to frame rate, but compression.

Other recording systems are still digital but may be computer- or server-based. These record as a DVR does, but store the data on servers that are linked. When one server is full, it switches to the next, and so forth. One or more servers can be used as a backup and either simultaneously store data or begin storing when another fails. This system is called a network video recorder (NVR).

REPORTING SOFTWARE

The second most important job of a Security Department is documentation. (Prevention is first.) All activities of the Security Department must be documented to show evidence that those events occurred, how they occurred, and why they occurred. Daily logs of patrol activities and incident reports of unusual events are the most common and most important of the events that we document. Logs are used to research incidents, show evidence of pre-ventative patrol, and track performance of officers. Incident reports provide a summary of an event to upper management, present our side of the story of an incident in court, and track events for later risk assessments.

The traditional way to document activity is a paper log. A standard table or spread-sheet of date/time, location, officer, and activity is the general structure of this log. Incident reports generally consist of a fact sheet with the statistics of the event and those involved, a narrative, supporting statements, and summary of evidence. (Report writing is covered in Chapter 11.)

Since the personal computer became prevalent in business, we have turned to the word processor to write our reports. The software does not matter—as far as the final product is concerned—because our legal system still uses paper documents. Thus, the selection of using pen and paper, word processor, or reporting software really does not matter from a legal standpoint. This is a business choice and is dependent on the conve-nience of the users.

In the past 20 years, software companies have produced reporting software specifically for the functions of security. This type of software generally integrates several modules, such as daily logs, incident reports, Lost and Found, personnel management, and others. There are three big advantages of using this software over the standard word processor.

Searching is one advantage of reporting software. Looking up a previous incident by a guest's name or date becomes much easier and faster. Another advantage is statistical data reports. You can determine crime trends, costs of incident management, total losses incurred, and whatever is important to you. An archive is the final advantage of reporting software. Data obviously saves room over paper documents, but is also safer because it can be backed up and filed in different ways.

Because reporting software does not really improve the quality of the final product, your decision to purchase and use it will depend on whether it saves you time and money. A smaller hotel may not save very much time on reports and logs in this type of system, but a large hotel that produces massive amounts of data will find that an integrated system will save time and labor on inputting data and exporting it.

TRACKING SYSTEMS

The justification for tracking systems was discussed in Chapter 8. The tracking system takes the place of manually logging the patrol routes and frequencies of our officers. Instead of relying on the integrity of these logs and the inherent "fudge factor," the tracking system proves that our officer was where we said he was. This section discusses the tracker's technical aspects and how they are operated.

History

Tracking systems date back to the middle of the last century when night watchmen would tour a building. They wore a large clock on a strap around their neck and each time they came to a designated check station, there would be a key hanging there. They would insert the key in their lock and it would log that they were there at that time and place. Over the years, the concept has hardly changed and the two components have only changed in their size and technology. As you might imagine, our biggest challenge is the human component that seeks to defeat the system, which feels like they are carrying around their own supervisor.

Today

Sixty years or so has taken us from keys to magnets to magnetic encoding to barcodes and radio frequency. Most devices now use an RF chip that is read by a handheld reader the size of a couple of rolls of quarters. The RF chips or buttons are placed in those strategic places around the property that you want inspected on a regular interval. Hotel stairwells and linen rooms are common hotel patrol points. Boiler rooms, swimming pools, laundry rooms, and kitchens might be other applications.

Buttons

The buttons are placed with glue or screwed into mounting plates and then the location has to be logged into a database. Buttons can be as small as a dime or as large as a cigarette lighter depending on the type of reader, but should be mounted out of the way and in an inconspicuous spot where the decor of the area will not be compromised. Be aware that the location of and around this button will become worn and unsightly. Constant contact from hands, fingers, the reader, and so forth tends to wear out wallpaper, paint, and polished surfaces. It is best to hide it. The officers will know where it is and guests do not need to see it. Buttons will wear out over time and often become dislodged from the surface. This is to be expected.

The Reader

The reader is a device usually carried in the hand and may be used with a belt holster, a wrist strap, or carried in the pocket. Lately these devices have been made out of metal, as the plastic ones tend to break with abuse. I have seen these things abused like you cannot imagine. Security officers, regardless of how the trackers are justified as their "friend," absolutely hate carrying them. I suppose they see them as babysitters or supervisors always looking over their shoulder. I have caught officers beating them against the wall, throwing them off the building, dipping them in water, and even trying to electrify them. This piece of valuable equipment, like a car or radio, needs to be inspected at every changeover and those in possession of it held accountable for damage.

The reader, usually referred to by its brand name, reads, collects, and stores data from the buttons. The user touches or scans the button and is rewarded with a beep or a light. The data is stored in memory until downloaded.

More advanced readers are actually wireless GPS transmitters that send the data via an internal network. This is a great safety device, for location of the officer, if you can afford it. A cellular device with GPS is not practical for hotels because of their vertical locations. These are better used for wide area patrol. Some buildings have been equipped with an internal GPS or locator system. It uses internally installed transceivers to pin-point locations. This system can be integrated into your radios, phones, track readers, and dispatching system as one system. Imagine the benefits of knowing the location of your employees at all times.

Tracking Software

The reader, unless it transmits wirelessly, needs to be downloaded on a regular basis to a database. I recommend doing this every time the reader changes hands. This gives an opportunity to inspect the reader and save its data before it is accidentally lost.

Once the data is downloaded, the reporting software allows management to review the activities of its patrol officers. Never assume that patrol is going along fine without checking. Lazy officers will test you by not using it or using it incorrectly. Supervisors need to address gaps and inconsistent patrols on a regular basis.

Management will need to decide how many buttons need to be "hit" in a patrol route and how long the gaps between buttons can be. If you require one tour of your tower every hour and there are 20 buttons, then there should be no more than three minutes between hits and all 20 buttons hit. There will be exceptions if an officer has a noise complaint or a report in a guest room. This is an acceptable gap, but should be logged to explain the gap later. Some suppliers provide a wallet with "excuse" buttons for the officer to scan if he goes on a call. These scans in the data report can be matched with the dispatch log to make sure the officer is not abusing the process.

As mentioned in the Chapter 8, this tracking system can be your best friend. When the unthinkable happens in your hotel, this proof of your preventative patrol may be the only thing that saves you from an inadequate security ruling.

LOST AND FOUND

Lost and Found policies are discussed in Chapter 8. This section explores the systems used to manage the Lost and Found process. Many reporting software products offer a module that helps to log items left unattended by guests. Because we are unfortunately responsible for these items left in our possession, we protect these assets as if they were our own. Like our other logs and reports, we can do this with paper, a simple spreadsheet, or a commercially produced software program.

Unlike reporting software, the Lost and Found database needs to have some security functions. A simple spreadsheet would be difficult to secure so that other users could not delete entries or edit them. When creating a program—or purchasing one—keep the following features in mind.

Access Rights

Users of the property database need to have access rights depending on their duties. Be careful not to give any one person the ability to enter, modify, and return items. There needs to be a check and balance or dual security on these transactions to avoid theft.

Audit Trail

The software should include the ability to track every data entry, modification, or deletion. The report should include the date, time, user, and action taken. This will be a way for management to audit the integrity of the users and the process.

User Access

The system should be server-based so that the database can be accessed from various locations on the property. This is for guest service.

EMPLOYEE LOCKERS

Lockers naturally fall under the purview of Security because they provide asset protection. Many businesses buy lockers, install them, and let the employees use them as they please. These days, you need to regulate and administer lockers so they are not abused, used for criminal activity, or prone to be a nuisance for the company.

Lockers

Locks on the lockers need to be of a type where management can open them. Keyed padlocks with a master key are probably best. Combinations are too complicated for many employees and are difficult to track and change. Make sure the lockers are in open areas where theft can be kept to a minimum.

Locker Placement

Locker rooms should be avoided because you cannot install cameras and thefts are more likely where employees forget to lock them. These lockers tend to become health hazards with dirty clothes, old food, and other live-out-of-the-locker issues. Lockers are best placed in hallways where there is traffic to watch them. Encourage employees to take their items to the dressing room for changing. A public area naturally discourages employees from leaving their personal items, trash, hangars, etc., around their lockers.

Security for Lockers

You cannot place cameras in a locker room, but if they are in a hallway, cameras used for watching other areas can watch the lockers as well. Theft most commonly occurs when employees forget to lock their lockers, or when they are too lazy to lock them. Make this part of your back-of-house patrol to check lockers and locks. Employees who steal from fellow employees are about as low as you can get. Anything you can do to prevent or catch these thieves is best for your property.

> Problem: Employees leaving lockers unlocked in the men's locker room find their property stolen during their shift. Solution: You cannot put cameras in a men's locker room—or can you? How about a hidden camera inside a locker? Set up a camera that just sees the face of the person opening the locker and nothing else. Place some bait in the locker and wait. Anyone opening the locker is a likely suspect and if you cannot see them remove the item, that is okay because you know they are the only ones who opened it. Remember, we do not need evidence or all of the elements of a crime to terminate an employee for stealing. This is an easily justifiable termination and you never have to reveal to the suspect that you had a camera there.

KEY DISPENSERS

Key dispensers used to be security officers. It did not take long, after these automated devices were created, to justify them through labor savings. A key dispenser is generally a cabinet that securely holds several key rings until they are individually unlocked from the cabinet electronically. The access method can be a numeric code, print reader, magnetic swipe, or any type of access device you want to attach to it. Key dispensers can issue keys without having another human present, or they can require two or three people to be present (to enter their access code) to issue a high security key set.

Key sets used in key dispensers are of the type that cannot be opened without damaging the ring, so one of the keys cannot be removed without authorization. In fact, this type of ring should be used for all issued key sets, whether or not you use the dispenser.

The most wonderful thing about the key dispenser—okay, the second most wonderful next to labor savings—is that it keeps a permanent audit trail of keys issued. In fact, you can set alarms so that high security keys kept out past their curfew notify you so you can see what is going on. Key dispensers are expensive, but if you spend a lot of time issuing keys, looking for them when lost, or figuring out who has what and for how long, they may be for you. Key dispensers also can be modified to issue other items, such as radios, patrol track wands, etc.

10

Emergency Procedures

Plans are nothing. Planning is everything.

Dwight Eisenhower, president

This book will not be detailing plan writing. That topic is too specific to property and organization to address in a general fashion here. However, we will go over the basics and some things to consider if you are writing a plan. I completely agree with President Eisenhower when he said plans are nothing because I have seen numerous organizations spend a lot of time and money to produce plans that sit on a shelf. Plenty of credible, intelligent people can help write a plan, but without exercising, training, and testing, it is a huge waste of effort and expense. The first part of this chapter addresses Emergency Planning from a property perspective. The second part is Business Continuity or Continuity of Operations (COOP) planning. Specific emergencies and their best responses are covered last.

PLANNING

The purpose of a risk assessment is to identify hazards and threats and prioritize them so they can be addressed in order of importance. Hazards and threats can be natural, such as weather, earthquakes, and floods; or they can be manufactured, such as terrorism, robbery, and slip and falls. A newer category of threats is technological and includes computer server breakdown, power failure, and so forth.

Your first step is to identify potential threats or hazards and list them. If you are not sure what they are, contact your local emergency manager or their Web site and see what disasters they prepare for as a region. Most hazards that are potential to the region are also a threat to your property.

Once this list of potential emergencies is created, it is time to assemble a team that will help you analyze the threats and plan for them.

Up until the end of World War II, most major emergencies were handled locally. Transportation and communication were limited, so there was little for the federal government to do for a hurricane or major earthquake. The military had the most experience in planning huge deployments and responses due to the wars. During the Cold War, emergency planning turned to civil defense and the government became active in helping citizens prepare for disasters, such as nuclear fallout.

As the chance of war carrying over to U.S. soil diminished when the Cold War ended, FEMA (Federal Emergency Management Agency) started to focus on other hazards and natural disasters. When 9/11 happened, we went back to war (or security) mode and established the Department of Homeland Security, which took on FEMA. Then Hurricane Katrina hit and proved that the country really was not prepared for natural disasters of a major magnitude, so the pendulum swung back to disaster preparedness.

A simpler way of explaining our national focus is that people focus on whatever crisis is fresh in their minds. Unfortunately, this is not just a government phenomenon, but all of us are pretty much the same way. You may receive calls from your boss, who hears a news story, and asks, "What are we doing to prepare for that?" It is our job to be prepared for every potential threat, whether it is a hot topic or not.

Team

As with developing any policy, it is best to gather a group of stakeholders, such as department heads, safety or response representatives from each department, or even a focus group of motivated employees. This should include each department that is involved when you have an emergency. Most employees and managers are happy to help and be part of the solution during an emergency event. They realize the importance of the event and will do whatever they can. If, for some reason, you do not have this kind of buy-in from employees, you may need to evoke help from the big boss to get everyone into the game. Fire alarms, earthquakes, and hurricanes mean "all hands on deck."

Once you have your team, establish your authority. In the public sector, this is done through official proclamations or laws. In the private sector, it may be a verbal or written order from your boss. The team then establishes objectives, a timeline, and a budget if possible. Objectives may include a mission statement or a list of threats to work on. The timeline will be your meeting schedule with specific deadlines. The budget may be zero, or part of your current budget.

After this team-forming process, planning is straightforward. Start with the emergency (i.e., fire, flood) and then list your objectives. Objectives may include evacuation or shelter-in-place. When you have your objective, create a second list of procedures to accomplish that objective: announcements, checking guest rooms, staffing elevators and stairwells, directing guests to safe areas, etc. Remember, this is Emergency Response and not Business Continuity. We will take care of the assets in Business Continuity coming up.

Then each department lists its own procedures during the fire (or other emergency). Bellpersons cover the elevators during evacuation, housekeepers help direct guest to the stairwells, frontdesk personnel bring a rooming list to assembly area, etc. (These are examples, so each department list should be a bit more detailed.) This process is conducted as a group so there is no redundancy of duties and nothing is left out.

Evacuation Planning

As I have mentioned, and will mention several more times, do not create a plan that will sit on the shelf. The plan needs to be created by the ones who will follow it. If you hand out your plan to other departments expecting them to follow X, Y, and Z during an emergency, then good luck. The good news for emergency planning for your property is there are really only three plans that the entire property will have to choose from for every disaster or emergency: full evacuation, partial evacuation, or shelter-in-place.

Full evacuation is used for fires (not fire alarms), gas leaks, active shooter, and other situations where the entire building is temporarily or permanently uninhabitable or too dangerous to occupy. Partial evacuation is when any portion of the property has to be cleared, such as fire alarms, bomb threats, and minor fires. Shelter-in-place is used as a response to emergencies outside, such as a riot, extreme weather, or citywide disaster. Evacuations, partial or full, need to be kept simple. Either you leave or you don't. Employees should have to remember only where they are going, how they get there, and maybe one duty they have on the way out.

The first part of an evacuation plan is to select an outside assembly area. This is generally a parking lot, garden or pool area, or maybe a neighboring business. The area needs to be large enough to hold as many guests as your hotel does. Alternate assembly areas need to be chosen to be used in the event of inclement weather or, in the case of terrorist attacks, the possibility of secondary attacks. Security will be in charge of selecting and guiding everyone to the evacuation area.

The second part of the plan is emergency exits. These exits obviously differ for each department or area of the building. Each employee should be taught two exits from each area of the building. As discussed previously, this will be covered in department training.

The third and final part of the emergency evacuation plan is one duty that each employee will do as he or she leaves the building. It may be to secure money, take an employee roster, or gather nearby guests and guide them to the exits.

After the plan is fully prepared, training can begin. Each member of each department needs to know his or her duty during the emergency and where to look for guidance if he or she forgets or has problems. This training also can be accomplished as a tabletop at a meeting or shift briefing where each employee learns, discusses, and verifies his or her knowledge of the plan.

Once each employee in the department understands his or her part in the emergency plan, departmental exercises can take place. A departmental exercise is generally done under the supervision of Security or the coordinating department to make sure it coincides with the property-wide plan. This can be done at the convenience of both departments. This type of exercise is an actual physical walk-through and need not involve guests or disturb the business. It simply starts with something like, "Suppose the fire alarm starts ringing right now . . ." Each person walks through each task—grabbing the rooming list, securing money drawers, walking toward the exit, etc.

This can be done as often as possible until each employee can do it without assistance. Then, obstacles can be added. Suppose an exit is blocked, someone does not show up at the assembly area, or it is snowing outside. These alternate steps that are added in to address contingencies should be written into the plan.

Property-wide exercises require preparation and collaboration. Most office buildings do these at least annually, but in a guest-based business like ours, this is more difficult. We are apprehensive about inconveniencing our guests for the sake of a fire drill and chances are management is not going to go for it. I have some suggestions for compromise on this issue.

First, plan the drill on a day when occupancy is extremely low. Select a time when fewer guests will be affected. Noon, for example, finds most people awake and already out of the building. Once a date and time are settled upon, you can warn guests well in advance. Advising them upon check-in with a reminder notice under the door the night before might be best. Signs in the lobby, elevators, and room floors are also helpful. You may want to make this a marketing event, showing your customers how prepared you are, inviting their feedback, and even giving away flashlights with your logo on them.

In 1992, Rick Rescorla reasoned in his risk assessment of the World Trade Center that the building was susceptible to a truck bomb being deployed in the underground garage. His security plan included evacuation drills for the Morgan Stanley Company for which he worked in the towers. Only a year later, terrorists actually used a truck bomb as described and Rescorla's plan got everyone out of the building safely. In 2001, when planes were used to attack the same buildings, almost every employee of Morgan Stanley was safely evacuated. Rescorla had continued his periodic evacuation drills based on the foreseeability that another attack could occur— and he was right.

Management and employees whined and complained about the incessant evacuation drills that Rescorla forced them to do on a regular basis. He did not waiver in his insistence and it paid off for every single employee except Rescorla, who died making sure everyone got out safely.

Through the department and property-wide exercises, tabletops, training, and drills, you should gather some useful feedback and corrections that need to be incorporated into the written plan. This evaluation can be obtained at the time of the drill, or at meetings held afterward. Either way, the plan remains a living document that never has time to collect dust on the shelf. Because after it is corrected, the process starts over and continues. It is not correct to assume after a couple of revisions that the plan is complete. There will always be changes to the building, new employees, promotions, and other physical and organizational alterations that need to be adjusted in the plan. This planning cycle is illustrated in the section Business Continuity later in this chapter.

The Security Department had two responsibilities in this process. One was to coordinate the other departments and make sure they all knew their place in the plan. Second was to actually handle the emergency directly. Security may have life-saving, firefighting, or other vital duties during an emergency, so it needs its own training on those incidents separate from the property training. The security manager on duty generally assumes command of these incidents. Some of those responses are discussed in the final section of this chapter.

Remember, because you spend about a third of the day at work and take days off (sometimes), the chances that you are at work when an emergency occurs is only about 25 percent. Make sure someone can take charge in the event of an emergency and that everyone participates in the planning and training.

Success

Measuring success of your plan is achieved when some of the following indicators are noticed. Senior management buys into the program. Your plans are incorporated into financial and personnel procedures. Plans are mentioned in newsletters, other manuals, or mailings. Every level of employee has an awareness of the procedures.

NATIONAL INCIDENT MANAGEMENT SYSTEM

In 2003, President George Bush issued Homeland Security Presidential Directive 5 (HSPD 5), with the purpose "to enhance the ability of the United States to manage domestic incidents by establishing a single, comprehensive national incident management system." This was a corrective action based, in part, on the challenges associated with the response to the 9/11 incidents in New York, Washington, D.C., and Pennsylvania.

Although many things worked well that day, it was evident that some did not. First responders dealing with those major incidents were faced with such issues as a lack of interoperable communications, lack of standardized languages, lack of collaboration among jurisdictions, lack of clearly defined command and control, and excessive interagency rivalry.

HSPD 5 created the National Incident Management System (NIMS) (since revised to the National Response Framework), which is a system to improve communication, collaboration, and response across multiple jurisdictions. Since that time, our local and state emergency responders have been trying to get into compliance with HSPD 5 and NIMS and most are doing so. What does this have to do with hotel security? Plenty. Depending on whom you ask, hotels are a part of the critical infrastructure. Whether we are designated as such or just want to make sure we are consistent with what our first responders are doing, we have some valuable lessons to learn from this system.

The primary components of NIMS that are relevant to your operation are Preparedness, Communications Management, Resource Management, and Command.

Communications

Communications management involves several things that you can resolve easily at your property. One aspect of communications is language. If you call a certain emergency a "Code 13," another department calls it a "Code Red," and the police department calls it a "10-99," you can see where confusion can occur. Most public agencies are switching over to plain language on the radio to avoid this confusion. Your radio language can be changed with some training. If your local police and fire departments do not use plain language, consider switching yours to match theirs.

In the old days, the Los Angeles Police Department was one of the first major police departments to start using radios in their patrol cars. There weren't any 10 codes or 9 codes yet, so they created 10 simple codes: Code 1, Code 2, Code 3, etc. For everything else, they used the California Penal Code numbers, which everyone already knew from their academy days. These simple three digit codes numbers—459, 211, 502—made great shortcuts for radio language, while describing the elements of the situation being investigated. Plain language was used for anything that did not fit a crime. "See the woman," "traffic collision," and "runaway juvenile" were common phrases on the radio. To this day, although dozens of other agencies using various codes and radio languages surround LAPD, they continue to use the same simple "plain language" that they developed.

Radio traffic is not the only media where language needs to be consistent. In the hospitality industry and the security industry, we have our own terminology. Security officers tend to speak in this language even when talking to their families or co-workers. It is always amusing to watch cops and security officers speak to outsiders, forgetting that some people have no idea what they are talking about. Not so amusing is when a security dispatcher is speaking to a police dispatcher and there is serious confusion as each of them reverts to their "native" language. In reports, policies, and everyday speak, we should avoid nomenclature and stick to plain language to teach ourselves the habit of speaking in terms that everyone understands.

Another aspect of communication is the hardware used by each agency or company. In the past decade, governmental agencies have been scrambling to standardize frequencies, bands, and radio types used so they can talk to each other in major events or mutual aid situations. We have the same obligation to these first responders as we upgrade or purchase new radio systems.

In recent years, several jurisdictions have been working on creating a "Common Operating Picture." This technology operates under several different names, but its primary objective is to get real-time and predeployment information to first responders. Some systems allow police to tap into video cameras at a location from their car computer or smart phone. Other systems provide responding fire trucks with maps of the building and photos or schematics of where critical areas are. It is in our best interest to support this rapidly developing technology.

Resource

A component of NIMS with which you may already be involved is Resource Management. The objective of this is to identify and catalog all resources within a certain area so they can be called upon when needed. If Town A has a flood and needs more water rescue equipment, Town B would be called upon to loan its equipment. The database would save time. Resources are everything from humans to vehicles to radios. Hotels may be able to offer resources, such as shuttle buses, hotel rooms, meeting spaces, food, etc. If resources are cataloged in advance, one call to the point person at your facility might save time.

Command

The Incident Command System (ICS) has been in use by the military for decades and was adopted by fire departments several years ago to battle regional fires. The need came from multiple jurisdictions battling together on a fire, but nobody knowing who was in charge. As you can imagine, this caused confusion and many other operational as well as financial and political trouble. ICS provides for a unified command structure where the commander is established in advance. Each fire captain or chief has the same training, so anyone can assume command and each of the components of NIMS can be delivered in exactly the same way. More and more private companies are learning ICS and operating with it so that any trained manager can manage a major event. In fact, ICS can be used to manage a meeting, a party, or a company promotion.

ICS and NIMS classes are available free online from FEMA or your local agencies may provide this training.

BUSINESS CONTINUITY

Business continuity is the second part of your emergency plan, continuing where it left off. This plan is like the recovery plan once the emergency is over. The plans do overlap some, but once the fire is out, we have to activate our plans for keeping the business operating. While Security is really the main player in the emergency response plan, the business continuity plan is more specific to individual departments. Often, the responsibility for this plan falls on another administrative department.

If you are the lucky one who gets to create this plan, I suggest doing just as we did in the previous section with the Emergency Plan. Gather your stakeholders and use them to write their own department procedures for business continuity. The business continuity process should look like the one shown in Figure 10.1.

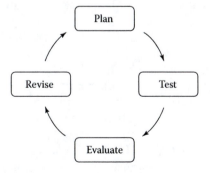

Figure 10. 1 The business continuity process.

Planning—The process described previously where stakeholders assemble to create and write the plan.

Training—Includes exercises, drills, testing, and other practice scenarios.

Evaluating—Postaction debriefs should be done by those involved, spectators, and local authorities invited to participate.

Revising—Corrections (lessons learned) need to be incorporated back into the plan and then the process starts all over.

Here are some things to consider as you work through this process.

Hotels and other entertainment venues are a little different from financial institutions, manufacturing plants, and others. If you were producing widgets, you would have to worry about an alternate manufacturing site and taking care of inventory. Banks are concerned with their cash, protecting their data, and finding an alternate customer service location. In our industry, you might say that if the building is damaged, there is no business. This is partially true, and your continuity plan may just be sustaining your data and communicating with customers. However, what if your shutdown is just temporary? You will have to relocate guests, continue to make reservations for the future, etc.

Employee loyalty is the biggest concern with most businesses staying in operation. After Hurricane Katrina, many employees fled the region and never returned. This is partially because they did not plan for it and partially because their employers jumped ship. It is, therefore, very important to take care of employees and help them prepare their own families before a disaster. Otherwise, even the employees who are onsite when the disaster strikes are likely to head home to check on loved ones. I have several ideas that will help with this and they are relatively free.

Contact other similar businesses or businesses in your market that have survived disaster and get ideas from them. They may have some plans for things that nobody thought of until afterward.

Create an education forum for your employees. This may be a newsletter, posters, classes, and even special events to raise awareness for disasters prone to your area. Show them how to prepare "go kits" for their home and car to sustain them for three days following a wide-area disaster. Use personal examples to which employees can relate to bring the message home. When major weather is imminent, put out reminders on what to do and how to be prepared.

Make your facility an emergency shelter. Let employees know that in emergencies their families can come to the hotel seeking refuge. If this is not possible, let them know where the closest shelter is so your employees will have a nearby meeting spot to regroup with family and then return to work. You can set this up with your local Red Cross or Emergency Manager.

Bring in free training from local authorities. The Red Cross, fire department, police department, and other groups are usually quite happy to address a meeting of employees and review emergency procedures, teach CPR, fire prevention, personal safety, etc. This is a great benefit to your staff and an even better way for you to maintain relationships with these groups in an emergency.

Make sure your Benefits, Payroll, and Human Resources departments are prepared to bring their services to employees after a disaster. These are vital services to all employees during difficult times and will keep employees nearby if you need them.

See if your Food Department is prepared to open on- or offsite services for employees during a crisis. Once again, this keeps them around and if they can invite their families down, even better.

During bad weather, invite employees to stay in the hotel. This will keep them safe and off the roads and there to work if you need them. Bring the spouse and kids. Why not? This costs so little for the return you get.

Be sure to include a succession plan. In a 24-hour operation, chances are the big boss will not be there to lead or even be able to get there in time to do anything. Make sure there is always someone qualified to run the operation and make those quick decisions in the boss's absence.

In a citywide disaster, assume that first responders and area resources will be committed to schools, hospitals, and government assets. They may not be there to implement their part of the plan, so plan with and without them. Federal assistance generally takes about 48 hours, so make sure your plan counts for this. Historically, employees also take about 48 hours to return to work after seeing to their families.

Allow for employee food and housing after a crisis. I mentioned this previously as a reaction to minor events like bad weather, but make sure these departments have it in their plans. Where are you going to feed people? Do we keep enough food on hand? Providing telephones or Internet to contact loved ones is vital for employees and guests. You will have very uncooperative victims on your hands if they cannot be assured their family and friends are safe.

IT is one of your vital departments, after life safety, for business continuity. They have unique issues and may require their own plan for network sustainability, offsite storage, data restoration, etc. If they do not have their own plan, include it in yours and make sure other departments meet their needs.

Forty percent of businesses struck by disaster never reopen their doors. Hotels, because they rely on their physical location, have an even higher failure rate. Business Continuity Management, as you have just learned, is a complex and time-consuming job. Many organizations have one or more persons assigned to this project exclusively. If you do not, it is unlikely that you will. I hope that you will at least get the buy-in from senior management to devote some staffing and resources to help you with this vital business function.

EMERGENCY RESPONSE

Just about any emergency that you can imagine, and some you cannot, can occur at your hotel. I have personally seen incidents, both manufactured and natural, that police officers and military infantrymen will not see in their entire careers. We have to be ready for anything that might happen at any hour of the day. Following is a list, in no particular order, of emergencies that you should be ready to encounter, and how to neutralize or resolve them. The list can probably never be complete, and even if it was, each situation has so many potential variables that it would still be incomplete. I hope to prepare you with these and get your imagination prepared for others not mentioned here.

Static post officers need to know in advance which posts can be left in the event of an emergency and which cannot. Certain access control posts will never leave their post unless the building is evacuated. Other fixed posts, such as the watch area, must be allowed to leave in the event of an emergency.

> In 2009, a woman in a restaurant was accidentally served a chemical cleaning solution instead of drinking water. After ingesting the chemical and feeling ill, a manager attended to her and began taking information for a report. The customer's husband repeatedly asked the manager the content of the solution and its medical remedies and his requests were refused, as the manager was more interested in obtaining information from the customer for his report. In court, the manager testified that it was company policy to gather report information first unless the guest was in a life-threatening situation. The customer was awarded $260,000 and was not permanently harmed.
>
> Written policy should *always* favor the safety and well-being of the guest first. Liability should be considered second. When these priorities are reversed, it can be costly, if not dangerous, for everyone.

Medical Calls

Medical calls are covered in Chapter 2.

Active Shooter

Prevention of active shooters is discussed in Chapters 2 and 7. This section addresses only the response to a person with a gun, whether it is a robber, disgruntled employee, crazed lunatic, or jihadist terrorist.

As I mentioned earlier, preventing these incidents is our job and should be our focus. However, some violent person may still make it into our workplace and we need to have a plan to react to it.

Warning: I am going to discuss armed security! I understand that this is a huge concern for some companies and I am not going to enter that controversy in this chapter. I did address the pros and cons of armed security in Chapter 2. So, wherever I mention first responders in this section, it will include whichever person is trained to respond with a weapon to an armed individual—Security or police.

Of the five stages of an active shooter (Fantasy, Planning, Preparation, Approach, and Implementation) Approach and Implementation are the ones most identifiable to us at the time of the threat. Fantasy, Planning, and Preparation are not identifiable unless we know the shooter and are around him before he acts. Therefore, except for the other chapters where we talked about prevention, here we will discuss the response to the action phases: Approach and Implementation. Just like other threats, a layered approach is essential to identifying and stopping an active shooter before he starts (statistically, most shooters are male). We can use Behavioral Recognition, Reporting Processes, Access Control, Employee Awareness, Training, and Physical Layers.

Behavioral Recognition

Profiling the behavior of an active shooter is not an exact science, but there are some signs that will tip us off if we are looking for them. As we learned in Workplace Violence, almost all shooters are seeking revenge. As humans, we know what revenge looks like. It is a determined, sometimes fixed expression, as opposed to a tourist who wanders or meanders. Most shooters actually enter the premises with guns drawn, so that is an easy one to spot. If not visible, they will certainly carry a backpack or some type of bag with extra guns and ammo. Those things are heavy and do not look like suitcases or computer bags common to hotel guests. The shooter who opened fire in a Las Vegas casino in 2007 walked the strip in a long trench coat in the summer for several hours "looking for someone to shoot." He expected to be confronted, but was ignored until he drew his weapon inside the casino.

Reporting Processes

Suppose a valet attendant or landscaper is the one who first notices the guy in the trench coat with a determined expression approaching the building. You need to have a method of notification in place to alert Security or other employees. Radios are the obvious solution, but maybe there are code words, hand signals, panic alarms, or other alternatives worth researching.

Reporting also includes the reporting of suspicious behavior when employees or guests are in the planning stage. Review Chapter 7 for reporting processes.

Access Control

Controlling access to a secure building is simple. In an open hospitality environment, it is complex and unorthodox. In Chapter 2, we talked about using layers of human and technological security to observe entrants. These should include plans for stopping or challenging a suspected intruder. In other words, even though your hotel or tourist venue is open to everyone, you have to observe, if not control, access.

Employee Awareness

Awareness of the measures discussed in this chapter is a good start. All employees should have a minimum of the "See Something, Say Something" awareness class.

Training

Security officers and others should be trained on the proper response to an active shooter. See next paragraphs.

Physical Layers

Physical layers were discussed in Chapter 2 and are vital to slowing or limiting the movements of a suspected intruder. "Choke points" are areas where movement is narrowed down to one small area of ingress or egress. This is where cameras should be placed, officers can intercept unwanted subjects, and profilers can see everyone who passes through. A revolving door in a hotel lobby and a hallway between convention rooms are examples of chokepoints in a hotel.

We have learned from such incidents as Columbine, Virginia Tech, Fort Hood, and others that active shooters want a high body count and rarely expect to be taken alive. We have to assume that someone shooting a gun cannot be reasoned with or convinced to stop killing. As protectors of the assets on our property, we have a duty to take reasonable measures with this in mind. If your security is not armed, your duties are simple: Evacuate guests and employees if possible, contain the suspect, and direct police to the scene. Step-by-step instructions are:

1. Assign one person to notify police (dispatcher, if you have one).
2. Monitor location and activity of suspect (video and witnesses).
3. Evacuate all persons from that portion of the building (if you can get to them safely).
4. Assign an officer to meet police at entrance. Prepare to tell first responder the number of shots fired, type of gun, description of suspect, location and direction of travel, possible exit and entry points to suspect location, and number of persons in danger (near shooter).
5. If possible, secure a perimeter from positions of cover to keep people out of shooting area and to monitor suspect's egress. If security is armed, maintain perimeter positions and engage only from cover and only if safe.
6. Instruct employees in harm's way to seek concealment and to stay put until police locate them.

Fire Alarm

Fire alarms are reliable and should always be treated as genuine. Operation of fire alarms is discussed in Chapter 9.

1. Assign one officer, preferably a supervisor, to "Fire Command" or your location of the enunciator panel.
2. Assign one officer to meet the fire department and direct them to Fire Command and the location of the alarm.
3. Assign one officer to respond to the location of alarm. This officer needs to provide an immediate cause for alarm: fire in a trashcan, water flowing from sprinkler, smoke on the floor, kitchen fire already out, etc.
4. Assign one officer to each floor above and below the location of the alarm. The alarm rings on these floors and guests will need to be directed to exits.
5. In a high-rise, assign one officer to each stairwell door at the base of the structure to direct guests to an assembly area.
6. Assign one officer to the assembly area.
7. Assign one officer to the base of elevators to keep guests from going into the building and direct the fire department to the proper floor. (Yes, firefighters take elevators.)
8. If cause of alarm is determined before first responders arrive, call them to provide an update.
9. Guests who ask what is happening should always be told that you are investigating an alarm and will advise when it is safe to return to the building.
10. If you have run out of security staff, use bell persons, valet attendants, and front desk personnel.

11. Update hotel operator as soon and as often as possible because he or she will receive many phone calls.

Actual Fire

Whether the alarm has been activated and you know a fire exists, your main objective is to evacuate persons. In addition to the applicable procedures above, do the following:

1. Manually pull or activate alarm if not already ringing.
2. Evacuate via door-to-door search. Knock once and open doors using security keys. Order everyone to leave. Do not force those who refuse. Advise fire department.
3. Obtain a list of disabled guests from the front desk.
4. Physically check every room.
5. Mark rooms that have been checked.
6. Check stairwells for stragglers.
7. Provide fire personnel with status of evacuation and fire.

Bomb Threat

Bomb threats are generally telephonic, but also may be in the form of a letter or even verbal. The vast majority of bomb threats are hoaxes. However, there are enough actual bombings with warnings that we must be prepared to act with public and employee safety as a primary consideration.

Bomb threats are made for two primary reasons: (1) the person has definite knowledge or believes that an explosive has been or will be placed and wishes to prevent injuries or property damage; (2) the person wants to create an atmosphere of anxiety and panic, which can develop into disruption of normal activities.

1. Personnel who would normally receive a threat must be briefed on how to respond to a threat, what to ask, and what to do. Obtain as much information as possible from the call-taker. Operators, secretaries, and dispatchers should have a copy of the bomb threat questionnaire available to help them obtain information.
2. Evacuation at this point should only be for a credible threat—one that indicates exact time, location, type, and reason for the bomb. See evacuations below.
3. Search. Whether credible or not, we will have to conduct a search of the property.
   a. Establish a command post. This is where all search-related information will be combined, processed, and planned.
   b. Prearranged search areas should be assigned with a checklist for each to ensure nothing is overlooked.
   c. Utilize other department personnel, such as maintenance to cover more area quickly.
   d. Do not use cell phones or radios to avoid radio-controlled detonations.
   e. Assign engineers to gas and electrical mains to shut off if necessary.
   f. Watch for common bomb containers that may be encountered: paper bags, boxes, purses, briefcases, wrapped packages, luggage left in a room after a guest has checked out.

g. Listen while searching. Identify all sounds in the area, such as electrical motors or other equipment, air conditioning noises, the hum of fluorescent lighting, and external noises. Noises unaccounted for should be thoroughly checked out and identified.

h. Check for unusual disturbances, such as loose air conditioning ducts or electrical panels. Check for the disturbance of dirt or dust in or around movable items. Check for doors that appear to have been forced or unlocked when they should be secure.

i. If an item is found and cannot be accounted for, that item becomes suspect and should be handled by trained personnel.

j. Priority search areas are:

   i. Exterior—Bushes, shrubs, and planters; plant beds for freshly disturbed earth; decorative facings and block work; drain spouts; trash receptacles; mail boxes and night deposit boxes; electrical panels; manhole covers and storm drains; vehicles parked next to buildings; roofs and ledges if low enough that a package may be thrown onto it; fire hose dry stand pipes. Roofs: cooling towers, elevator equipment rooms, roof vents, and ducts.

   ii. Interior—Entry or lobby areas: planters, display items, seats, ashtrays, news racks, stairways, and elevators. Restrooms: towel racks, trash containers, toilet bowls, supply closets. Trash or compactor areas. Receiving areas. Supply rooms. Linen closets. Janitorial storage. Offices open to the public. Guest rooms vacated and not cleaned and/or unoccupied during the last 24 hours. Basement: air conditioning and heating ducts, electrical panels, crawl holes, scuttle holes, sumps and drains, vital equipment areas, hallways not normally used.

4. Special caution: Often there is more than one bomb placed by a person who intends to do harm or damage. If a bomb is located, do not assume that the search should be terminated. The search may be suspended until the first device is handled.

As you can see, a proper bomb search is a tedious, time-consuming process.

In 1980, at Harvey's Hotel/Casino Lake Tahoe, a disgruntled customer smuggled in an actual bomb disguised as a copy machine. The device was delivered directly to the executive offices without any question and contained 1,000 pounds of dynamite with some very elaborate tamper switches. The FBI exploded the bomb and it damaged most of the casino/hotel and the hotel across the street. The actual text from the threat note is as follows:

TO THE MANAGEMENT:

STERN WARNING TO THE MANAGEMENT AND BOMB SQUAD:

Do not move or tilt this bomb because the mechanism controlling the detonators in it will set it off at a movement of less than .01 of the open-end Richter scale. Don't try to flood or gas the bomb. There is a float switch and an atmospheric pressure switch set at 26.00–33.00. Both are attached to detonators. Do not try to take it apart. The flathead screws are also attached to triggers and as much as ¼ to ¾ of a turn will cause an explosion. In other words, this bomb is so sensitive that the slightest movement either inside or outside will cause it to explode.

This bomb can never be dismantled or disarmed without causing an explosion. Not even by the creator. Only by proper instruction can it be moved to a safe place where it can be deliberately exploded, or where the third automatic timer can be allowed to detonate it. There are three automatic timers each set for three different explosion times. Only if you comply with the instructions in this letter will you be given instructions on how to disconnect the first two automatic timers and how to move the bomb to a place where it can be exploded safely.

WARNING:

I repeat, do not try to move, disarm, or enter this bomb. It will explode.

If exploded this bomb contains enough TNT to severely damage Harrah's across the street. This should give you some idea of the amount of TNT contained within this box. It is full of TNT. It is our advice to cordon off a minimum of 1,200 feet radius and remove all people from that area.

DEMANDS:

We demand $3 million in used $100 bills. They must be unmarked, unbugged, and chemically untreated. If we find anything wrong with the money, we will stop all instructions for moving the bomb.

INSTRUCTIONS FOR DELIVERY:

The money is to be delivered by helicopter. The helicopter pilot is to park at 2300 hours as close as possible to the LTA building by the light at the Lake Tahoe Airport. It is to face the east. The pilot has to be alone and unarmed. The pilot is to get out and stand by the chain-link fence gate. He is to wait for further instructions, which will be delivered by a taxi that will be hired. The driver will know nothing. They may also be delivered by a private individual or through the nearby public phone at exactly 0010 hours. At 0010 hours, the pilot will receive instructions about where and what to do. Before the pilot enters the helicopter, he has to take a strong flashlight and shine it around the inside of the helicopter so that it will light up the entire inside. We must be able to see it from a distance with binoculars. We want to be able to see everything that is inside the helicopter so that we can be sure there is no one hiding inside and that there is no contraband inside.

CONDITIONS OF THE BUSINESS TRANSACTION:

These conditions must be followed to the letter. Any deviation from these conditions will leave your casino in a shambles. Also, remember that even a very small earthquake will detonate the bomb so do not try to delay the delivery of the money.

(1) All news media, local or nationwide will be kept ignorant of the transactions between us and the casino management until the bomb is removed from the building.
(2) The helicopter will be manned only by the pilot. He must be unarmed and unbugged. We do not want any misunderstanding, which might cause us to have to take lives unnecessarily.
(3) Fill the helicopter up completely with gas.
(4) The helicopter pilot after he receives the first instructions cannot communicate with anyone except the necessary instructions given and taken by the tower. All channels from 11.30 to 17.00 will be monitored.

The designer of this bomb will not participate in the exchange so it will be completely useless to apprehend any person making the exchange because they will not know how it works. They perform their duty for reward. And again, if you don't want to be stuck with 1,000 pounds of TNT do not allow any investigation by local agencies, FBI, or any other investigative agency action before the bomb is removed. If the instructions are violated in any way by any authority, the secret of the handling of the bomb will definitely not be revealed. If the money is received without any problems, six sets of instructions regarding the removal of the bomb will be given to you at different times. The pilot will receive the first set of instructions. He can carry it back with him. If the money is sold to the buyer without complications, you may receive the remaining five sets of instructions one by one via the Kingsbury Post Office by general delivery, or you may receive them all at once. The extent of your cooperation will make the difference. If you cooperate fully, it will ensure a very speedy exchange. We don't want to burden your business opportunities or cause more loss of money than is necessary.

ATTENTION:

There will be no extension or renegotiation. Demands are firm regardless. The transaction has to take place within 24 hours. If you do not comply, we will not contact you again and we will not answer any attempts to contact us. In the event of a double-cross, there will be another time sometime in the future when another attempt will be made. We have the ways and means to get another bomb in.

TO THE PILOT:

The helicopter has to be filled up with gas. Do not come armed with any weapon. Do not bring a shotgun rider. All radio channels will be monitored. You are to have no communication with anyone after you reach the airport. Do not try to be a hero, Arlington is full of them and they can't even smell the flowers. Follow the orders strictly. You will make five stops, none of which will be at an airfield. You will have ample lighting for landing. All sites are fairly level. One has about two degrees pitch. There will be a clearance of more than 200 feet radius. We don't want any trouble but we won't run away if you bring it.
Happy landing.

Bomb Evacuation

If a device is found, an area relative to the size of the device will have to be evacuated and cordoned off.

1. Evacuate 100 yards just to be safe for most portable-sized devices (briefcase, pipe bomb, etc.)
2. Use fire alarm as necessary to get everyone's attention.
3. Evacuate away from the device. If device is near an exit, evacuate toward opposite exit.
4. Leave doors and windows open.
5. Turn off electrical appliances and machinery.
6. Turn off gas to area, but leave lights on.
7. Note the following to provide to first responders: size of object, exact location of object, type of container or wrappings, any sound coming from object, anything leading from the object or connected with or to it, and anything in the immediate area of the object that might create additional hazards or dangers (near gas main, air conditioning room, Freon™, ammonia, acids, etc.).
8. Have key personnel standing by to consult with fire department, such as Engineering, Maintenance, Security, Health, and Safety.

Bomb Threat Call-Taker Instructions

1. As soon as it is realized that the call is a bomb threat, start recording all information about the call.
2. Stay calm and listen carefully to each word.
3. Try to keep the caller talking, asking questions as to the location and timing device. Although the caller may not respond, the more he or she says, the more we will learn.
4. Note the following:
   a. Gender of caller.
   b. Apparent age.
   c. Accent, if any.
   d. Speech impediments or voice characteristics, such as lisps, drawls, slurred words, etc.
   e. Attitude of caller—calm, excited, rehearsed, etc.
   f. Pay particular attention to background noises, street noises, motors running, or anything that may be a clue to the origin of the call.
5. Remain available for interview by police and fire department.

Explosion

We have seen enough explosions caused by terrorists overseas to be concerned. This is a very real threat and is not always accompanied by a warning. We need to maintain our sensibilities if this happens. Look at all of the times one explosion has been followed by second and third explosions. These secondary explosions are either meant to go simultaneously with the first (and were late) or are purposefully activated when first responders are arriving. Even though the explosion is over, there are several potential problems to deal with.

1. The explosion may be of a biological, radiological, or chemical nature (dirty bomb, for example) so the immediate area is not safe. Evacuate everyone, including the injured if possible.
2. There may be a secondary explosion in the same area awaiting first responders. Evacuate immediately.
3. When evacuating, keep the secondary explosions in mind. They are likely to target the response locations, such as the main entrance or the normal evacuation rallying point.
4. Everything is part of the crime scene. Do not allow persons (witnesses or suspects) to leave or remove or damage evidence.

Suicidal Subject

For some reason, people like to go to hotels to commit suicide. Maybe they don't want to dirty up their own residence or want to make sure someone finds them (housekeeping). Once you are around hotels for a while, you will see suicide by drug overdose, gunshot, cut wrists, and fall from a high place. The "jumper" may not be the most common, but it is certainly the most visible to the public. Whether from the roof of the hotel, the window or balcony of the hotel, or the garage, this event is often messy, public, and resource-intensive.

An onlooker or a relative on the phone will likely notify you of a jumper. Procedures for handling this are as follows:

1. Obtain as much information about the subject as possible: name, address, cell phone, exact location, reason for suicide attempt, doctor's name and number, etc.
2. Notify police. Provide exact location so they can respond discreetly if they choose.
3. Establish a perimeter that will prevent persons from entering the landing area, the take-off area, and anywhere in between.
4. Extend perimeter to limit vantage points by onlookers.
5. Do not approach subject. Gather information for police.
6. Let police handle everything else. You become their support.

Earthquake

Most buildings designed after the 1970s were built to withstand moderate to strong earthquakes. Find out from your engineering department the structural specifications of your building and use that to help you design your response. Whenever an earthquake occurs that is strong enough to be felt by guests, do the following (you will not have time to advise anyone what to do during the shaking, so these procedures begin when shaking stops):

1. Initiate a brief inspection of the building to determine damage and injuries. Engineers should check for foundation and structural damage. Security should inspect public areas for loose fixtures, items about to fall, and cracks.

2. Engineering will advise if the building is unsafe to occupy. Generally, the safest place is inside the building because items may fall outside.
3. If an evacuation is recommended, use the fire alarm to notify everyone to leave.
4. Conduct the evacuation to the assembly area as discussed in the section "Fire Evacuation."
5. Remember, authorities may be swamped with other calls. Call them only if you need them.
6. Guests may want to leave the building, regardless of whether it is necessary. Assure them they are safer inside, but never refuse someone's egress.

Weather Emergency

The majority of disasters affecting businesses are weather-related. The specific emergency depends on your geographic location. Hurricanes, tornadoes, blizzards, and floods are hotel killers. However, a properly prepared hotel can be a place of refuge and assistance instead of another unprepared victim if you stay informed. For weather-related events in your area, stay in touch with local authorities who provide warnings, information, and assistance for your type of climate. Here are some general guidelines to keep in mind.

You no longer need to watch the evening news to stay on top of the weather. There are so many Web sites and notification services available that you can know instantly when weather changes. Even if you are not on property, you should track these events and keep your staff notified and prepared.

Make sure your facilities staff has a protocol in place to secure doors and other outdoor items for windstorms, hurricanes, and tornadoes. There may not be enough warning for you to call a meeting and give people assignments. These responses should be automatic.

Implement a communications method to keep your guests informed. Most travelers use the hotel as a home base as they hit tourist spots in your 100-mile area. You want to have warnings in such a place as the bell desk that tells guests if lightning is expected at the water park or the golf course or if a tornado touched down in the next town.

Even a simple rainstorm can cause power outages and leaks. Each officer and employees from other departments need to know in advance what is expected of them when these events occur—someone checks escalators and elevators; flashlights are available in key areas; generators, even if automatic, are monitored; automatic doors and other devices are placed in manual mode. Leaks cause slip hazards and should be attended to by someone setting out barriers and buckets.

Riots

We see riots in urban areas for the craziest things these days. Whether it is a sports team win (or loss), a controversial police shooting, politics, or an over-crowded concert, angry mobs can pop up just about anywhere for any reason. Your hotel, amusement park, or nightclub is a beautiful target for vandalism and may be right in the way of the riot.

Your plan, worked out in advance, needs to protect guests, employees, and property—in that order. Throughout this book, I have stressed keeping track of what goes on outside as well as inside your property. Riots are a good reason. If there is one in your neighborhood, you need some time to prepare, so you want some advance notice. I hope that you have worked out a communication network with your neighbors to let you know. Your outside patrol officers are your next best bet for a warning. Even if there is not a full-blown riot, you want to be kept advised of trouble brewing nearby. Following are some key elements of the plan and your response, starting from outside.

1. Your outside officers (who should be the first to know) are the first concern. Bring them inside. If other employees (valet, landscapers) are outside, the outside officers will bring them in as well.
2. Notify the police, if they do not already know.
3. Activate your internal notification system or phone tree. Advise department heads to keep employees and guests inside and keep off of phones unless it is an emergency.
4. Assign officers to secure all perimeter doors. Doors that do not lock should have some sort of barrier or lock made for them in advance.
5. Post officers at each entrance (inside) to prevent anyone from leaving the building. Guests who insist on leaving should be warned that there would be no re-entry. Allow no entry by persons unless they have a hotel key. Others who are escaping the violence should be allowed in on a discretionary basis.
6. Be aware of doors and other street-facing glass that could be broken by rioters.
7. Do not attempt to arrest troublemakers unless necessary. The mob mentality will target the uniform and overwhelm you.
8. Direct all video cameras to the riot, attempting to scan faces of perpetrators. This video will be used by the police to make arrests later.

Riots generally last only a few minutes while the police deploy extreme measures such as gas or nonlethal weapons. Be prepared for this and shut down air intake vents if they are at street level. If there are injuries requiring advanced medical care, call the paramedics as usual. They should have police escorting them. If not, you may have to provide first aid while you wait out the worst of it.

Gas or Chemical Leak

The street maintenance crew outside your building got a little carried away with the backhoe and ruptured a natural gas pipe. The nature of most gases is that they are just a bit heavier than air, so they travel along at ground level with the wind. That means the gas comes through open doors and windows, through air intake vents, and any nooks and crannies in the building. Other gases in your neighborhood, or traveling through your neighborhood, will act very similarly and require an evacuation. Here are the procedures to follow:

1. Notify the fire department. They should respond to your fire command area unless it is in the danger area.
2. Do not allow anyone to smoke in the immediate area.
3. Evacuate guests and employees to a place that is upwind or even on a higher floor, depending on the gas direction of travel.

4. You may have to set up a triage area to treat persons with difficulty breathing or other signs of exposure until local emergency medical personnel get organized. You should have oxygen with your AED (automatic external defibrillator) equipment. Bring it and use it generously.

Bioterrorism

Bioterrorism includes any toxic substance that occurs naturally or derives from a natural substance. Generally, these are bacteria, viruses, or toxins. Botulism is a widely available bacterium and Ricin is an easily produced toxic protein. Anthrax, another disease caused by bacteria, was used shortly after the World Trade Center attack to terrorize postal employees and a couple of senators, so its use is not out of the realm of possibility. Secretaries and mailroom clerks around the world still shudder to imagine opening an envelope with a white, powdery substance inside.

The response to a bioterror attack of this nature is to evacuate the surrounding area and isolate the substance and anyone who touched it. Ventilators should be turned off and doors and windows closed. Notify the police and fire department to handle and evaluate the substance.

Labor Strike

If you have union employees or deal with union employees from vendors (produce delivery drivers, window washers, etc.), you should have a strike contingency plan. Work out this plan using the method described in the section Business Continuity Planning above in this chapter. Nevertheless, you also need a response plan described here.

Most strikes are planned well in advance and management should know about them way before they happen. Security acts as an arm of management, but still performs its primary function of protecting the company's assets. This is a stressful and delicate situation for everyone, so it is important to follow procedures to the letter. Here are some things to put into your response plan.

1. After notifying your General Manager and Human Resources Director, call the police. The police will respond to help keep the peace and make sure both sides know their legal rights and limitations. (These vary slightly by state.)
2. Even though you represent management, you will get much farther if you treat strikers fairly and professionally. Never comment on the labor agreement in dispute. Just remind your people and theirs that you are there to make sure everything is legal, safe, and fair.
3. In most jurisdictions, strikers cannot block a public sidewalk, an entrance or exit to your facility, or interfere with the business in any way. Have the police issue these reminders if violations occur.
4. Direct any available video cameras to record the actions of the strikers for use later if necessary (not for revenge, but for criminal or labor violations).
5. Make sure employee vehicles and their ingress and egress are safe. You may have to assign extra security to parking areas and entrances and exits.
6. Follow instructions from your Human Resources or labor counsel.

Power Failure

Your facility, no matter the size, probably has one or more backup generators. These are generally gas- or diesel-powered engines that come on automatically when the power goes out. You also may or may not have an Uninterrupted Power Supply (UPS) that keeps power flowing to critical systems for that few seconds or minutes between when the power goes out and the generator energizes the circuits. The UPS works with many large batteries connected in series so it cannot power large motors and like those found on escalators, elevators, and heating and cooling units. It is designed to prevent surges and maintain constant power to computers, servers, cash registers, and video and alarm equipment. Despite all of these technological marvels, a power failure, even a "bump," can cause some problems that require your response.

It is doubtful that your generators can power every single circuit in your facility. Usually, a small percentage of lights and certain necessary equipment (possibly elevators and escalators) are connected to the generators. This means there will be some darker areas inside and outside the property that require an officer to stand by and assist guests. Even if escalators and elevators can run on backup power, it is likely they will stop and need to be restarted depending on their age. Security and Engineering should physically check every elevator to make sure they are running and nobody has been injured. Most elevators installed in the past 20 years have a video display of elevator location and travel. Escalators should be monitored with cameras.

Did you know that casinos connect their slot machines to the backup generator? The reason is probably obvious to you: revenue. However, there are two other reasons for this. Slot machines provide most of the lighting inside a casino. Without overhead lighting, the slots need to keep running so people can see where they are going. The second reason is for the machine. Each slot machine, with its own computer, is worth about as much as a new car, so losing a circuit board to a power surge would be a bad thing.

If you do not have generators or if they do not work, your staff will be very busy. You should always have flashlights and battery-powered lanterns available. Battery emergency lights—required by code—will come on and provide some light, but there will be dark spots. Make sure officers know in advance the key areas where they should be stationed in a power failure (front desk, elevator banks, retail store, etc.). Don't forget if you have a repeater for your radios or if you use cell phones, they work on electricity, too. Is your repeater connected to backup power? Your cell site? Battery chargers?

Escalator Accidents

Escalator accidents are more common than you think. The several hundred that I have responded to in my career usually involved kids or adults playing around, intoxicated persons who should not have been walking, or those with bad eyesight (depth perception).

In other words, they were almost all the guest's fault. Unfortunately, because an escalator is a big piece of moving equipment on an incline and with very sharp surfaces, injuries can be substantial.

The first response on an escalator emergency is to stop it as soon as possible. There should be an emergency stop button at the top and bottom. The second priority is to stabilize the injured person. He or she may be lying precariously across several sharp steps. The victim will be in pain, likely bleeding, and precautions for broken bones should be taken. If in doubt, stabilize and call paramedics.

Once the initial emergency is over, gathering witness statements and evidence is very important. This guest will at least seek reimbursement for medical bills from you and, at most, sue you for defective equipment, poor signage, or unsafe conditions. Many properties place cameras over the escalator to record these incidents. This is a small investment considering the cause is usually "driver error." To cover yourself further, have the escalator inspected before returning it to service. Many escalator maintenance companies have to assume some of the liability for accidents, so they may be willing to do this for you. In some states, the government inspector must be notified of major accidents on escalators before returning them to service. See if this is required in your jurisdiction.

> In 2005, an escalator at a Denver, Colorado, ballpark stopped while carrying passengers at the end of a ballgame. The escalator stopped and abruptly restarted at full speed causing several people to fall and become injured. The switch that is supposed to gradually bring the escalator back up to speed malfunctioned. One woman who received several surgeries because of her injuries finally had to have her leg amputated. She sued the park and the escalator manufacturer. Ballparks all across the country had a negative impact to their business for the rest of the season.
>
> Does this change the way you respond to escalator emergencies or what you do postaccident?

Missing Child

Over 2,000 children are reported missing each day in the United States. Of course, some of these are runaways and family abductions, but enough are endangered that it is everyone's concern. Besides the heartache to the family and to your staff, this is not something you want happening on your property. There is a best practice response to a report of a child missing and you should train on it and use it each time. Code Adam, named after Adam Walsh (see textbox below) is a program used by thousands of businesses to respond to a report of a missing child. The concept is simple. On the first report of a child missing, the facility is locked down and all employees are directed to the search. This is simple to train and practice and is worth every minute.

Your staff and all employees on your property should be trained to listen for a report overhead or on the radio of "Code Adam." Some employees respond to a designated location (all exits and hallways covered) and stop every child who leaves until a description is

On July 27, 1981, 6-year-old Adam Walsh and his mother Revé went to a department store about a mile away from their home to shop for lamps. When they entered the store, Adam saw several children playing video games on a television monitor and asked if he could stay to play. His mother let him stay and went to the lamp department, which was about 75 feet away. Because the lamp she wanted was not in stock, she returned rather quickly, less than 10 minutes later, but couldn't find Adam. After looking for Adam on her own for two hours, someone finally called the local police department. By the end of that week, thousands of fliers with Adam's photograph were distributed through the local area. Sixteen days after Adam disappeared from the store his body was found and identified.

given. Others assist in a methodical search of the building. This continues until the child is found.

For more information, contact the National Center for Missing and Exploited Children.

11

Investigations

It used to be a good hotel, but that proves nothing—I used to be a good boy.

Mark Twain, author

The first hotel security personnel were referred to as "detectives" for a reason. Losses are recovered and prevented with investigations. You just cannot operate a hospitality Security Department without investigations. Most incidents require some follow-up and you need some behind-the-scenes people turning over stones to see what is really happening on your property.

PRELIMINARY INVESTIGATIONS

Most of this book focuses on prevention and being proactive to maintain a safe, secure, and comfortable environment for everyone. In this chapter, we focus on the reactionary side of the business. Response is probably the most visible aspect of the Security Department and likely the place where we can make the best impression on our guests even though most of these types of interactions are negative. Fortunately, if done properly, a good security officer, following good procedures, can turn this negative into a positive.

The purpose of the preliminary investigation is to gather and document as much information as possible while the guest is still present, or while the incident is still "fresh." Every incident has some sort of investigation, even if the responding officer at the scene concludes that investigation. We will start with that initial response, gather evidence, and then begin the investigation itself.

Response to Calls

The investigation of any incident begins as soon as the first officer arrives on scene. The officer has already begun the process as she approaches and mentally records the scene. This recording includes what the scene entails: persons present, their actions, placement of objects, condition of the area, weather, lighting, etc. It is up to you to train the officer to memorize and document these important pieces of data. Granted, not every piece of data is relevant to every scene, but rather than try to distinguish in advance which ones are, it is better to go for the entire thing. Sorting through too much information is better than later wishing that you had it. Providing the officer with tools will allow her to do this preliminary investigation completely and efficiently.

Training

Training, as usual, is the first step. Start with an awareness of the goal of the investigation. Most officers do not take the time to be as detailed and thorough as they could because they do not understand the criticality of the investigation. It has to be explained to them that even though maybe 1 of 100 of these investigations do little more than get filed away, that one could cost the company hundreds of thousands or millions of dollars. This is not an exaggeration. There are many cases throughout this book that could be used for this training.

Once the awareness is engrained, technical training must be provided. (Training is covered in more detail in Chapter 6.) Officers should be shown to document everything as they see it upon arrival. If possible—if it is not an emergency—the first officer should look carefully at the overall scene. In a guest room, he should note the condition of the door, the items in the bathroom, signs of struggle or accident, other persons present, etc. A camera is the best way to document and can be a good way to jog an officer's memory later, but notes should still be taken. The camera will not capture sounds, verbal statements, smells, and even lighting conditions. Taking notes is not that simple. It is difficult for anyone to know what he or she should write. As mentioned previously, just write down everything. It helps to have another officer who can take statements and discuss the situation with the guest while the first officer concentrates on documentation.

Photography

Anything that supports the statements should be photographed. Anything that contradicts the story also should be photographed. In other words, the entire scene must be photographed. Start with an overview of the scene. This shot should put the location into context. The second shot is generally an overview of the specific location, showing placement of objects. Then take individual shots of each object from different angles. Close-ups should be taken if possible. A full and facial shot of everyone involved is important because the investigator will use these to identify people on video.

Interview

Once the scene is "preserved," at least in memory and in photos, the next step is to reconstruct what happened. This is accomplished by first obtaining a verbal account from the "victim" and then from any witnesses. Allow them to verbalize the story, separately if possible, and before they write it down. As they recount their experiences, let them speak uninterrupted as you take notes. After the verbal statement is given, ask questions to clarify or understand. Then repeat it back from your notes. "So you used your key, walked in the room, and saw the suitcase lying upside down on the floor right about here." If they then change the story, note the change. Then have them write the statement. Once you have the statement, compare their verbal and written statements for clarification. "You told me that you used your key to open the door, but your wife said you lost your key and used hers." (We are not interrogating, just asking for clarification.) Once you have their statements down, compare the story with the evidence. "You said the suitcase was upside down on the floor, but it is now on the bed." This goes on until we have his story, her story, the maid's story, and our story (what we saw). These will be put together in the report.

Evidence

Evidence is everything that supports or disproves the incident. Your legal counsel has to decide what physical evidence she wants you to gather and retain. The police handle criminal evidence. Our evidence refers mostly to accidents, noncriminal incidents, or even criminal incidents if the police did not want the case. Included in these categories are stools from which guests fall, broken glasses in which their mouths were cut, or a bottle of cleaning fluid that burned their eyes. If your counsel finds these items unnecessary, then do not save them, because once you do, you are stuck with them.

Gathering evidence is a process that has to be taken seriously. Handling must be done in a way that does not damage or alter it. Packaging should be done so as not to further damage or contaminate the item, and it must be sealed so there is no question as to whether it was tampered with. Storage must be secured and access limited to one person, such as the investigator.

There may be external items to be retained, such as video, computer data, reports, lock interrogations, and so forth. These must be labeled and preserved with the report.

Once the statements, photographs, and evidence are gathered, the preliminary investigation is complete.

REPORT WRITING

A report is simply the documentation of an incident to preserve the information for later use. Reports may be seen by supervisors, department heads, police, lawyers, prosecutors, juries, and judges. This needs to be stressed to the report writer so that like the preliminary investigation, the report is thorough, detailed, and accurate. Report writing is arguably one of the most important functions of the Security Department, so even though you have given and received training on it, I am going to go over the important stuff.

Officers should be hired and trained with the objective that they will write reports based on incidents that they see. Having supervisors or specialists write the reports works for some, but is awkward. It is difficult to write a report in the first person if one is not at the scene. Supervisors are trained and paid to take more responsibilities than this frontline duty, so this process is inefficient. Hiring officers who can already write is a big help.

Format

Whether you use report-writing software, a word processor, or write by hand, these elements are standard. First is the statistical stuff, and second is the narrative. Last are the attachments.

Report Data

This statistical information is placed in a certain order and format for several reasons. First, it allows the reader to discern the basics without reading through an entire narrative. Anyone can pick up Page 1 and see who was involved, what the loss or injury was, and what the value was. Second, it makes the job of the data entry person easier. If you have to enter data manually, these fill-in boxes make it much faster for the clerk and reduce errors. Third, including all of this information in a narrative format makes it cluttered and difficult to read.

Almost every incident has photos. We already discussed how and where to take them; now they have to be documented in the report. The photos should be listed before the narrative with a number that corresponds to the photo or file name. A brief description, name of photographer, location, date, and time taken should be included in this list.

Video is also included in many reports. You may choose to have your investigator review video for the officer, but the reporting officer should really do it. This helps the officer put the story together and saves the investigator time. It also ensures the video is pulled and saved before it goes stale or is recorded over. In the report, video should be listed similar to the photos, and in the narrative a summary of what the officer saw on the video. This is included in the narrative because not everyone is going to have time or even the original video to review, so the narrative will help them decide if they even need to bother looking at it.

Narrative

This part is much easier than everyone makes it out to be. The narrative simply tells a story, in chronological order of what the writer did from start to finish. It should be done in the first person (use "I" instead of "Officer Jones" or "This officer"). These are outdated forms of writing and are difficult for a layperson (like on a jury) to read and understand.

The narrative starts at the beginning (from the writer's point of view): On this date at this time, I was dispatched to... Or: On this date at this time, I saw.... As the narrative continues, it is easiest to tell the story from the eyes of the officer as it happened. "When I arrived I saw this, I did this, and this person was doing this and then I did this. Mr. Guest said that this happened, then I spoke to Miss Customer and she told me this happened." On and on it goes until the officer leaves the scene. Then she continues writing whatever follow-up she did—gathering statements, room information, lock interrogation, etc.

Corrections

Officers should correct their own reports by proofreading them. Spell check is a good tool, but the wording and grammar should be their own. Using big words or words they don't understand will cause problems later if they are deposed. Their own wording should be used as long as it is accurate. I am not saying to use slang, profanity, or gibberish, but it is not necessary and does not sound like normal conversation to use words like "approximately" and "expedited" when "about" and "hurried" will do.

Hint

Officers who are self-conscious about their writing ability will sweat, stall, and struggle through this process. Ask them to stop writing and tell you what they did on the call. They will likely tell you a story like the one I related before. Perfect. Now write exactly what you just told me. They are likely stuck on the big words and what they think we want to see. When it dawns on them that a story in their own words is what we want, it makes it as easy as writing in a journal or diary. When they get to that part, we just fine-tune the edges with such things as photos, video review, etc.

Attachments

Numerous documents having relevance to the report should be attached directly to it. Do not presume that other departments will hold the info for you or that it will be attached later. Some attachments that are common in hotel reports are the statements from guests and victims, the room folio, lock interrogation report, reports from housekeepers and engineers, and any other paper document that is necessary to support the report.

The written report with supporting video, photos, statements, and other evidence concludes the preliminary investigation. I hope that you have an investigator who can follow-up on it if necessary.

INVESTIGATIONS

Investigations in the Hospitality industry are usually considered somewhat reactionary, where the investigator follows up on certain reports to "solve" them. This is only partially true. If you limit your investigators to follow-ups, you are severely limiting their capabilities. These are some of your most well-trained, highly skilled employees and their talents can be put to work in other ways that benefit the property. In this chapter, we will not only discuss how to recover assets, but also how investigators compile data, analyze it, and enforce vulnerabilities.

Unlike police detectives, the objective of a hotel investigator is not to prove (or solve) a crime, but to protect (or recover) assets. Call this your "Loss Recovery" unit to keep the focus on the objective. Recovery, in security, is most often accomplished through report follow-up. In most cases, security officers generate reports. (In some cases, investigators will initiate a report from information they received directly. This is discussed later.)

Report Follow-Up

It is the investigator's role to review reports for thoroughness, extract statistics, and monitor incident trends. He should not be looking for grammar, punctuation, and sentence structure (that should be done by a supervisor), but needs to flag reports that are lacking in information he might need for an investigation. If there is video missing or a witness statement that was not included, these need to be attended to immediately even if the investigation has not started.

The investigator extracts statistics that will be important for crime analysis and risk assessments (later in this chapter) on all reports. As for follow-up, this is done on those reports that meet certain thresholds set up in advance with the director of security. Thresholds (or triggers) are established based on the staffing levels—how many investigators to handle how many incidents—and what reports are worth solving. If there were 10 missing property reports per week and only one investigator, you might raise the loss amount up to reduce the number of reports to investigate. On the other hand, if your claims representative were going to automatically pay claims less than $50, it would not be worth investigating values less than that. This is not to say that these losses are ignored. You will still track them to see where they fall in your Risk Assessment and to see if there are any commonalities, such as the same valet attendant or certain room numbers and so forth.

Thresholds may get more complicated depending on whether there is enough evidence to conduct an investigation, the workload of the investigator, if the suspect is an employee, if there is liability on the hotel, etc. Whatever the thresholds are, they should be documented so the investigator may apply each report he sees to the criteria and make a quick decision to close the case or leave it open. There also should be a regular meeting, perhaps weekly, between the investigator and the Director to discuss the cases and determine whether they should be investigated based on workload, other investigations that have occurred, or input from the General Manager or Risk Manager. Triggers are discussed in further detail later in this chapter.

Some incidents will be investigated every time, such as sexual harassment, employee theft, discriminatory offense, or law enforcement (criminal) involvement. Set those criteria in advance as well or handle them on a case-by-case basis so they are not overlooked. Types of investigations vary depending on the incident, so we will go through each type you are likely to encounter at your property.

You will likely be investigating five types of incidents:

Internal—Any incident involving an employee as the suspect (offender) or as the victim (complainant). This would include most property losses, damage, employee theft, and guest complaints.

Criminal—Any incident where the police or a law enforcement agency will bring charges against an employee or guest.

Accident—Guest accidents and injuries. This includes food poisoning claims, bed bugs, etc.

Workers' Comp—Employees injured in the line of duty and work-related illnesses. Food poisoning, carpal tunnel, second-hand smoke, etc.

Personnel—Incidents involving employee misconduct, such as sexual harassment, intoxicated on duty, and employee complaints.

The investigator will have to determine the type of incident, who will do the investigation, and the type of investigation. These types are based on the expected outcome:

Personnel—Might result in disciplinary action or term

Criminal—Could result in criminal charges

Workers' Comp—May result in claim denial

Guest claim—Determine fault of company

Personnel Investigations

The first consideration of a personnel investigation is who will do it. Many HR departments prefer to conduct their own investigations. This is fine, but make sure their investigators are trained in interviewing skills. Smaller organizations hire an outside investigator to conduct these. I prefer Security to do all investigations, not only because of the training they have, but because it is a "third party," which allows HR to make an unbiased decision. A second consideration is consistency and fairness among all employees. HR and some department heads will think they have an easy case (two or more witnesses saw misconduct) and will make a termination decision without an investigation. This is often not a problem, but this employee may have a case against the company if he can show you required a full investigation by Security with other employees and not him. On the other hand, the employee who is terminated after a thorough investigation with interviews and an interrogation may claim discrimination because the other employee was not subjected to the same treatment. Establish a system with your HR Department that puts all employees through the same type of investigation so your actions are perceived as fair.

In 2008, a restaurant worker, who had been sexually harassed by her boss, sued the restaurant for hostile working environment. The restaurant had completed the investigation within two days of the first report and fired the harassing boss. The court ruled in favor of the restaurant because they had taken thorough and quick action against the offending supervisor.

A consistently enforced policy and thorough investigations can help a company defend itself from these types of suits. Sloppy or slow investigations can lead the victims to believe that management does not buy into their own policies or that management is trying to cover for its unacceptable behavior.

Written statements are usually the first step in any investigation. Statements should be obtained from all parties in the incident. This is a common way for the investigator to receive the investigation. A manager hands him the statements and he does the rest. (Don't complain about this—the less done on your behalf, the better.) The initial statements will likely be from the "victim" or the one making the complaint. There also may be a "suspect" or offender statement. If these statements have not been written yet, do not obtain them. A good interviewer will get better information verbally and nail it down with the written statement afterward.

It is common, in our culturally diverse environment, to get statements written in a foreign language. Do not trust other employees to translate this for you. Friends and co-workers will not provide an accurate translation and will insert their own opinion of what they think the victim should have written. Have a prearranged Security or Human Resources employee to do this for you.

Verbal translations should be handled in the same way. Do not use the employee's supervisor or co-worker to translate for you. You will need a qualified translator—at least an unbiased one.

The next step in an investigation is to gather evidence. Evidence includes any item or piece of information that will prove or disprove any part of the incident. This may be video, email, personnel files, policy excerpts, and prior cases. Each of these items needs to reviewed, documented, and filed with the report.

Video may or may not show the incident as described, but it also may be used to prove that the incident did not happen as alleged. It is useful as well for identifying witnesses that can be interviewed and to prove witnesses actually saw anything at all.

Email and other computer data are invaluable in many types of cases. This information should be saved in its data form and on paper to include with the report. Do not rely on the department or Information Technology (IT) to archive this for you. This data can be easily misplaced and your case lost.

Personnel files may or may not show previous related incidents, such as a pattern of behavior or a tendency to make false reports. They also may contain policy memos that were signed by the employee prohibiting that behavior.

Policy excerpts are necessary to justify your case. If you are investigating sexual harassment, include that policy to show what your case is proving.

At this point in your investigation, having reviewed the available evidence and statements, it is time for a management conference. This is usually between HR, the department involved, and the investigator. This is a chance for everyone to understand how much proof will be needed (this is discussed later) and what type of proof—a confession, two corroborating accounts, certain wording in an email—and what the expected outcome will be—termination, suspension, discipline, remedial training, etc. The investigator can also pick up some negotiating tools to use in his interrogation. "If you admit to this and undergo some counseling, I might be able to get you off with just a suspension."

Interview

An interview is simply asking and answering questions. Notes are taken, but it should be audio and video recorded with the camera facing the subject. There are interviewing and interrogation skills that require specialized training and every person who conducts these processes should have that training. We will touch on some of it, but this chapter does not replace that training and a lot of practice.

Victim

We usually start with the victim first. This is not vital, but it just makes more sense to get the original complaint directly from the complainant so you understand exactly what you are investigating. The interview is nonconfrontational and a chance to get the victim's side of the story. Just as was done in the preliminary investigation, questions are asked and answers repeated to clarify. Note: I have seen many company investigators perform this initial interview like an interrogation, accusing the employee of causing the problem, and deriding them for wasting his time. You do not want this type of rapport with employees. Let them know you are trustworthy and sympathetic. This will earn their respect and trust, and word will travel quickly that you are one they can go to for help or to report someone else's misconduct.

During the interview, the investigator is doing several things. First, he analyzes the written statement and compares it to the statements made verbally. Second, he examines body language. This is not quite the same as what you see on TV. The concept is to determine someone's truth-telling style by noting their body language and mannerisms when they are telling the truth, then comparing that style to answers given later during questioning. Third, he is deciding what questions to ask to extract more information on certain points that arise.

During the interview, the investigator also will introduce questions that arose from reviewing evidence. You said it happened here, but the video shows it happened elsewhere; tell me more about that. Your statement says that there was nobody else around, but an employee told me she was there the entire time and saw nothing; tell me more about that. Once again, there is some great comprehensive training available on this topic and it is highly recommended.

In conclusion, always tell everyone involved in an interview two things: (1) false accusations or false statements and refusal to cooperate with an internal investigation can result in termination, and (2) the interview and investigation are confidential and revealing the content thereof is a violation of policy.

Witnesses

Witness interviews are handled the same as the victim interview. Either their story will corroborate the victim or it will not, so you will need to delve into those conflicts. They may reveal important details that the victim left out. A witness can turn an investigation upside down, revealing a conspiracy to get the suspect in trouble, so keep an open mind and cull the facts. Witnesses should be admonished just as the victim was on disclosure and cooperation.

Nonwitnesses

You find these people without the help of the victim. A nonwitness is someone who was at the scene, but says nothing happened. These people can also reveal a conspiracy and have no motive to lie.

Character Witness

A character witness is someone who can vouch for the validity of the incident or the history of any one of the subjects in the investigation. They may be able to tell you if the two employees had a previous relationship if you are investigating domestic violence or sexual harassment. They may be able to tell you about their financial status if you are investigating an embezzlement case. Although they may not have witnessed any misconduct or an actual incident, their historical information may be relevant.

Suspect Employee

The last person to be interviewed (at least in the first round) is the suspect or the accused employee. If the employee has not yet written a statement, it is better to hold off until the end of the interview. The reason for your interview is to get their side of the story. So, this interview should start out and remain friendly. The interviewer needs to build some trust and some integrity by reminding the employee that he is just doing his job, just wants the truth, wants the employee's side of the story, and may be the only person who can help him.

The employee should tell the story uninterrupted. During this time, notes are taken with careful attention to truth-telling style; gaps in mental time line, at which points in the story the mannerisms change, parts of the story that do not match; and parts of the story that are left out from the witnesses' or victim's story.

The truth-telling style was explained briefly before, and I cannot stress enough how important it is to have extensive training in these techniques. For the sake of the Security Director who needs to know what his investigator is doing in those interviews, I am summarizing it here. The interviewer pays close attention to the subject's telling of the story. It is better to have him start at the beginning of the workday and tell what he did from the moment he arrived on property that day. This gives a chance to identify the subject's truth-telling style. This style is displayed as he tells the truthful part of his day (where he parked, what he had for lunch, etc.). The interviewer notes his body movements, posture, facial expressions, etc.

As the dialog gets to the point of the alleged incident, we watch for changes in the body language, voice inflection, and so forth. These may indicate lies. We also listen for gaps in the timeline. There may be much detail as he recounts each hour of his workday, then breezes through the 15 minutes when he was in the storeroom drinking beer. It is more difficult to recall a lie, so people tend to leave out detail so they are not caught up in the lie. Once again, this may be an indicator, but it will be worth more investigation.

When he finishes his story, the interviewer goes back to the areas of concern. Whether it was a gap in the timeline, a different body language, or a difference between his story and the victim's, probe that area and repeat back what he said and say, "Tell me more about that." Do not tell him which part interested you; just ask him to talk more. This is done several times, continually narrowing him down or leading him through a complicated lie that he cannot get out of and that you know is not true.

Once this process is concluded, there should be some idea in the investigator's mind of whether the subject was being truthful. That is when you have him write his statement. This often puts him at ease that he is out of trouble because you could not get anything out of him. Do not prompt the statement; just say you need him to write everything that happened between 3 and 4 p.m. or everything he did in the storeroom up until he went to his locker.

Postinterview Conference

At this point, there is a pause in the investigation as the investigator reviews his findings. He either knows the employee is "guilty" or has learned new information that needs to be checked. If the latter is the case, the investigator goes back to evidence or more interviews until he has resolved all doubts or questions. If the investigator has already reached his conclusion, he will need to consult with his director, the HR director, and possibly the department head. This conference is used to review all the findings and determine the next steps. (See "Burden of Proof" later in this chapter.) Someone will decide if there is enough evidence to stop the investigation and issue discipline or termination, or whether it will go unresolved with no discipline. It may be determined that everyone believes he did the act of which he is accused, but they want a confession. This is done through an interrogation.

Interrogation

The interrogation is somewhat different from an interview, and only necessary if there is not enough evidence. To begin an interrogation, the interviewer knows the subject is guilty, but does not have enough evidence. A confession is the goal of an interrogation. The interviewer does almost all of the talking and spends some time telling the subject how much evidence he has against him—statements, video, witnesses—he just wants to know why the person did it. Or he just wants to recover the money, or some other secondary concern. This takes some time to engrain in the subject's mind that guilt is no longer a doubt while he will deny it. Good interrogators use several styles to achieve the confession. They may use guilt, such as "What is your family going to think?" or they may be empathetic, "I know you just needed the money to feed your kids. I might have done the same thing in your position." Or, they may try promising them leniency, "If you just tell me how you did it, I can talk to my boss and maybe we won't press charges." There are many techniques and you may have to use them all for hours until the subject finally sees no way out.

A California employee of a large manufacturing company was called into the office and accused of theft of company parts. He was forced to drive the investigators to his home and submit to a search for the missing parts. The man sued for false imprisonment and invasion of privacy and was awarded $214,000.

Investigators have no authority to search a person and his property without consent. Care should be taken not to hold someone against his will and certainly not to physically force him to do anything. During an investigative interview, the only authority an investigator has is over the employee's employment.

Resignation versus Termination

Many companies will accept a resignation in lieu of an employee being terminated. HR Directors prefer this for many reasons. One is that their unemployment insurance may not have to pay on a resignation. This is hardly true anymore because employees can claim they resigned under duress. Two is that they believe they will save time and money if the employee decides to challenge his termination with a labor agency. This is also no longer applicable for the same reason. Three is that they are not comfortable with the evidence provided. It is generally not up to Security to make this decision or to accept a resignation. Whatever your HR Department decides, make sure your investigation is complete and accurate and includes all of the evidence even if you think you will not need it.

In 2010, a warehouse worker at a Connecticut beer distributor was being questioned about stolen beer. Investigators showed him video of the theft and offered to let him resign. The man calmly refused, asked to use the restroom, and came out with a handgun he had hidden in his lunch box. Nine people died.

Investigators should remain calm and friendly, but never let their guard down despite an employee's demeanor. This situation was avoidable and may have been prevented with some of the policies discussed in Chapter 7.

Conclusion

Remember that confessions are not necessary to prove or resolve your case. Later we will talk about the burden of proof required in a hotel investigation and restitution, which is our main objective.

Cooperation

When the police interview a suspect, they have to advise him or her of certain constitutional rights. We sometimes have to remind ourselves that we are not the police and do not have to do that. Our interviews are with employees and their participation is a condition of their employment. You should have a policy to this effect in your company policy manual, and you should remind employees of this when talking to them. Of course, they are free to leave at any time, but doing so will be cause for termination. It is advisable to tell them that before beginning an interview. This is a good time to remind them that lying or refusing to cooperate also may be cause for termination.

Having provided these admonishments, make sure the interview scene is nonthreatening. Do not back your subject into a corner where he feels he cannot leave. This could come back to you as false imprisonment or unlawful detention. There is nothing wrong with offering water, tissues, and restroom breaks. The old tales of the wobbly chair, bright lights, and threats of violence are reserved for the movies.

Unions

If your company has any employees in bargaining units, chances are they have wording in their contract allowing a shop steward to be present during interviews. A rule derived from The Weingarten Act provides any employee who is questioned by any member of management, where the questioning might lead to disciplinary action or termination, to have an employee witness present. The details of this agreement depend on the specific contracts in place at your property, so you should consult your HR Department. Failure to provide the shop steward during your interview may invalidate the information received and cause a union grievance to be filed, or worse—an unfair labor complaint. Once you establish this procedure with HR, make sure you follow it the same way each time you interview a union employee. In most contracts, the steward is not allowed to give advice or even talk, so it is not a big deal. In fact, you may be able to select the steward.

Translators

We mentioned earlier, regarding statements, that the translator you use should be one of your choosing who has training. What I have seen in most instances is the translator plays lawyer and speaks on behalf of one party instead of just translating. You can imagine how this can botch an interview where you are trying to reveal lies in the wording or certain statements that make the employee nervous. Even with a good, trained translator, it will be very difficult to do a good interview or interrogation. In a perfect world, you would have a bilingual trained investigator.

Burden of Proof

In a personnel investigation, we are not proving a crime, only a policy violation. We do not have the same burden (beyond a reasonable doubt) that has to be proved in a criminal setting. This is why we go for violations of policy rather than breaking of laws. For example, if you are investigating a theft (loss) from a storeroom, you only need to know that your suspect was in an unauthorized area, did not follow requisition procedures, etc. If you had to prove the actual theft, you would need a video camera or a witness who saw the suspect put the item in his pants. Suppose a guest complained that an employee shoved him. This may be a criminal battery. To prove that the battery occurred, you would need a witness, video, or something more definite. Unsuccessfully prosecuting an employee for battery does nothing for the hotel (or anyone else), but we can easily prove that he violated a guest service policy, was out of his work area without permission, had inappropriate contact with a guest, or any number of policy violations.

Because policy violations are not misdemeanors, they do not have to occur in our presence to terminate the employee. Since our property is not a court of law, we do not have to prove beyond a reasonable doubt that he did it.

In O.J. Simpson's murder trial, the prosecution was not successful in proving beyond a reasonable doubt that he committed the crimes, so he was acquitted. In the subsequent civil trial, he was found to be responsible for the murders. Civil trials have a different burden of proof called "preponderance of evidence." This is substantially less proof required, and is therefore easier to prove. For the sake of this illustration, suppose Simpson was our employee and we wanted to terminate him because his involvement in the alleged murders was damaging our reputation. We would have many policy violations, not even related to the murder, that we would use to successfully terminate him.

Criminal Investigation

During an interview of what you suspected was a personnel investigation, the case may turn into a criminal investigation. For example, what you thought was a sexual harassment allegation might turn out to be an alleged battery or even sexual assault. Naturally, you would notify law enforcement as soon as you find out. The danger in continuing a suspect interview may cross a line of acting as an agent of the police. All kinds of legal ramifications come into question, including should you now "Mirandize" the suspect; is the information you receive now protected by the Fourth Amendment; and is the suspect still free to leave. Better safe than sorry—inform the suspect you are calling the police and turn over everything you have to them. If you have enough to arrest the suspect to keep him from leaving, do so. The investigation now becomes a police matter and your HR Department can make a decision based on their outcome.

Keep in mind that your investigation may have to continue—without the suspect—to cover any civil liability. Even though law enforcement action may seem to take this to a certain level and out of your hands, the company may still be liable for a hostile work environment or something else depending on the original allegation. So, you will want to stay in touch with the detective or prosecution as it relates to company liability.

In order to stay in contact with the investigating agency, you should develop a supporting role. This means supplying video, handing over statements you already have, and seeking witnesses and evidence. Be sure to consult your counsel on what level you will cooperate with police. There may be proprietary information that must remain private and is subject to subpoena. Finally, make sure to keep copies of everything you give the outside investigators. If their case falls through or even if it does not, you may have to run a continuing, or parallel, investigation of your own.

Private versus Public

Many people in both private and public sectors have trouble distinguishing the difference between private and police investigations. The objective of a police investigation is to prove that the suspect committed a crime. Even if the investigation objective is to find a suspect, it is done knowing that a crime occurred. While there may be crimes occurring at your property that require investigations, keep reminding yourself that you are not the hotel police department. Your objective—your only objective—is to protect the assets of the company. After a loss has occurred, the only way to protect assets is to recover the loss and to prevent future losses from occurring. This is a novel way of thinking for some of us who have been engrained to solve crimes and catch bad guys.

If a guest suffers a loss, it is the investigator's job to either prove that it was not the fault of the hotel or recover the loss. For example, if a guest is missing his or her laptop from the room, and we can prove that no employee took it, and there was no responsibility for the loss, such as a faulty lock or no security, then the hotel has no exposure.

Restitution

We have talked throughout this and other chapters about recovering losses. This is commonly done through restitution. Restitution can be a valuable interrogation tool and a metric for showing security's contribution to the bottom line. It is generally a negotiated amount up to or equal to the amount of the loss. It can also include administrative, labor, investigative, and other costs associated with the loss.

During an interview, a common tactic is to use restitution as a bargaining tool. An employee who thinks he is facing criminal prosecution may be very willing to pay back what was stolen or damaged. The investigator can negotiate on the amount and even payment terms in return for other information provided. Remember, this is a private agreement and has nothing to do with the crime or the police. That also means it will be harder to collect. You should try to get the majority of the amount out of the employee's final check because it is not likely you will see him again.

Court-ordered restitution is also a very viable source of recovery for the Security Department. An employee who is being charged with embezzlement or a "guest" who is being charged with theft can be responsible for restitution. This will depend on the initiative of the police officer making the arrest report, the detective who prepares it for prosecution, and the prosecutor. If all of them work with information you provide, the judge is likely to order restitution if the suspect is found guilty. Your department should have restitution letters that are filled in when an arrest is made. Include the loss amount and any associated costs with the arrest. Don't forget the labor costs of the arrest, the administrative costs of processing the report, and any other department costs. It is best to have these costs itemized in a list in advance, so the arresting officer can put these into a letter to go with the police.

Workers' Compensation Investigation

Security is not always the department dubbed to do employee accident investigations. I believe it is only natural for Security to use its trained investigators for this, especially because it may reveal employee misconduct. The Workers' Compensation Department, HR, or the insurance company usually initiates these investigations. If the explanation of the accident appears doubtful, if there are some suspected safety or policy violations, or if the employee is suspected of insurance fraud by making a false claim, an investigation is likely to be requested.

The process is very similar to the one for personnel investigations discussed earlier in this chapter. There may be different forms and report formats and the burden of proof may also vary, but the fundamentals are the same. As we proved a particular policy violation in the personnel investigation, for accidents we focus on four main conclusions:

1. Is it work-related?
2. Are there any safety violations or recommendations for future safety policies?
3. Was it caused by the employee, the company, or a third party?
4. Was there negligence on the part of the employee?

Each of these can cause a claim to be denied, partially paid, or deferred to another party. The insurance company will generally direct you to its main concerns. Regardless of what the insurance company decides, you may be directed by HR to find policy or safety violations that they will address.

Guest Claims

The fourth type of investigation involves guest claims. These claims (whether there is an actual claim or not) include guest accidents, loss or damage of guest property, food-related illnesses, and company-wide complaints.

Guest accidents are, by far, the most costly claim your property will handle. A slip and fall that involves back surgery or long-term loss of a bodily function or limb can cost hundreds of thousands of dollars. If the case goes to a jury, your little investigation might save or cost the company millions. This is not an exaggeration as the examples throughout this book have illustrated. Liability, safety, and prevention of accidents are addressed elsewhere in this book, so we will focus only on the investigation here.

Triggers

Your department may not have the work force or the time to investigate every guest report that comes through. If that is the case, you need to develop triggers that automatically start an investigation. For reports involving guests, here are some examples of criteria that would trigger an investigation.

Loss or damage greater than $250
Any guest injury
Complaints that are serious, such as discrimination
Where the return is greater than the cost of the investigation (sometimes it is cheaper to pay)

Statements

We discussed gathering statements in the section entitled Preliminary Investigation. The investigator will put that statement to good use because it is unlikely that there will be an interview or further contact with the guest. The investigator can use the information in the statement and see where it differs from the verbal account given to the officer. For example, when the watch was first missing, it was worth $100. When the guest wrote the statement later, it was valued at $500. When the guest calls your claims representative, it is now worth $5,000. We use the statement as we did with interviews, but in lieu of getting to speak to the guest.

Witnesses

Witnesses are handled differently depending on whether they are guests or employees. Employee witnesses are treated as they are in a personnel investigation: Obtain and evaluate statement and interview as necessary to gain more information. Guest witnesses can be contacted after they leave, but it is not likely to be in person if they are tourists. Phone interviews do not work well for discerning the truth, but are perfectly acceptable for following up to clarify what the guests wrote in their statements.

"Suspect" employees should be investigated exactly as with a personnel investigation. Remember that with a personnel investigation, the objective is to prove a policy violation. In a guest loss, we are trying to prove that we have no responsibility for the loss. These two objectives seem to conflict because if we prove an employee was responsible, then the hotel is vicariously liable for the loss as well.

Your Risk Manager or Claims Department may not want to investigate certain incidents because they can more easily deny the claim and responsibility if there is no evidence of hotel responsibility. In the old days, Security departments would keep their investigations confidential for that very reason. That way the claims person could pick and choose the investigative reports that favored the hotel. We all know this is wrong and no longer even true. Any documentation can be called into court, if it goes that far.

ANALYSIS

As I said at the beginning of the Investigations section, investigators are the most skilled employees you have. They can and should be used for other important functions than just loss recovery.

Metrics

"Metrics" means "to measure," which is why it applies to the socket set in your toolbox as well as the measurements of your department. In fact, toolbox is a good allusion for how Security uses metrics.

Measurements of the department come from a wide variety of data sources and are used for just as many reasons. One metric you are already using is your daily labor report. This report, from the company's timekeeper, tells you how much you spent on labor, how much overtime, how many hours, and so forth. The time clock is the data source, and the report is the metric. Someone put that metric together for the managers in your company based on what metrics he or she was told you needed. You could expand that report to include other measurements if you knew how to access the data and how to create the report. You probably do not "own" time clock data, but you do own other Security data, so all we need to work on metrics is a data source and a reporting tool.

Data Sources

Let's determine the types of data sources, then what metrics we want, then how to get from A to B. However, even if we do not know what metrics we need, the sooner you start collecting data, the more data you will have to work with when you are ready.

Most reporting systems (discussed in Chapter 9) create their own database and even have their own metrics. Some limit your reports to the metrics they created, but others give you access to the raw data and allow you to download it into a spreadsheet or reporting software. This is great, but you may still have to create some data for yourself. For example, not all car burglaries in your parking lot are reported to Security. Some people know that you are not going to reimburse them for a loss, so they make a police report and go through their insurance. In that case, you may download the raw data from your reporting software, which will give you dates, times, locations, value, etc. and then manually add the information you get from the police department. (Remember, we did this as part of our Risk Assessment in Chapter 1.)

241

If you do not have reporting software—by that I mean you do reports in a word processor or by hand—you need to create your own data source. This is not so difficult if done on a daily or weekly basis, which is why I mentioned starting now so you do not have to go back and do it when you decide you need to know everything that happened this year. Decide how you are going to work with this data. Excel® allows you to work with other reporting systems, so I would suggest Excel or similar spreadsheet software. Handwriting a table or spreadsheet will not allow you to format it for use in Excel, so avoid this wasted step if you can.

Creating a Spreadsheet

The secret to getting the most out of your data is to separate data into as many different categories as possible. In a spreadsheet, these data are the columns, such as date, time, location, names, etc. You could have 20, 30, even 50 columns if you include victims' names, witnesses, addresses, employee numbers, etc. In database lingo, this huge spreadsheet is called a flat table or database. A relational database is one that divides data into different tables and links them together by common fields. That is just some background information to understand the process. If you are going to do this manually, stick with the flat spreadsheet.

With manual entry, the hardest part will be setting up the spreadsheet columns with everything you want. As mentioned previously, get each column down to the smallest detail. Do not combine date and time or first and last name in the same column. It will be easier to sort and work with those columns if they have just one value. Once the blank spreadsheet or database is created, someone needs to enter the data daily or weekly. This should only take a few minutes as the person doing it starts in row one and enters the information horizontally for each report or incident.

A spreadsheet like Excel allows you to do most things like sorting and adding, but a more advanced system like Access or Crystal lets you combine data sources called "tables," create formulas for working with the data called "queries," and format it into a presentable report. You can get most anything from your raw data with these programs. As we get into crime analysis, we may want to know which housekeeper is common to the most room losses, what times of day most of our vehicle burglaries occur, or if the number of patrol routes has any effect on slip and falls.

Crime Analysis

It is the responsibility of the Security Director to be preventative more than reactive. Even police departments that traditionally focused on reacting to crimes and trying to catch criminals on the back end are now using crime prevention techniques to reduce the chances of a crime occurring in the first place. We already know physical prevention techniques and they are discussed throughout this book, such as layered security, preventative patrol, and behavioral analysis. Another important method that you should be using, and may already be using to some extent, is crime prevention analysis.

The concept is to use data, as we did in our Risk Assessment, to prevent crime by investigating patterns. As you analyze crime statistics, you will notice trends that suggest certain commonalities. Burglaries may occur on certain hotel floors, at certain times of the day, or by certain methods. Crime (or incident) analysis is the sorting of data to reveal patterns, exceptions, and trends. Now that we have a spreadsheet with some data, or a reporting system that provides us with presorted information, we can start to see what we have. There are many ways to look at the data and you really need to look at all of it for it to be of any use.

Location

You may start by dividing your property into general locations, such as garage, guest rooms, nightclub, and lobby. These areas are so different that there probably will not be any overlap of crime or incidents. In other words, statistics that you derive from the garage or parking area will not likely be related in any way to crime you have in guest rooms.

Once you separate these areas, you can work on data from each one separately. In each of these areas, you will want to have sublocations, or locations that are more specific. These may be floors in a garage, or quadrants in a parking lot. In the hotel, it would likely be floors. In the public areas, you have the lobby, each restaurant, bar, etc.

When you sort by these areas, you may already see patterns, such as one particular floor that has problems over another. In Valet, or the nightclub, of course, every incident is in that location, so skip this step for those specific areas. If you notice a trend or something unusual about a particular location, there must be a reason and that is what we are here to solve.

Crime Type

The next "sorting" method of analyzing crime data is by type of crime. This will show you at a glance if you have more of a problem with damaged cars in Valet, rather than property loss; or property loss in guest rooms, rather than assaults or robberies; or more fights in the nightclub than missing purses.

Time

The next sort option is date and time. Here you are looking for commonalities related to time of day, day of week, shift, etc. Perhaps most car burglaries occur between 7 p.m. and midnight. Maybe room losses usually happen during the day. Fights in the nightclub occur most often on Wednesdays. (This seems very elementary to most of you, but you need to follow the steps to ensure that you do not overlook anything. We will get further into the analysis shortly.)

Suspect

Another sorting option of our crime data is the suspect. The obvious pattern might be a housekeeper who has coincidentally cleaned all the rooms where losses occurred. Less obvious are profiles of suspects. You probably do not have suspects identified in most cases. However, in nightclub fights you should have descriptions. Do white males in their early twenties start all the fights? The same goes for losses in the kitchen. You can rule out a bunch of staff members if the suspects all had grey shirts and the kitchen staff has white shirts.

Other Sorts

If you find commonalities in your data, it will be worth it to drill down deeper into other categories. These may include specific room numbers, approximate times, etc.

Crime Triangle

Three of the categories we just talked about make up the crime triangle. This triangle is a useful illustrative way to solve and prevent crime.

The crime triangle consists of three components of a crime: location, victim, and suspect. Every crime must have a victim, one who suffers from the crime; a suspect, one who commits the crime; and a location where the crime occurred. (The location may be virtual, such as the Internet or telephone.) Take away any of the three components and there is no crime.

Suspect

The suspect leg of this triangle is traditionally the one we go for. The suspect is the bad guy, the one breaking the law, so that is generally where we concentrate our efforts of solving crimes. If a neighborhood is having a rash of car burglaries, the police try to catch the bad guy and, thus, eliminate future crimes. Of course, this is great if you can do it, but it is best to let the police do that and for us to concentrate our efforts on preventing the crime from occurring again. Catching the suspect may prevent the suspect from committing the crime again, but it is only one third of the prevention. Someone else can come along and commit the same crime, theoretically.

Without getting too far into psychology of a criminal, it is important to understand a little bit about his/her thought process. When most of us make a decision between good and bad, we use rational judgment that takes all of the factors into account: How will this affect the other person? Will I be caught? What will happen if I am caught? How would I explain that to my loved ones? And so forth. Most of us choose not to commit the crime because of the way we answered those questions. (This may explain why alcohol turns normal people into criminals.)

The criminal mind generally works a bit differently. The thief or assailant does not ask himself those questions (until afterward, maybe). He sees the immediate gratification of possessing the item, committing the violent act, or the thrill of the bad act. This makes most criminals opportunists and shortsighted thinkers. It helps us to know this because we know that if we decrease the opportunity or make it more difficult or time-consuming to commit the crime, we can prevent many of these acts.

For example, a wallet lying on a counter unattended is too tempting for someone who does not ask himself the questions. He sees an opportunity and takes it. If the owner is standing near the wallet, it becomes less of an opportunity and less tempting because the immediate gratification becomes less likely because the person may fight him. If the owner is holding her wallet, that makes it far less tempting. The gratification is now out of sight to most (unless they are a skilled snatcher and do not see the person holding it as a deterrent).

One exception to this theory is the criminal who "justifies" his actions. It should have been mine anyway; they don't deserve to have it; they can afford to lose it; she hurt me so I will hurt her; he fired me so I will show him who is boss; etc. Since we know there are criminal minds out there, and plenty of justifications, we have to limit the opportunities.

Victim

Of course, if we get rid of all the victims, we can certainly prevent crime. That is not very conducive to the hospitality business. Seriously, we can have some influence on potential victims to prevent them from becoming victims. We do this all the time by warning vehicle owners to lock their cars and not to leave valuables inside, providing awareness training, posting signs warning patrons, etc.

Anything you can do to get hotel guests out of the "tourist/victim" mentality and make them more self-aware is a way to prevent crime. We want our guests to have a worry-free stay in our establishment so we have to find a reasonable balance between paradise and prison.

Location

Naturally, if you change or eliminate a location of a crime, it will not happen again—at least not there. This is also a common prevention technique we use. If crimes are happening in a certain area, we beef up or patrol, install cameras and locks, etc. Consider these measures in your hotel.

The crime triangle is something you were already using, and maybe did not realize it. However, when you approach crime prevention using the triangle model, you will focus on all three legs, rather than just one. This gives you three times the opportunity to prevent the crime. As you review crime trends from the data you compiled, determine which leg provides the commonality. Location is easy. More car burglaries are occurring on the fifth floor of the garage or door pushers keep hitting the same room, which has a faulty closure. These are easy crime trends to address.

Sometimes the trend is not location, but suspect. For example, if you have a problem with graffiti, it may happen all over the property, but you can develop a profile of the suspect easily. It may be video, or you may know what gang the suspect comes from. Then your prevention step might be to identify those persons and watch them or exclude them.

Finally, the data may show that the commonality is the victim. The obvious example would be little old ladies who keep getting robbed of their purses. You may want to put more resources on watching little old ladies with purses, warning people not to carry cash in their purse, or providing awareness training.

Off-Property Incidents

In Chapter 1, we mentioned the importance of gathering outside data for performing the Risk Assessment. Investigators or analysts are usually the likely persons to track this activity. Besides assessing risk, we need to know what is happening at other hotels (or similar properties) and at neighboring businesses and streets. The criminal activity in our neighborhood has many affects on us. It makes or breaks our reputation, makes our guests and employees feel threatened, and determines what types of security measures we will take.

Street crime near your property may prompt you to install lighting, locked gates, fenced parking, etc. Other hotels with a propensity for crime may encourage you to take preventative steps to avoid those crimes on your property. Gang activity in your neighborhood will decide whether you have dress codes, controlled entry, or even armed security.

For all of these reasons, track activity on a spreadsheet just as you do for internal incidents. List the major incidents specifically, such as with a news clipping, and other incidents by category and location. If applicable, list the security measures you took to reduce the chance of those crimes happening.

Reacting to the Data

Measuring the incidents we have, sorting the data, and analyzing it not only provide nice reports for the boss, but also can help solve the problems, thereby protecting the assets even better. The traditional method was to go after the bad guy. But, the crime triangle shows us that the bad guy is only a third of the problem and not necessarily the easiest side of the triangle to remove. Remember that our job is to protect the assets. The most efficient way to do that is through prevention. Arresting people, or even firing people, does not always prevent the loss.

So, what else can our crime analysts recommend to prevent future crimes or losses? The answer is in the data. Look at the information you have and determine the most efficient method of preventing it from happening again. Lighting, cameras, locks, patrol, training, awareness, and special operations are just a few of the tools at our disposal, and the solution should be obvious in the crime data.

SPECIAL OPERATIONS

After performing a crime analysis or beginning a specific investigation, it may be determined that the suspect leg of the triangle is the one we need to remove. As long as we admit that this will not be preventative in nature and will likely cost more, it is perfectly justifiable to go after the suspect, especially if it is an employee. These temporary operations are designed specifically to target one suspect or a group of suspects. Operations include undercover officers, outside agencies, or covert cameras. They may include targeted area patrols, new procedures, or training.

Undercover Operations

Undercover operations encompass a wide variety of plainclothes, covert, or discreet investigations depending on the objective. I find that either Security Departments do not use them enough or they use them too much. The advantage of a discreet operation is that it addresses those offenders who are privy to the visible security measures. Disadvantages are that they are not very preventative in nature—more reactionary—and often take resources away from other necessary areas.

Outside Agencies

It may be appropriate at times to ask local law enforcement agencies to conduct a special operation on your property. Naturally, this method can only be used for suspected criminal activity. If your problem is a policy violation or anything less than criminal, the police cannot be of much help. However, they may be very interested in working a known problem with prostitution, drug dealing, or fraud.

If police detectives are assigned to work your property, you will be placed in a supportive role. You should provide whatever information they need and whatever technical support you can. See the section on Prostitution in this chapter. Suggestions for law enforcement investigations include prostitution, organized crime, drug sales, car burglaries, etc.

Private Outside Agencies

Other loss investigations should not be handled internally. A complicated internal fraud case is an example of an investigation that requires a great deal of resources, an unknown undercover employee, and a perspective that is strictly unbiased. Even if you are confident in the ability of your staff to perform this operation, and to do so without favor, remember that perception is reality. The outcome may be questioned morally or even legally if there is even a hint that your relationship with co-workers affected the investigation.

There are many very qualified private investigators to use for such an investigation. If you do not know someone who can give you a personal recommendation, go through your local security association or police liaison. Your company law firm may have a reliable company that they have used in the past. This is not a job to be chosen from the yellow pages.

Like the police, you will have to hand the entire matter over to this outside person. As with any secret, the more people you tell, the less likely it will be a secret. Every executive wants to know and thinks he has a reason to know, but it is better if only one person knows.

Use the guidelines set out in the Personnel Investigations section of this chapter in defining your objective, what the expected outcome will be, if there will be charges filed, a term, etc. Suggested uses for an outside employee investigation include fraud in the Accounting Department, bartenders stealing, Receiving Department losses, nightclub doorpersons stealing, employee drug use, etc.

In-House Operations

It is almost impossible to have your investigators operate undercover if targeting an employee. Use an outside company if your investigation is internal and requires undercover personnel. Some internal investigations can be done with video. This process is generally like fishing. You place some bait, get the right equipment in place, and wait for someone to come along and bite.

One common place we do this in hotels is guest rooms. This is a huge waste of time unless you have narrowed down a suspect to a housekeeper. Let's do some math.

Suppose you have an average of 500 hotel rooms occupied every night. And suppose you average one room loss per day (night). Further, suppose you have time to set up a room two days per month with an investigator, video camera, and bait. That is a 1 in 7,500 chance that you will be at the right room on the right floor where the right housekeeper is tempted by the right bait. Unless you narrow down those odds, you are throwing away resources. Recall our crime analysis previously in this chapter. First, make sure it is a housekeeper. It could be a door pusher or a cohabitant of the room. Second, see if any housekeeper is common on more than one room loss. Third, narrow down the bait by determining if there are commonalities with the property taken (cash, jewelry, etc.).

If you have a suspect employee, a probable day of the week, a preferred floor, and type of bait, then you have a better than 1 in 10 chance. That is worth it, but still not guaranteed to catch anyone.

How to conduct this operation is the easy and fun part. You will come up with some neat cameras and other equipment to do this because your motivation will be there. I just want to make sure you put the proper preparation into selecting the location, victim, and suspect to target before you begin.

Covert Cameras

Covert cameras are those that are hidden from view or disguised as something else. Before you even think about using hidden cameras, check with your legal counsel on issues such as expectation of privacy and wire-tapping laws. There is no specific law about where to put cameras. The precedents are set in federal and state case law about what is reasonable. We also follow different rules than the police do because we are private. There are now very specific laws in each state about audio recording. These laws come from older wire-tapping laws. Some states are keeping up with technology (to include video) and others are not. So your state might forbid recording an audio conversation and allow (by lack of any laws against it) video recording.

> A New York jury awarded a man $3 million after he sued his employer for discrimination. The man had made several complaints regarding ethnic slurs from his co-workers. There was no apparent investigation of the slurs, but a camera was placed in the man's work area to watch him, presumably to retaliate for his complaints.
>
> Cameras are a good way to document misconduct or criminal activity, but should never be used in this manner. The Security Director or Human Resources Director should authorize such use of cameras to ensure that employees are investigated fairly and that labor laws are not violated.

To keep you out of trouble, here are some rules that should cover you in most states. Do not place a video camera in a place where someone would expect to have privacy. This includes bathrooms and dressing rooms, but also may include a private office or even a storeroom. Make sure you have a documentable reason why you need a hidden camera there. Reasons include a rash of thefts from the area, reports of misconduct, such as sexual activity or sleeping, and suspicion of fraud on a computer. Do not place a hidden camera in an occupied guest room. Consider a general policy about video surveillance for all employees. Do not audio record someone in secret.

Some great ideas for camera placement have been used in hotels by clever investigators. Your networking with other directors and investigators will give you good ideas and save you from duplicating mistakes.

Room Losses

Set up two rooms—one with bait and camera, the other with video equipment and investigator. Use bait as discussed previously, depending on the potential for loss, and check the integrity of everyone that comes into that room. This will include the housekeeper, bell person if you make a reason for them to be there, engineer if you call in some maintenance request, and security for lost and found. After you have tested those with access, try leaving the door ajar. This will attract what are called "door pushers" (opportunistic thieves who look for open doors in hotels). You can arrest them if they steal something or 86 them if you prefer. This will test security and other employees as well to see if they take action when they spot an open door.

There is much folklore surrounding the origins of the term "86." We know 86 as the popular term for trespassing someone from our establishment. Nevada hotels are the most notorious for this service, which occurs many times every day in casinos and bars throughout the state.

One origin of this term comes from the Old West days. When a bar patron was becoming too drunk or creating a disturbance, they would serve him alcohol that was 86 percent (172 proof). That would pretty much knock him out. I doubt that is your policy now. Other explanations for the term come from addresses of famous bars on the East Coast, section numbers of liquor laws, and a cross-out method used for taking items off menus. The F-86 Sabre aircraft had many notable "kills" and other successes throughout history.

There are numerous camera options available these days due to their smaller size. Cameras can be secreted in almost anything and if you have a technician available with a little imagination, she can probably put a camera in just about anything.

Suggested uses for in-house operations include losses from guest rooms, storerooms, valet vehicles, and lockers; employee vandalism; safety violations; and harassment.

Bag Checks

The ideal policy would be to have a security officer inspecting every employee who leaves the employee areas (back of the house). This is often considered not worth the labor required, or not practical due to the layout of the basement or employee area. Twenty-four-hour inspection posts are certainly expensive, so it may be worth it to do random bag checks.

The unfortunate fact is employees walk off your property with company merchandise every day. Whether it is shampoo, towels, and soap, or alarm clocks and hair dryers, or even alcohol and guest property—chances are there are some thieves among us. A simple deterrent to this is to do bag checks daily at the end of shift or at least randomly.

Bag checks are simple and can take less than 30 minutes. Station two officers at the employee exit and inspect every purse, backpack, and duffle bag that comes through. Do not target housekeepers. Require every employee to go through this process to be fair.

Make sure the second officer is watching for employees who see the inspection site and head back to their lockers.

A hotel had an employee inspection post that ran 24/7 for many years. During hard financial times, that post was closed. A few months later, the director of Security decided to institute random inspections. On the first day, the very first employee who walked past the inspection area was a housekeeper with an alarm clock in her purse. Several more were seen turning around and heading back to their work area.

Investigators can assist with bag checks and take the opportunity to specifically watch certain employees who appear in their metrics more than others do. They also may want to set up an integrity check of storage areas and use the bag check to check for stolen products.

Make sure your company has a policy about employees being subject to search. Signage is a good reminder.

DRUG TESTING

According to a study performed by George Washington University, the hospitality industry employs the largest number of workers with alcohol problems. Alcohol is just one part of a nationwide drug problem that is woven into the fabric of our workforce. Whatever the statistics on substance use or your own personal feelings, we can probably all agree that it has no place at work. Besides, if the company has a policy against it, it is your job to enforce it.

Companies generally do drug testing in four different circumstances: pre-employment, postaccident, random, and cause. I will assume that you have little to do with the pre-employment screening, so we will discuss the other three, which are almost identical processes. First, a brief discussion about drugs.

For our purposes, we can classify mind-influencing or psychoactive drugs as either stimulants or depressants. (This is over-simplified for illustration only.) These "controlled substances" are alcohol, marijuana, prescription drugs, and street drugs. Each of these substances affects judgment and physical skills and, therefore, can cause accidents and poor work performance and place a company in a bad light.

Most drugs take effect on the mind and body within about 30 minutes. Their effects can last up to four hours in most cases. (That means someone who is under the influence in the second half of his or her shift most likely consumed the drug while working.) Testing methods include urine, blood, and saliva. (Hair testing does not work to see immediate effects so it is used for pre-employment screening. Sweat, or patch, testing is used to check for usage over a long period.)

Your HR professionals, legal counsel, and company medical provider should decide testing methods and policies. Some bargaining agreements have special stipulations about testing methods that must be followed. Whatever your procedures are, these are my recommendations and you can adapt them to meet your requirements.

Random Testing

Most companies do not allow for random testing (except for regulated employees like bus drivers, airline pilots, and sports figures). The accusations of discrimination and favoritism are too difficult to defend for normal workers and it is difficult to administer. If you do have random testing, it is likely that Security will not be involved, but if you are, follow the procedures in the next section.

Postaccident

Almost every company requires a drug test following an employee accident. Your company will have to decide if this is done for every reported accident, those that just claim injuries, or those that require medical treatment. I would suggest any accident where an injury is claimed gets a drug test. Before any testing is done, the employee should be required to sign a policy statement with a witness. The policy should state three things:

1. The company requires the test and refusal to take it will result in termination.
2. If the test comes back positive or has to be sent for further testing, the employee will be on investigative suspension.
3. If the test is positive or requires further testing, the employee will not be permitted to drive home.

To save time and money, I recommend using a swab test that can be given by Security. These tests are a few of dollars per use, test for a wide variety of drugs, and give immediate results. If this test is negative, it is finished. If the swab were positive, I would have it corroborated by a professional lab. This will avoid a $10 test that was administered by an untrained security officer being challenged later. Swab tests also do not have thresholds, which means someone on a legal, prescription dose of valium would come back as positive.

They make swab tests for alcohol or you can use a breathalyzer, which provides a blood/alcohol percentage. This may be important to your HR Department because it is written into most labor agreements.

Lab or clinic testing should be of the type recommended by your medical provider. They may want to do urine, blood, or both. Urine testing means the employee has to pee in a cup. The clinic will tell you all sorts of stories about how these are defeated by guilty employees, but the clinic personnel know how to spot deceptive tricks. The blood method involves drawing a blood sample. Different substances stay in the urine and in the blood for various durations and at varying levels. The comparison of blood and urine helps the lab technician decide the level of effect that the employee has. If you have a local medical clinic that is available 24 hours, you will have to have someone drive the employee to the clinic for testing. Most clinics will provide preliminary results immediately. If there is a suspected positive, they will send the sample to a lab and results may take one to three days.

If prescription drugs are indicated in a test, the lab will usually contact the employee to justify these medications and provide prescriptions. The level in the body must meet the amount prescribed. Most lawyers will not allow a termination for prescription drug use.

Cause Testing

Testing an employee for "reasonable cause" is quite a bit more subjective than postaccident. The justification is not as clear, but with the right policies, we can make it simple. You should start with a policy that allows for drug testing if there is reasonable suspicion that

251

an employee is under the influence. Then require a manager to have that reasonable suspicion. No special training is involved if you use the "reasonable person" test. Assuming your managers are reasonable, they know what behavior is unusual or possibly related to substance abuse. To avoid accusations of targeting, require the department manager or supervisor to get a second opinion from the Security Supervisor. The two supervisors should be able to agree that they smell alcohol, note strange behavior, hear slurred speech, and see dilated or constricted pupils or a staggering walk.

The testing procedure after that point is the same as for postaccident. Fortunately, the swab testing is noninvasive and does not take the employee off the job very long if it is negative.

PROSTITUTION

As mentioned throughout this publication, prostitution is a big problem for hotels. When I was a young Security Manager, my very experienced hotel manager told me, "Prostitutes are good for the hotel business." He was obviously referring to keeping guests happy and bringing in new business. Unfortunately, the sex industry is not glamorous, far from it, and the criminal negatives far outweigh any business positives. These next few sections on prostitution are my opinion, but they are based on factual experience.

If you have no experience with the criminal side of prostitution, forget about the movies and the stories that glamorize it. Prostitutes are not working their way through college, they are not aspiring actresses, and they are not engaging in a victimless crime. They may have started that way or may have even been lured to this way of life with those promises, but 99 percent of them are motivated by drugs. If the pimp (or "daddy") does not bring them into the business, he will take over their business by force. Drugs are used as a reward and create a dependent relationship with the male. The male pimp uses violence to force a submissive relationship where the female is rewarded by pleasuring him. This reprogramming turns the prostitute into a drone seeking money for sex, which earns favor with the pimp, which earns her more drugs and membership in the pimp's "family" or "stable." The pimp, who is grooming his own interns of his trade, sends young men to be the escorts of the prostitutes. As you can imagine, this dysfunctional network has huge potential for violent crime. Here are some examples seen in hotels.

The pimp ("chulo" in Spanish) will rent a room for the prostitute to work her business. She will work the hotel bar, club, or even the street and bring men back to her room for the transaction. Often, this deal goes off without a problem. Occasionally, the protector, who gets greedy, will "roll" (rob) the client ("John" or "date") in the room, taking his money by force before or after the sex. A certain percentage of the sex deal has to go back to the pimp, so the intern is motivated to make some money on the side. The room also can be used along with the Internet to be a home base for callouts. Callouts are appointments made by phone or Internet where the prostitute is called to the client's hotel room.

A prostitute may be called to a guest's hotel room on a callout as described previously. In that case, the pimp or protector may accompany the female and wait in the hall or even the lobby or bar until the deal is complete. A harmful version of this is when the prostitute leaves the door ajar for her male friends—or just lets them in—and they come in and rob the victim. This is often a very violent robbery because the pimps need to show their hookers and others that they should not be messed with. These "guerrilla" pimps rely on the fact that most victims would not dare report this crime.

The classic and most common prostitute crime is where the prostitute goes into the wallet of her victim while he sleeps and leaves before he notices. This turns into an expensive lesson for the salesman from out-of-town who would not even dream of reporting he got ripped off by a prostitute.

Preventing and watching for these types of criminals involves a lot of experience and behavioral profiling.

Front Desk

Clerks at the front desk are experienced at this type of profiling and can spot a prostitute or a pimp immediately. Local IDs, young males or females traveling alone, provocative dress for the female and street clothes for the male, big handbags, but no luggage, and interest in Wi-Fi service are all possible indicators. Combine those indicators with the instinct of dealing with them regularly, and the Front Desk clerk can be a great resource. Have the clerks tell you when they check in suspicious guests so you can keep an eye on these folks and their activity.

Bell Desk

It is universally known that bell persons are the ones to go to for prostitutes. If they are not acting as a direct agent, they definitely see what is going on and can be a good resource. Enforce your policies and get them on your side in keeping trouble out of your hotel.

Suspicious Persons

Security officers should be alert for males loitering around hotel rooms, in the lobby, or at bars, especially if they came in with a woman and are now alone. Women who frequent bars alone, drinking very little, and especially leave with different men work inside hotels and are usually perceived as a bit classier than streetwalkers. Streetwalkers entering the hotel almost always carry a large shoulder bag where they keep cosmetics and a change of clothes to get ready for the next date.

Hotel Rooms

Housekeepers can usually tip you off to a room that is used for prostitution. Cosmetics without luggage and sex paraphernalia, combined with a laptop and drugs are positive signs. Of course, Housekeeping may notice the clientele coming in and out. Pimps and other members of the stable may use the room to sleep during the day after working all night. Housekeepers (and most employees) do not need awareness classes on prostitution. They know what it is and what it looks like. They do need to know it is a concern for you, so that they will tell you when they see it.

Homosexual Prostitution

Same-gender prostitution is just as prevalent but not necessarily as visible. There is usually not the same level of violence and drugs, but they are still present. Transvestites are sometimes called "dragons." Lesbian prostitutes ("jaspers") are very difficult to spot because they do not wear the flamboyant clothing associated with a heterosexual prostitute. Their behavior, like any other "freelancer," is obvious when working your bars or when accompanying clients or "marks." A pimp-less prostitute is called a "renegade."

Outside

I doubt you have streetwalkers working the corner in front of your hotel. Take a drive around your town, or just ask the police, until you find the nearest "track" (street where prostitutes await clients). Get a look at these persons so you can identify them when they come in your hotel.

Intervention

If you do find a prostitute, either known to you or from her behavior or a tip, never approach her with her client. This is extremely embarrassing for your guest. First, you may be wrong and then you end up accusing his daughter or girlfriend. Second, he will be embarrassed to the point of leaving your hotel and blaming it on you. She will not be embarrassed at all and will accuse you very loudly of profiling or discriminating. Third, he may defend her and embarrass you. I have been in all of these situations and will never repeat them.

Instead, approach the woman when she is alone. Simply trespass her from the property. Never give a reason, mainly because you cannot prove it. If you just want to interview her, that is fine too. This will let her know you are aware of her and will know who she is if anything happens. Talking to Johns is not recommended. It does absolutely nothing to protect the hotel and, as mentioned previously, just embarrasses all involved.

Many hotels that have a big problem with prostitutes working their floors and bars find it worth the time and expense to devote some effort to this problem. First, you should attempt to get your local authorities to run an "operation" in your hotel or at your bars or both. They may have a special unit that works these cases and can do the work for you. Most police departments understand the sensitive nature of these operations and will sincerely try not to disrupt your business or damage your reputation.

One method is for them to use two or three rooms that you provide. One is the bait room, another across the hall is within sight, or where surveillance equipment can be monitored. The third may be a holding room or processing room. The police may use certain Web sites where prostitutes advertise to lure them to the room. When the prostitute comes to the room, the deal is recorded, and then the arrest is made. The suspect is then taken to the holding room for processing and transporting off property. I suggest providing police access to service elevators and any other facilities to avoid mixing with guests. Police are generally sensitive to this and will cooperate in exchange for you making it convenient. You also can arrange to photograph and trespass the suspects. Remember that the prosecution does not matter to the hotel. The fact is that the suspect came to your hotel on an invitation from a Web site and is not wanted there. Sometimes you can find the pimp nearby, whom the police cannot arrest, but you can trespass. Note: Do not cooperate with the police who want to target Johns. This does not benefit the hotel and is likely to snare a hotel guest or two. You want the word to get out to the prostitution community that they could run into a trap at your hotel, but not the salesmen from Iowa. That just hurts business.

Another operation the police can do is one that is a little easier for your staff to do as well. This involves a decoy at the bar to attract freelancers. For the police, they have to complete the elements of the crime, which include the arrangement of the transaction. As agents of the hotel, we need absolutely no reason at all. So, if someone comes up and says, "Looking to party?" then that is enough for you. Either way, especially if the police are involved, do not make an arrest or approach in public. This looks very bad. Accompany the suspect away from the bar and take care of the situation there. Once again, discourage the police from conducting operations that target Johns at your bars.

ABANDONED LUGGAGE

A Security Department could drive itself crazy if it overreacted to every suspicious bag. To avoid the anxiety and work force drain that these incidents can cause in a post 9/11 world, take these basic steps.

Risk Assessment

In your initial Risk Assessment, you should have determined your likelihood for a terrorist attack or bombing. A hotel in Islamabad has a much different expectation and reaction to an abandoned bag than one in Billings, Montana. In Israel, for example, every citizen notices suspicious packages and they are programmed to immediately clear the area and call the authorities. You will adjust your response accordingly, but the rest of this section outlines reasonable steps for most U.S. hotels.

Back Track

The more people you have watching for suspicious activity, the better. This was explained in Chapter 2. The sooner a suspicious item is found, the easier it is to find its owner or who left it, and what their intent is. First, make sure employees are watching for guests leaving their items unattended. Forgetfulness is very common for people on holiday, so reminding them not only protects them from theft, but also the hotel from a long ordeal. Second, check with employees or even guests in the area to see if anyone saw who left the item. Third, look for clues on the bag before touching it: nametag, plane tag, or any identifying marks. These can be checked through the Front Desk. Fourth, if necessary, look at video. If you have adequate camera coverage, you should be able to see who left it and whether it was an accident. If you do not have coverage of that area, you may at least have coverage of the person bringing it in the front door or out of the elevator.

Internal Procedures

We have learned from terrorist history that there is usually a dry run and surveillance before an actual incident. A dummy bag may be left and then the action taken may be observed. A bomber who is leaving a bag obviously wants to get far enough away to be protected and avoid capture or he would just detonate while he is holding it. Following this logic, it is best to have a quick, efficient procedure for dealing with unattended bags. Besides the identification process described previously, provide officers with a basic bomb awareness class. This will help them notice the obvious signs of a bomb such as smell, stained fabric, protruding wires, etc. Train security officers to remove the item immediately—after a cursory check—and take it to an isolated area.

Official Response

If your bag or package has made it this far in the process, you have a genuine ordeal on your hands. Your likely next step is to call the police. By the way, this should not be the first time you discuss this scenario with police. Find out in advance how they want these situations handled and what their response will be. It will likely be to send a patrol officer who will make his own assessment. He will call a supervisor who will make her assessment and call the fire department or bomb squad. I guarantee none of them wants to err on the side of being blown up, so they will always take it to the next level. By this time, the area will be evacuated for hundreds of yards and your business will be closed during the investigation.

Large hotels such as those in Las Vegas and New York that consider themselves likely terrorist targets find it is worth the extra expense to conduct their own investigation prior to calling law enforcement. Shutting down a hotel in Las Vegas for two hours not only causes hundreds of thousands of dollars, but it will make world headlines. By that time, bomb or not, you have a PR nightmare. The expense mentioned involves proprietary bomb dogs, electronic sniffers, and x-ray equipment. These are costly items, but when placed against the costs mentioned, they provide a good return on investment.

(See Chapter 10 for more on bomb threats.)

INTERNAL CRIME

It is said that while you are trying to prevent one thief from entering your front door, there are six leaving out the back door. That is not a statistic on doors, but on internal theft and fraud.

We prevent and detect internal crime a few ways. First is patrol, which is discussed in Chapter 8 and in this chapter. Regular, uniformed patrol helps prevent some general theft but rarely catches a thief in the act. Second is internal audit. Internal audit is generally an Accounting or other oversight body's function and not ours, but we will talk about it as an overview. Third is the Security audit. This is not to be confused with the special operations discussed earlier in this chapter. I will explain the difference shortly.

EMPLOYEE CRIME STATS

75 percent of employees steal once—50 percent of those steal again
20 percent of revenue is lost to employee theft
38 percent of shrinkage is employee theft
Workers spend an average of 7 hours per week goofing off
1 in 6 workers drink or use drugs at work
50 percent feel one gets ahead based on politics, not hard work
25 percent expect to compromise their beliefs to get ahead on the job
Only 20 percent are "very satisfied" with jobs

Internal Audit

Let's face it, a uniformed security officer (or even an undercover one) has no chance of detecting an accountant who is transferring money to his own account, or a department head who commits payroll fraud. This is done through checks and balances performed by the company. In fact, new accounting regulations enacted after Enron and other scandals now require outside oversight in most businesses. So, sometimes we see independent accounting firms going through the books. Frankly, these people are looking for major book juggling and are not likely to catch a kickback on a mattress.

However, accountants are on the same side as Security and we are all trying to protect the assets. Rather than work independently of them, we should work as partners. This is a relationship and a process you will need to develop through your general manager if you have not already done so. Your Auditing Department (accounting, compliance, whatever you call it) is auditing all day every day. This is a routine designed to catch and fix mistakes, prepare reports for the boss, and generate tax reports. These auditors may not be looking for fraud and might not even notice it unless someone tells them what to look for. In the payroll fraud example below, a fictitious employee is created and paid. An auditor is looking to see that hours on the check match the time clock, that the amount of the check is correct, and that the proper department was billed. If you ask them to look for duplicate addresses on checks, employees who always have the same hours, or checks that are always mailed (to name a few), they could alert you to these exceptions and you would do a follow-up audit. More on this later.

Security Audits

Security has the unique ability to watch employees. Observing an employee perform his job is the only way to prove he is stealing. Accounting or their boss may suspect theft, but the only way to catch it is to see it. An investigator performs an audit by watching an employee for a certain period and observing that procedures are followed and that the transactions are accurate. Procedures are developed to prevent loss. Examples of procedures are counting out change twice to a customer, closing a cash drawer between transactions, and checking ID on credit transactions.

When procedures are not followed, the employee will make a mistake, be taken as a victim, or commit a theft. Unfortunately, the chances of catching a thief in a one-hour audit are slim, but catching the procedure violations is common. Correcting the procedure violations will prevent mistakes, prevent robberies and thefts, and let the employee know he is being watched.

Establish a procedure with each department (not just cash handlers) so you can perform effective audits. You will need their procedure manual, schedules, and what they want audited. (You can audit smiles, uniform appearance, and time of transactions also). Once you have this information, set up a form or medium where you can get the audit information back to the department for follow-up. Of course, if you do catch a theft live on video, you will need a predetermined procedure for pulling the offending employee and conducting an investigation.

Types of Audits

Regulatory—These are not common in most hotels, but if you have departments that have to conform to certain governmental regulations, you will need to audit them to ensure they are following those regulations.

Performance—A performance audit is designed to evaluate employees doing their job. The topic may be guest service, number of guests served per hour, or duration of breaks.

Integrity—This audit is the type described previously to check for procedures that prevent loss.

Guest service—Most hotels have specific guest service policies, such as eye contact, smile and greet, providing directions, offering assistance, etc. Video audits are the best way of evaluating compliance with these policies.

Performing Audits

The first and best way to decide who gets audited is based on tips. Tips may come anonymously or they may come from a manager who suspects misconduct. They also may come from internal audit or some data where a strange pattern or exception has been identified. In the absence of any suspicions, the next way is to perform audits randomly. You may already decide that you will do one audit per week for each department. Then try to hit different employees on all shifts and in all areas. You cannot be truly random, but avoid picking on one department, gender, race, or union.

Most audits can be performed in about an hour unless there is a specific reason for going longer. If you are looking for specific types of transactions, frequency of breaks, or opening and closing procedures, you will need to adjust duration accordingly.

Next, we will review some common areas of theft and fraud that you can audit or at least be aware.

More internal (and external) theft can be prevented by strong controls and procedures rather than security investigations. There are two important components to a strong internal controls program. First is developing the proper controls. There are industry practices to follow for each job type. For example, cashiers are trained to follow several routine procedures, such as counting out change twice, checking counterfeit bills, and how money is

FRAUD DETECTION

Tips from employees (26 percent)
By accident (19 percent)
Internal audit (19 percent)
Internal controls (15 percent)
External audit (11 percent)
Tips from customer (9 percent)
Tips from vendor (5 percent)

These stats lead us to several solutions and one conclusion: Most initial detection of fraud comes from tips. Reduce "accidental" discoveries by increasing intentional discoveries. You need an anonymous tip line. You need to develop management communication channels (listen to employees). You need to develop an informant program. If you can, reward tipsters. Follow up with informant with results from tips. Maintain regular and consistent controls. Review controls based on prior incidents, including other hotels. When in doubt, check it out. If it just doesn't look right, it probably is not.

placed in the till. If you have departments not following these procedures, suggest them to the department head. The manager will save money that is lost through theft and errors and your internal crime will go down. Second is the enforcement of the developed controls. Employees need to be audited (watched) regularly and their violations addressed. Addressing procedure violations tells the employee that he is being watched and that if he is testing us we are going to catch him. Do not hesitate to modify controls that are lacking or missing. Better to fill the hole late than not at all.

Your Accounting Department or whomever does your internal auditing will help with enforcing these controls and suggesting others.

Accounting

Payroll scams—many large businesses are victims of payroll scams. There are several variations on this, but the most lucrative is to create a fictitious employee. The department head or manager fills out the paperwork to hire an employee who does not exist (or it could be a friend or relative who does not work there). Once the employee is in the system, they clock him in and out every day and have the check mailed somewhere. If this sounds easy to do, think of the controls you can establish to prevent it. Another department (like HR) should meet and enter the employee in the system (can an HR clerk pull off this scam?), have checks picked up in person from another department, random checks of employee time record and duties performed, and camera on the time clock. Other variations of payroll scams are real employees who clock in and out, but do not work, managers who manipulate time records and take a cut of the extra money, employees clocking each other in and out or using job codes with higher pay (if you have an automated system).

Collusion—The most common form of internal theft is where two people from different departments work together to steal. Since a basic control in any money-handling operation is to have two signatures or verifiers of funds, both of those verifiers working together defeats the control. This is common in casinos, but also occurs in any business between employees of one department, employees of opposing departments, and manager and employee. The best control for this is to have a third verifier. If that is not possible, use cameras. In accounting, a common collusion is between a purchaser and an accounts payable clerk (or similar relationship). One buys the product and the other pays for it. Use your imagination: If you buy fruit for the Food Department, how hard would it be to buy a pallet of oranges from yourself and have your friend in accounts payable pay you for that pallet? He could send the check to your cousin's house payable to Darrell Clifton Produce. This is why you need verifiers, such as the receiving clerk who receives the shipment and verifies all the information on the invoice before it is paid.

Credit card fraud—The Payment Card Industry (PCI) Council has made great strides to protect credit card holders. These are not laws, but requirements set forth by Visa, MasterCard, American Express, and others on businesses as a condition of accepting their cards for payment. They are very strict now and if you have not heard of PCI, go to your Controller's office and say, "What in the heck is PCI?" and watch them all jump out the windows. I exaggerate, but only about the windows—they are locked, right? Up until about 10 years ago, any busboy or guest could go through your trash and pull up a receipts containing credit card numbers. This is no longer the case. In fact, your credit card receipts now have most of the credit card number masked and it has to be masked from the time it enters your system until all electronic or paper traces of it are destroyed. However, there is likely someone in your business (probably an Accounts Receivable clerk) who has access to these numbers. If so, this type of theft is hard to prevent. Make sure PCI is followed strictly in your facility.

Identity theft—similar to credit card fraud, a lot of unprotected personal data of customers are floating around your Accounting Department. Several people can access names with addresses and other ID information. Are you doing background checks on every employee?

Charge-offs—Another function of Accounts Receivable is collecting on bills. Denied credit cards, under payments, room damage, and normal bills for goods and services go through this department. Once again, use your imagination to figure out ways to steal if you are an A/R clerk making $12 an hour. Pay me a little extra and I won't report this delinquent bill to the credit card company. Send the money to my house and I will make this bill go away. Send a mattress to my house and just add 1 percent to our bill. Nobody would ever know. Controls like oversight and verification are keys here.

Fake vendors—Just like payroll, it is very easy to set up a fake vendor and pay yourself for services not performed. For example, take window washers. How would an auditor know whether we actually had a vendor washing the windows every month?

Cashiers

Voids—A very common source of extra income for cashiers is a false void or manipulation of voids. The oldest trick in the book is to sell something, collect the cash, void the transaction, and pocket the money. Most departments will require a supervisor approval for voids, but in the interest of guest service, they are sometimes approved after the customer has left.

Returns—Another old trick is a false return. A cashier grabs an item from stock, scans it as being returned, puts it back in stock, and pockets the money. Sometimes these require approval and sometimes not. Patterns and trends should be watched and audits may catch returns and voids.

Coupons—A cashier obtains a coupon and applies it to a transaction after the customer pays full price. The cashier pockets the difference.

Credit cards—As in accounting, theft of a credit card number is the easiest and most common. It is very hard to trace. Another possibility, especially in restaurants is to over-charge and pocket the difference. A more advanced trick is to use a pocket card reader. Many phones and electronic devices have attachments that do this. Imagine the possibilities.

Restaurants

Besides the common credit card thefts and false voids mentioned in the Retail section of this chapter, there are some losses unique to restaurants. Almost every food server in the world takes the guest's credit card to the back room to process the payment. That food server has temporary possession of the credit card number, the security code from the back, and even the zip code from the customer's driver's license used to verify many credit card thefts. Unfortunately, the guest does not notice the scam until he gets his statement. The credit card company will rarely investigate these crimes and the hotel will never know about it.

Even with PCI rules (credit card company compliance) protecting credit card numbers left around on receipts, technology has made it easier for nefarious frontline employees to obtain credit information. Magnetic and RF card readers can be attached to cell phones or other pocket-sized devices on a food server. Imagine a waiter swiping the customer card on his iPhone on the way to the cashier. How would anyone know? Few controls will mitigate this type of crime. One option is to limit cell phones and other devices while at work. Otherwise, you will have to wait for a report from the guest or possibly the card company that you can investigate. Camera patrols and audits may catch this behavior.

Another popular employee scam is over-charging on the bill. If the server acts as the cashier, then it is a simple case of adding an amount to the bill or entering a higher amount on the authorization and pocketing the difference. If the waiter is not the cashier, he may just add extra items to the bill to raise the total and increase the gratuity. This is more likely in large groups where the payer is not likely to verify the charges on the bill.

A final scam for you to look at is the food cashier who works in a snack bar or deli-type food outlet. Guests often use credit cards in these establishments but are likely not to leave a tip. The guest presents his card, the cashier prints the ticket for the amount, and the customer signs it, leaving the tip line blank. After the guest leaves, the cashier adds a couple of bucks to the tip line and re-authorizes the amount in the register. The cashier pockets the tip amount. The guest is likely not to notice on his statement that he spent $14 instead of $12, so nobody finds out.

Receiving

Receiving has many points in the process where theft can occur. This area generally encompasses the dock, storage areas, and any place where goods are taken into the property. Receiving is where the Purchasing Department connects with the Food Department and other users of these purchased items. As we have discussed throughout this book, theft is most likely to occur when cash and merchandise change hands. Because this is the main function of this department, controls need to be created, followed, and enforced strictly to protect the assets.

The basic process of receiving goes like this. A department, such as Food, places an internal order for more items. Purchasing places the order with the outside vendor. These orders are sent to the dock where they are used to verify that we received everything we ordered and everything that was delivered was ordered. Those verified deliveries are placed into internal storage where they are again ordered by the department on an as-needed basis. You can see where controls at every step of the process prevent theft if the controls are audited.

Outgoing Theft

One of the most common forms of internal theft does not involve receiving at all. It is usually very easy for employees to obtain merchandise that is in their control, such as meat, liquor, or other valued items. The theft occurs when they try to get it out of the building. Trash is generally associated with the receiving dock because they are in the same part of the building. It is important to keep the trash area separate and its access supervised so that items from the building are not brought out, and received items are not transferred over to, the dumpster for later removal. Security should be present when trash is removed from the locked trash area.

Receiving Theft

Merchandise is most vulnerable after the receiver has verified that all items on a packing slip have arrived. Now the property is owned by the company and in the possession of the person moving and storing it. A trash diversion as described previously is common here. Simply grabbing a bottle of liquor and putting it in a locker, delivering a case of extra meat to your friend in the kitchen, or even consuming a six-pack while working can easily go undetected here. Security patrols and audits are good deterrence, but an additional control of having the internal store receive the items from the dock is better. The store's supervisor or audit control should be doing inventories to make sure that what we think we have is what we have. Do not wait until three cases of tequila come up missing from storage to learn how the process works in your hotel. Sit down with the Purchasing Manager or controller to understand the safeguards already in place and to make sure they are adequate.

False Orders and Return Thefts

A slightly more complicated theft is the false order. The receiving clerk says we are all out of steak so he has Purchasing place the order. When the steak arrives, he can do several things. One is he can receive it, sign the driver's paperwork, and throw it in the back of his truck. Two, he can receive it, signing that it arrived and was placed into inventory, and then take it. Three, after receiving it, he can fill out a return slip that it was bad and had to go back, and then steal it. All of these thefts can be caught in the audit process, but can sometimes take weeks to process. By that time, everyone has forgotten about the delivery and because they cannot find the stuff, they just chalk it up to a mistake. Dual controls or a second signature help prevent these problems.

Lost Merchandise

Not all losses in Receiving are intentional. Items are lost or misplaced regularly. Security may or may not get involved in investigating or even mitigating these losses until it reaches a certain dollar amount and someone wants some answers. So, it behooves us to make sure controls are in place to protect against loss, and that those controls are strictly followed. You are correct in that Receiving management and Accounting are more responsible, but they may not see the vulnerabilities that you would see in an assessment of that area.

Do not wait until the big investigation to learn the process. Right now, there are deliveries being made without invoices or signatures, receivers signing without verifying, and shipments not being fully opened and verified. To make it worse, nobody is reporting these losses. They will probably write them off as unknown losses or as items consumed.

I hinted at some of these controls previously, and the department knows which work best, but you may have to help enforce them. This is part of the job of protecting assets.

Housekeeping

Guest-room attendants normally do not handle cash, so internal theft comes in the form of guest property or company property. Strict lost and found and key control policies are important here.

Security

Yes, security officers steal also. Collusion is one common way because Security is often used as the verifier on transactions and they see how all the processes work. Security also has the ability to take from lost and found or make false returns on property. Another one that I have seen too often by officers is a "drunk roll." An officer may accompany an intoxicated guest to his room and then take the guest's money without him knowing.

There are many other internal theft opportunities. If it is possible, someone will find it. The best way to prevent it is with strong internal controls. Keep an eye on other properties. If someone thinks of a way to steal something at another hotel, he or she is bound to try it at yours—or maybe already has.

BACKGROUND CHECKS

So which departments should have background checks on their employees? This is a trick question. And the answer is, all of them. I have seen many hotels that decide the only employees at risk of stealing are Security, housekeepers, and maybe managers. Even if that were true, stealing is the least of our concerns. First, any employee can steal—kitchen workers, receivers, cleaning staff. Second, workplace violence, sexual harassment, drug sales and use, and even poor work performance can be larger risks and create more losses for the property than simple theft. Any employee can participate in these illicit activities, so it is not logical to pick and choose who will have their history investigated.

Many organizations task the Security Director with doing background checks for all employees. If you do this, you know how time-consuming it is. I strongly recommend finding a contract provider to do this for you. It is well worth the price to have an outside company do your background checks. Criminal history is important and you need to check each state in which the applicant lived. This is time consuming and may be costly. This will actually cost you less if you compare like services. The background company knows what and where to check, but make sure the service includes what you want. Consistency—a common theme throughout this book—is key to your fair hiring practices. Imagine trying to defend why you spent hours checking the background of a person of one race, then spent days on a person of another race.

Timing of background checks is just as important as the complexity. In the last century, when a background check required a lot of legwork, many organized crime rings knew how to take advantage. Groups of immigrants from Mexico and Asia, knowing that background checks from their native countries took longer or were almost impossible, would come into a hotel filling those difficult-to-hire housekeeping positions. In cities where hotels were being built at an incredible rate, such as Las Vegas, managers needed housekeepers in quantity and they needed them immediately. They would hire them first, and worry about the background check later. Housekeepers clean about 16 rooms a day and have access to others, so 10 housekeepers in one day could "clean up" 200 rooms and be out before the background check even started.

There are two morals to this story. One is that backgrounds should be completed before an employee starts working. Second is the hiring of immigrants. Legal immigrants go through a long process of obtaining a work visa or resident alien status so they can work legally in this country. Therefore, they should have some work history in the United States, even if it was under-the-table or as a student. If they have a Social Security number, it should be traced to determine if it was newly issued or whether someone else may have had it before. Once again, this is a complex issue and should be given to experienced professionals.

Section 4

The Security Executive

12

Executive Skills

I always wanted to be somebody, but now I realize I should have been more specific.

Lily Tomlin, comedian

EXECUTIVE GROWTH

This chapter is 100-percent subjective. It is my opinion, but that opinion is based on observing, working with, and interviewing Security Directors worldwide. I have taken the good traits from those I admire and those who are successful and outlined them here. (I have even used a couple of the less successful ones to prove my points.) Everyone has their own style and these suggestions may not be part of yours, but I ask that you take some advice from the experts. That advice is presented for you here.

As the director of Security for your property, you need to decide what role you want to play in your corporate organization. One observation I have made is that Security Directors fall into two general categories. First is the passive response agent who is called up to the executive offices whenever anything happens related to Security. This director is generally told how much money he can spend, what size staff he needs, where his cameras will be placed, and when he needs to do something different. This director prefers to fly low and avoid problems and just wants to appease everyone.

Second is the director who takes a leadership role in the executive team. He presents himself as not only the Security expert, but becomes a spokesperson for the guests and what is best for them. He realizes that Security is everyone's concern and collaborates with all departments to make sure his needs are actually the needs of the entire organization. This director is seen as the expert on property and nobody would think of making decisions without him.

As you might imagine, my preference is for the second director. He or she will be more productive, more effective, and will be better compensated and more successful in the long run. Ironically, this proactive approach goes right along with the preventative nature of our industry. These are my observations and solutions for attaining this level of leadership at your hotel.

You have three responsibilities as an executive in your company. One is to your boss and the executive team. Two is your responsibility to your staff and their development. Three is the responsibility you have to yourself and your personal growth. This chapter will devote itself to making your company, your department, and you as successful as possible.

FINDING YOUR PLACE

I have noticed that the office of the Security Director is placed somewhere in the hotel away from the "C-suite." Marketing, Sales, and Operations are all there in the executive cluster, but Security is down in the basement. There is probably a practical reason for this, but it is also symbolic of the pecking order in a hotel. There are advantages and disadvantages to this separation, so make the best of the positives and reverse the negatives.

COOPERATION AND COLLABORATION

Let's talk about your place in the grand scheme of things. The perception everyone has of you and what you do is based entirely on you. Without a proactive approach to becoming a part of the team, the other department heads and even your boss may consider yours a supportive role. Worse yet, they will consider you and your department a necessary evil. This image probably comes from our predecessors who were perceived as gorillas, called in as the muscle to take out the trash. We need to put as much distance between us and that horrible, negative image as we can.

> Allen Pinkerton was born in Scotland and became a successful businessman in the mid-1800s. His unwavering ethics and appreciation for protecting business from those who would harm it soon earned him a reputation as the first private detective. Spying against the Confederate Army and protecting industry from some of the dirtier union organizers built his reputation into a formidable business of its own—the Pinkerton Agency. In 1871 when the Department of Justice was formed, it did not have the budget to train and staff full-time investigators, so it contracted with Pinkerton. This relationship lasted about 20 years and was terminated by federal law. So you might say that the country's first organized police agency was really a security company. Many of us in industrial security still trace our beliefs and our philosophies back to Mr. Pinkerton. Pinkerton's legacy lives on as a division of the worldwide Securitas Company.

Start with your place in the organization. If your current situation allows a department head to tell you to install cameras in a certain location or provide security for a particular event, you are not being a director. You need to get yourself into a position where you collaborate with your colleagues and come up with solutions together rather than being told how to run your department. You have to bring yourself up to an equal playing field. This is not a competition; it is about a well-rounded team where each member has his or her expertise. Your expertise is security.

Expertise is the key. Building your expertise is discussed in the personal growth section of this chapter. In this section, we detail how to offer it to the team. Start by playing offense instead of defense. Get out in front of situations instead of waiting for the call that tells you what to do.

If you can get up to that level where you are an equal—one of the executives who has an equal seat at the round table—take it a step farther. With security in your blood, you have an advantage that you need to impart to your colleagues. You are used to operating within a team, where everyone operates toward the same goal—the company. Your fellow executives—Sales, Marketing, Operations—have made their way in the business by competing with each other. They probably think and act more vertically (some call this "kissing up") than they do horizontally (as a team). Your security DNA is of a different type. You realize as a team player that competition with your colleagues, even if it is only for attention from the boss, is counterproductive.

As you excel at the collaborative model, you will be known as a team player, one who is comfortable with his or her place and does not feel a need to compete for attention. I guarantee your boss will notice and will start using you to team-build and problem-solve. Are you still fuzzy on this concept? See if this example hits home: There are a couple of department heads that are so busy worried about what the other is doing, who will get their idea to the boss first, who gets a bigger piece of the budget, and who will blink first, that they are not getting anything done. You explain to your boss that you have already put together a team of select department heads to solve a certain problem. Your boss will notice this behavior and will reward you with more responsibility. When he or she has a new initiative or sets up a new working group, you will be the likely the first choice. Your boss wants global thinkers and not those who operate in their own silos.

EXECUTIVE MEETINGS

Chances are, you are involved in some regular staff or operations meeting. If not, you should be. Study the agendas of these meetings and come prepared. Take note of plans to host special events, celebrities, and public officials. Use the contacts you made in your networking (see next) and investigate places where they have stayed before. Someone else has already managed this security issue, so take advantage of his or her experience. Your value increases when you come to a meeting prepared to discuss security concerns that Marketing has not considered.

Once you become a member of these collaborative sessions, make your input positive. The reason you were probably not considered initially is the perception that you will be an obstacle. Frankly, we in Security do tend to make ourselves obstacles by saying, "It will not work," "I don't have the staff," or "It will cost too much money." Look, think, and present yourself as a company person. Offer your objections only if you have a solution

269

(e.g., we may have to spend a little overtime, but it may be worth it to get our name out there. Or, that group tends to cause trouble at conventions, but that is why you have such an effective Security Department). Instead of saying no, you are saying yes and are providing valuable input.

Set up individual meetings with the departments you work with most. Risk Management, Human Resources, and Facilities, for example, are probably the departments you support. Work out problems before they occur. As mentioned previously, do not be an obstacle. Be willing to do anything you can to make their job easier and they will return the courtesy. Once you get comfortable with this process, try it with departments with which you may not work as closely. Go over upcoming events with the catering manager. Let him or her know you will not be an obstacle, but a resource to make the events run smoother.

You don't like hearing on Friday that there is going to be a group of 500 fraternity students staying in your hotel on Saturday. The Sales Department doesn't tell you because either they don't consider your opinion important or they fear you will throw up barriers. Work with these event planners so that they will tell you far in advance so you can make your own plans. Explain your point of view and that if you have time to prepare, you will not be an obstacle, but a willing participant. Either the fraternity group can trash the hotel or they can provide a lot of revenue, depending on how much time you have to prepare for them. As you offer your expertise, such as segregating the group from other guests, adding officers here and there, closing the pool, and so on, you will become known to those event planners as a resource.

Nothing is more frustrating than having the rest of the team plan a remodel or new addition without consulting Security. As they design and build a new bar, for example, they get caught up in the architecture, hiring, marketing, and menus and take for granted the placement of cameras, access control, type of clientele, etc. Approach this as with the meetings discussed previously. Get in on the initial planning and become a resource instead of an obstacle. Instead of whining that a bar will bring fights and problems and ruin our business, explain how some basic, cost-effective controls can reduce many problems. Show how properly placed controls will prevent theft and reduce loss.

COMMUNICATING WITH THE BOSS

Set up regular meetings with your boss. This is a chance to let him or her know what is going on in Security. Concentrate on what Security brings to the bottom line—losses recovered, losses prevented, and situations resolved. Do not wait for this meeting to notify the boss of important incidents. You never want him to hear from someone else what he should have heard from you. Establish in advance the types of notifications to provide (fires, fights, internal thefts), by what means they will be given (phone, email, in person), and when (immediately or the next day). I have seen how department heads will race to the boss to reveal some juicy information just to receive favor for being first to report. Do not let this bother you, as you will be following a protocol that your boss prefers.

Without dipping too much into your own personal style, I want to stress the importance of your relationship with your boss. We Security Directors tend to be quiet but honest, reserved but capable. Unfortunately, it does not matter how good you are if the boss does not know it. You may need to manage your boss a little so that she knows you exist, trusts your judgment, and has you in mind when raises, bonuses, and promotions come along.

Start by keeping regular meetings with your boss. Have a weekly regular time set up (every Friday at 2 p.m.) and have some ammunition ready for those impromptu meetings. Come to the weekly meeting with your own agenda or notes on what to discuss. Bring a brief summary of your payroll, expenses, or financial status. (She already knows, but wants to know if you know.) Lay out briefly what you are doing to reduce expenses or overtime (before she asks). Summarize any big investigations, major incidents, or ongoing problems that your department has solved. Do not sugarcoat. The boss wants to hear your challenges as well as your successes. If you do not have the answer, ask for advice. Most executives want to hear that you will seek help when needed. Perhaps it is a problem manager or a rash of vehicle burglaries.

In addition to the weekly meetings, always have something ready for the "elevator meeting." You may run into your boss in an elevator, the parking lot, or the lunchroom and you need to be prepared to speak of something besides the weather. We caught the guy stealing towels off the maid carts, or I think I found a better source for DVRs—I will have a report for you Friday. Better yet, be ready to answer his questions about overtime, who parked in his parking spot, or what the occupancy is.

Keep track of your personal and department task list. If you were given an assignment, or you mentioned at a previous meeting that you would see to some project, keep a mental list of that progress. Have this information ready and keep the boss updated. I completed the background check you asked for, compiled the stats of how many towels were missing year-to-date, and got prices on the new uniforms. I have not yet completed the yearly loss report, but I will have it Monday. Your secretary has the other reports. Keep your accomplishments on the top of her mind so that when the big assignment or even promotion comes up, the recollection of your performance is positive. Remind yourself that in Security, your achievements are not always obvious and you need to blow your own horn.

I mentioned in the beginning of this section that you want to avoid getting too comfortable. This is not where you want to be because others will resent you and your time will be short. Nobody likes to see someone kicking back, skating through the day, while they are working their tail off. If you find yourself with nothing to do, or that you are spending more time at work socializing and butting into everyone else's job, you are too comfortable. I am not telling you to fake being busy because you cannot sustain that. You need to challenge yourself constantly. First, you are fooling yourself if you think your property runs perfectly and is crime-free. There is always a project you can initiate to further reduce crime or increase guest satisfaction (see Chapter 11 for some hints). Self-motivators are successful executives. Keep running, keep challenging yourself, and keep making your job better.

COMMUNICATING WITH YOUR STAFF

Other departments actually expect Security to be the experts at communication. We developed the preshift briefings, we use radios, and we document the important stuff in our reports. Make sure you practice this good communication both ways between you and your staff. Let them know what is going on with the property as soon as you can, before they get the information elsewhere. Security officers like knowing things first—everyone does. Take notes at the meetings that you attend and create a process so you can get that information to your troops immediately.

Create a process where you know everything your staff knows as soon as it happens—24/7. Whether it is phone calls at all hours, text messages to your company phone, or emails to your iPhone, you should be available at all times. Do not feel bothered when you are called late at night. You are happy to hear it in real time rather than from your boss in the morning.

Many say that the success of a good leader is dependent on those with whom she surrounds herself. Your managers and supervisors need to have the same work ethic and be as smart as you. Some leaders are tempted to promote those who are good, but not good enough to pose a threat to their own job. When you think about it, that threat only exists in your own motivation. If you are following some of the traits and habits in this chapter, you will stay ahead and set the example for your subordinates. If they are biting at your heels to get your job, that is the best thing that can happen. You will have a stronger team and you will have some encouragement to stay current and energetic. Usually the lazy manager fears his subordinates. He deserves what he gets.

Remember the secondary duty you have in any position in the company is to prepare your successor. This is often called grooming and is a requirement more than a luxury. How are you protecting the assets of the company if something happens to you and the department is left with no clear leadership?

First, you need to select one or more likely candidates. Do this by asking them what their aspirations are. If they are comfortable and just want to finish out a few years before retiring, or have their sights set on another career, they are probably not your best choice. However, do not forget that many of our best Security professionals were on their way to another career when they came across this one. After all, how many kids in the fifth grade dream of becoming a Security Director?

Second, engage in some casual training. This type of training includes discussing certain factors in the decision-making process. Explain how you make decisions, prepare the budget, communicate with the boss, and handle difficult decisions.

Maintaining Morale

Transmitting news back and forth is one thing, but maintaining constant, open dialog is more complicated and, for some, more difficult to achieve. Many managers claim to have an open-door policy, but keeping everyone satisfied takes a bit more than that.

Security officers may be some of the most difficult employees to motivate. Many, by their own admission, are either finishing out their careers, waiting for a better opportunity, or just plain lazy.

In my experience, Security officers are motivated in several ways. First, just as they said in their interview, they want to help others. Most of us feel a sense of satisfaction and accomplishment when we help someone through a difficult situation and use our unique resources to resolve it. Second, they may not have admitted to this one, but most want some action. That 1 percent of the time we get our adrenaline pumping is often the most satisfying part of our job. Third, and I really doubt anyone will admit to this one, is respect. As Security officers, in a position of authority, we like to be looked up to, give orders, and walk around looking handsome and professional.

Ask management if these motivators fit into their profile of the perfect Security officer, and they will definitely like number one (helping others), but probably are not too keen on numbers two and three: providing action and bossing others around. Most business operators want a Security force that is helpful, loyal, honest, and efficient. Imagine if you could combine the expectations of employees and management so that everyone is happy. Actually, you *can* give the officer those three things he wants (and more) and achieve a highly successful Security Department (and more). That is our job as Security professionals—to provide for the employee *and* the executives and operate a highly effective department—and here is how it is done.

Officer Empowerment

Employees who are treated like drones and expected to follow orders blindly will never reach any level higher than that of a guard force. I am hoping that you would rather have officers who make decisions, protect the property as if it were their own, and enjoy their work enough to pass that attitude on to guests and the bottom line. In Chapter 6, we discussed officers making decisions and learning from them.

One comprehensive way to experience the advantages of empowerment is to get officers involved in the decision-making processes of management. Assemble a cross section of officers into a focus group. This group needs to be managed closely and have strict guidelines. Use a manager to facilitate. If you think your managers are part of the problem, use a manager from another department. The objective of a focus group, in this application, is to solve problems, create new procedures, or address some specific issue. This is a step-by-step process that will certainly get you some positive results.

1. Select the group members. Take a good cross section of age, experience, and schedules. Quiet or loud, it does not really matter as long as you think each person will be honest and reasonable. This is a great way to reward those who always make suggestions and those who tend to complain without a basis. Be sure they are volunteers and that you pay them for their time.
2. Outline the rules. Facilitators keep the group on track so that the meeting does not become a gripe session, everyone participates, and the results are not outrageous. This is explained next. Meetings should be about an hour. Two-hour meetings become ineffective and tiring.
3. Start with an objective, such as "How to improve guest service," "Improve our training program," "Reduce turnover," etc. The group will tend to go off on tangents and start solving other problems. The facilitator will keep the group focused on this objective. (By the way, use one of those easel pads, write this stuff down, and post it on the wall until the focus group is disbanded.)
4. The Perfect World. This is different from the objective in that it is the manner in which you would achieve the objective. For example, if the objective were to

improve guest service, some of the items in this category would be "Every offi-cer would greet every guest by name," "Officers would smile," "Officers would accompany guests when they ask for directions," etc. This is a brainstorming ses-sion, so almost anything goes. Do not write the crazy stuff: "Officers could read the guests' minds." That is not possible or reasonable, so leave that stuff off and keep focused. Post this on the wall also. This will take one or two meetings.

5. The Current World. Yes, we are working backward for a reason. Now we list the facts of how we operate currently. "Some officers smile some of the time," "Officers often do not greet guests," "Officers point to the bathrooms instead of escorting guests," and "Management does not know which employees do greet guests cor-rectly." These are all current facts. Leave out the negatives like, "Officers do not have enough training." This is reaching for a solution and we are not ready for that yet. Post these on the wall also. This will also take one or two meetings.

6. This might be a good time for homework and field trips. Send the group to other departments, other hotels, or other service businesses to see how others do it. This is very enlightening. Have them bring back their findings for the next step.

7. Connect the dots. Now the fun part begins. Up to this point, everyone was prob-ably trying to solve the problem. Just ask them to write their ideas down and set them aside. The reason for avoiding this premature problem solving is if they have not seen the Current World, how do they know their idea solves a current issue? Continue with the brainstorming format as you look at a way to get from each of your bullet points in Current World to your bullets in Perfect World. Presumably, you will come up with a training program, an evaluation process, and so forth. Some of the answers may surprise you. Disney developed its concept of being "on stage" to improve guest service. The smile and attitude becomes part of your "performance."

The focus group (known by whatever name you want to call it—Security Circles, Round Tables, etc.) is not only a great way to solve a problem, but it also creates that impor-tant "buy-in."

There are also simple ways to maintain and improve morale.

Image—Everyone wants a positive image. The officer wants to look good, smart, effec-tive, and professional. What a coincidence! That is what *we* want, right?

Let's start with uniforms. Uniforms are dependent on the type of business, and even geography. First, decide on the message your uniform is trying to convey based on the objec-tives of the department. A "high-class" hotel may want to present proper ladies and gentle-men who dress similar to the clientele and the other employees. A motel may need something more utilitarian. An amusement park may need a distinctive law-enforcement look to pre-vent criminal activity, relate to children, and provide visibility. I suggest asking your employ-ees what they want. What are they comfortable wearing? What do they think gets them the most respect? What uniform allows them to use their equipment more effectively?

After one property began allowing employees to wear Hawaiian shirts on Fridays as part of a promotion, the director asked the officers if they wanted to try something like that. He thought he was being generous allowing them to dress casually. He was surprised to find that the overwhelming majority said "No way!" and begged him not to make them wear colorful shirts. They felt that nobody would take them seriously, respect them, or even be able to pick them out in the crowd. What he expected to be a reward or a motivator turned out to be a punishment, so he did not do it. Try asking your employees what they think.

Title—What do your employees want to be called? This is a very big deal for most security officers. A guard is someone who stands by a door controlling access at best and a piece of metal that keeps the chain from falling off your bike at worst. We expect much more from our officers than guarding, such as rational thinking, discretionary decisions, and some personality. This is a couple of steps (at least) above a guard and your employees should be recognized for this skill. Try calling them "officers" and see how their morale and self-confidence improves. This is a big change for the rest of the organization as well. They will require some time to acclimate to this way of thinking. This morale booster costs you nothing except a little effort.

Recognition—Officers enjoy the satisfaction of doing a good job and solving problems for others. Most do not require financial reward, although that is nice, but love being recognized in front of their fellow employees. A memo on the board does not quite do it, although it is better than nothing. Try mentioning something an officer did well in your daily briefing or other meeting. Alternatively, take it a step farther and have the officer explain what he or she did and make it a training process. What could be more rewarding than having something that you did being used to train others? Whenever you get a letter or comment from a patron or other employee acknowledging the efforts of one of your officers, write the employee a thank-you note. Hand-write it and throw in a gift card for coffee or a burger. Have the shift manager deliver it in person with his own thank you because it makes him look good. This is guaranteed to foster "Aw shucks" embarrassment all around. They will probably cowboy-up and toss it aside as "just doing my job, ma'am." I bet they will take it straight home to their significant other and gush through dinner. This is also low-cost and worth taking out of your own pocket, if necessary.

Proper training and equipment is very important to your officers. This improves their confidence and gives them more tools to help their guests and employees. Look at some of your equipment, especially the basics like radios, uniforms, and so forth. Spend the money to make them work correctly. Nothing is more frustrating, and likely to cause more damage, than radio batteries that are worn and do not hold a charge, dead spots when transmitting and receiving, worn uniforms, and anything else that does not work well. Your officers consider all of these things, especially the radios (and weapons if you use them) important to their safety, so take this issue seriously and ask them what they think. In the end, you will save money because good equipment is usually better cared for than the bad stuff.

Open Door Policy

Everyone claims to have an open door policy. (I have seen many a manager write their open door policy behind closed doors.) This is the notion that you are always available and always willing to listen. This "policy" seems shallow when the employee has to come to you with a problem. As stated previously, the best way to stay in touch with your employees is to get out there and talk to them. By the time someone gets up the nerve to come to your office with a problem, it may have gotten out of hand. Some will never come to your office unless you make them. Unless you want your office known as the place where everyone goes to be fired, invite officers in just to talk. Tell them they did something well and it was noticed. Ask their opinion on the issue of the day or if they have suggestions for the property. Then your office really does become an open office.

PERSONAL GROWTH

Third of the responsibilities of a good executive is to yourself. Start with education and experience. If you are lacking in experience, you must network and learn from others. If you lack education, it is not too late. Most employers are happy to support continuing education if it benefits them. Obtaining a certification like Certified Protection Professional from ASIS is the best example I can think of to advance your education in security. There are also certifications and classes provided through your local university, FEMA and DHS, and many other organizations. Do these on your own time if you need to. Classes not only make you more knowledgeable, but also you will find that they motivate you to think of and try new things. They also are a great networking experience, which I will discuss more in length later.

Once you get your personal growth on the right track, you need to start attending meetings and conferences relative to your industry and to your market. This will do several things for you. You will network with other professionals in similar situations. They will learn from you and you from them. These will become your resources when you need advice for a challenge that is new to you. You will find that whatever it is, someone else has already experienced it and can help you through it. Conversely, your peers may come across something in which you have experience and you can return the favor.

Your Work Ethic

Another thing I have noticed with Security Directors is that they are usually overwhelmed or lazy. Maybe lazy is too harsh of a word, so let's call it "comfortable." You can probably see yourself in one of these two categories and I hope you see the disadvantages of each.

The overwhelmed director runs on a high level of stress because he does not delegate enough, has inadequate staff surrounding him, or takes on more than he can manage. The comfortable director tends to have plenty of time for golf, takes weekends off, spends time talking with colleagues (nothing to do with work), and appears a little too confident. Ideally, you find your place somewhere in the middle of these two stereotypes. Look at the following suggestions for finding that middle ground.

Stress

The more responsibilities you have, the higher your stress level. It is not all about work; we all have bills, car troubles, family problems, and other stresses at home. Add to those layoffs, downsizing, bad economy, revenue drops, and grumpy bosses. Don't forget that you manage a staff with all the same problems you have. The way we handle or reduce our stress not only affects our own family and work, but also it sets the tone for our employees to deal with their own issues. If, for example, you yell at others to cope with your stress, that behavior snowballs downhill until the entire department handles all conflict this way.

This entire book is devoted to making your job easier, which is definitely a stress reducer, but here we will talk about ways to avoid and diminish that stress if it does pop up. Before we begin, acknowledge that stress, and even anger, are natural emotions. Do not feel bad, or less of a manager, if you feel them.

I am not a doctor, so I will not pretend to advise you on your physical or emotional health. Take these on with a psychoanalyst, physical therapist, or dietician. What I can do here is help you keep those causes of work stress down. It is true that rest, proper diet, and exercise are huge factors in reducing stress.

Time Management

When we run out of time, we have to neglect (or we forget) something we have to do. Keep a schedule, such as Outlook, so you do not double-book or overlook important meetings or events. Put everything in your calendar or you may forget even routine things like "walking around talking to employees" or "read incident reports." This will hold those places to keep you from blowing them off to go to a meeting. If a meeting is scheduled during your email reading time, reschedule the emails. When you get to the point where you have so many meetings that office or floor time is impossible, something has to go. Delegation is a positive way of duplicating yourself.

The stress is not generally caused by one event, but usually not having the time or resources to deal with that event will contribute to it.

Delegation

If you go to so many meetings that it exceeds your work time, you have too many meetings. Decide which ones can be delegated to a manager or administrative assistant. Delegation not only duplicates you, but it empowers and trains those who answer to you, to learn your job and how to run your department. If you spend a lot of time on interviewing job applicants, maybe you need a hiring manager. If you attend many meetings to coordinate special events, perhaps you need a special events manager.

When delegating, make sure you take the time to train that subordinate on the subject matter, the limits of his authority, and the background he needs to properly address the situation. Make sure he reports to you, but also make sure the report of the meeting is not as long as the meeting itself. That saves you no time at all.

PERSONAL HABITS

Visibility

The Security Director should be the most visible person on the property. It is your responsibility to know every employee on every shift, especially your own staff. Set a time each day to get out and meet the employees and the guests. Set time each week where you work a different shift. Seeing the boss is a real morale booster and makes you part of the team, rather than a memo writer in an office.

Besides being visible to everyone, your demeanor at all times should be above reproach. Visiting the bar after work, flirting with employees during work, and driving erratically through the parking lot all look bad and set a poor example. Remember that everything you do will be watched and scrutinized more than anyone else. This is partially because you are an executive and partially because you are Security. Employees will look for a double standard and assume one exists even if it does not.

Punctuality is a trait of a good leader. If you tend to be late, it shows that you do not manage time well. Awake earlier, leave for meetings earlier, and account for problems on the way. Do what you need to do to get to work on time and keep appointments.

Respect

One of the hardest personal traits for managers to achieve is respect. Many mistakenly place the desire to be loved over the need for respect. When decisions are made because a manager wants to be nice instead of what is best for the department, personal ego is now running the department. Some decisions will be difficult personally, but if they are in the best interest of the company and everyone understands the mission is to protect the assets, then the decision becomes clear to everyone.

When everyone is treated fairly and equally, respect will be almost automatic. Not everyone will like every decision, but if it is made for a good business reason, they will respect and understand it. My advice here is treating everyone you encounter, employee or not, as you would treat your mother, your boss, or someone whom you respect. You will feel better about yourself and those around you will respect you for it.

Attitude

Attitude is a big part of being overwhelmed. We have all seen how the exact same event affects people in different ways. Everyone looks upon your behavior so you need to be the model. Panic is a big stressor for people who feel overwhelmed. Being in Security, you probably have this under control. Perfectionism is another personal habit that leads to stress. If you expect perfection from everyone and everything, you are going to be disappointed often. You will never be satisfied, always stressed, and never get anything done if you expect perfection. I have seen this consume ineffective managers. That is not to say that you should not expect tasks and assignments to be completed correctly. Just cut down on being so "nit picky."

Negativity is an attitude that seems to permeate an entire organization when just one or a few people practice it. People choose to be negative. As mentioned previously, the same situation can be accurately perceived as a positive by one and a negative by another. Just prior to writing this paragraph, I told two people that I was having new shelves installed to store office supplies. The first person was very excited that her job would be easier and it would take less time to find supplies. The second person commented that it would probably take a week for our engineers to install and paint the shelves. Then he complained about having to learn where everything was. Two people. Same event. One positive and one negative. Think about the attitude that you model for your employees.

Breaks are important enough that we make our employees take them. They reduce fatigue and allow the mind to clear. Make sure you take breaks as well. Avoid lunch at your desk and take time to walk away from a problem, if you can, to relax and clear your mind. Overwhelming stresses can seem much less significant the next day. Besides, break time is a great time to interact with your employees.

Another method to deal with stress is to talk things out with peers. Avoid sharing problems with subordinates. Perhaps another department head or someone away from work can provide advice, but also be a sounding board as you vent. Be sure not to vent to those on your team. This is explained in another section.

Your personal demeanor is important to everyone. Being seen intoxicated, even off-duty, or in your grubby clothes can tarnish your image. How do you expect your boss to be dressed? What would you think of her if she were not dressed to your expectations? What do you think your employees expect? Decide on an image you want and stay with it. Imagine a major incident occurs at your property late at night and you decide to head down there and take charge. Maybe the media shows up and you need to make a statement. Decide on the image you want for you and your property and present yourself in that way.

NETWORKING

Earlier, I mentioned personal growth, and networking is part of that. Many of us security types are not comfortable with this process. We are somewhat private individuals who do not sell ourselves well. If you ever watch a salesperson network, it is almost sickening to people like us. We conjure descriptive words like "ass-kissers" and fakes. Believe me, I was the same way, and I am still somewhat uncomfortable with "small talk." Some Security Directors keep to themselves, talk to no one, and mind their own business. I do not consider them successful. Recall that example from the beginning of this chapter about the director who is more of a sheep dog.

One day, I realized that I did not need to sell myself as these salesmen do, but I did need to sell my hotel and my department to get what I wanted. Perhaps I felt like less of an idiot knowing that it was part of my job and not for my own career building. After that, I found it easy to network, make small talk, sit and converse with strangers, and build my address book. So, let's go through the networking process methodically because methods are our nature.

First, we need an objective. Why network? Your reason for networking is to share information. Unlike that camera salesperson who asks you how you are doing at every association luncheon, you are not selling widgets. You are selling anything you have to offer in exchange for anything you need from the other guys. Here are some examples.

When metal thieves steal your brass sprinkler fixtures, chances are you will file a police report. It goes to detectives, and it may or may not get assigned to a human, who may or may not go looking at the scrap yards for your brass. However, if you call that sergeant from property crimes who you met at the security chiefs' meeting last month, he will likely put some emphasis on your report. By the way, he also needs a favor. He needs to get a photo of a known car burglar out to as many security departments as possible. Suppose you send his email to all of your colleagues in the entire city and save him some legwork. There is nothing illegal, unethical, or immoral about this transaction of information, but it could not be done without a little networking.

Now suppose you are planning an exercise to test your new evacuation plan and you want the fire department involved. Call the chief who you met at a city council meeting last week. If they bring their engine to the hotel and spend a couple hours helping you evacuate your employees, you can let them use your penthouse floor to do some high-rise drills next month when the hotel is under construction.

Call or email your fellow hotel security directors and invite them to send a few officers to the CPR training that you are hosting next week. They will reciprocate when they have training classes of their own. If they cannot host some training, maybe they have some other amenities they can offer for the good of the group.

Information is our objective and we have some tools we can use to trade and to open up conversations. It is now time to start. I have found the best way to network is to get involved in as many organizations and groups as you can.

Government meetings—City councils, committees, county commissioners, and any other governmental group is the best place to find police and fire chiefs, inspectors, code enforcement, city attorneys, etc. These people are much friendlier when they have met you and they know you are one of the good guys.

Associations—ASIS has a local chapter in almost every city and is a great way to meet like-minded people in your business. I always find it amazing that security professionals in other industries (retail, contract, utilities, manufacturing) have many of the same problems and solutions that we have. Other associations may have chapters in your town.

Local trade groups—I have mentioned Security Directors' Associations, but there may be other security groups focused on retail, fraud, or other crimes. These are a must-join because this will be your base of contacts and where you give and receive all of your information.

Nonprofit groups—There are always some community groups in every town that fight drug abuse, domestic violence, crimes against kids, etc. There may be a crime-stoppers or other citizen tip group that meets and exchanges information.

Public/private groups—In the past 10 years or so, local and federal government has really reached out to the private sector to battle issues of joint interest. Two that come to mind are emergency preparedness and counterterrorism. Every city or county is required by the federal government to have an Emergency Manager. Meet this person and find out what he or she does. They are usually very excited to get cooperation from private entities, especially hotels that can provide resources in an emergency. There are also fusion centers in every state that deal with terrorism among other things. They may have an advisory board or a communication group and they want to exchange information with the private sector.

Online—Finally, there are many groups on the Internet that network and share information. Engage these to your comfort level, but I find that I learn more from these people than anywhere else. The best way to get your feet wet is to log on and observe the conversations until you feel comfortable.

Regional Training

I mentioned several groups and agencies where regional training is a benefit and is probably already being planned. Airports, school districts, and fire departments do all kinds of regional training. Start by observing these exercises and using those network skills. Find out what your hotel's role would be in a disaster and which one of these agencies would respond to your facility. You can learn some valuable emergency training skills from these people and maybe offer some resources in return.

Regional Communication

Two of the groups I mentioned previously are keys to your regional communication trees. Your local Security Directors Association and Fusion Center are all about communication. The Directors group should have a listserv of email addresses that can broadcast information instantly. This is invaluable and necessary in every community. If you do not have a group like this, start one or join one in the next town. The Fusion Center will usually proclaim itself as the focal point for dissemination of official government information of importance to the private sector. Make sure you are on its mailing list.

COLLABORATING WITH OTHER PROPERTIES

Mutual Aid

The concept of mutual aid is generally considered a government relationship. Fire departments have aid agreements to assist each other when their resources are overwhelmed. Police departments call the next county when they need specialized training or equipment for a hostage situation. Private enterprise has actually been using mutual aid for years. You might be surprised to find that your own hotel probably has agreements with other hotels to "walk" guests in the event of an over-booked situation or a catastrophe.

These agreements between companies tend to be verbal, which have no teeth. In the event of an emergency, what will be your recourse if that other hotel decides it doesn't want to participate in the agreement? What if the other hotel doesn't even know what its responsibilities are to your organization? This agreement that was based on a handshake might cost millions of dollars if someone breaks it. Your insurance company and lawyers are going to be looking for someone to blame. You don't want to be the one who made the handshake with no documentation. Therefore, you need a written agreement.

Written Agreement

This is a step-by-step process to create a Memorandum of Understanding (MOU) for mutual aid. Start by determining your needs. What is the agreement about? (Evacuation space, food for displaced guests, hotel rooms, etc.) Then meet with the key personnel of each property that makes those decisions. When a verbal agreement has been made, document it as "the purpose." Next, on the document state the authority by which it is made. (This is normally for governmental entities, but we can state that it is between management of each property.) Then we specifically list control and coordination of the agreement. This means who will be in control and who will coordinate these mutual activities. In other words, who is responsible for adhering to the agreement? Then specifically list the responsibilities of each department and each person if necessary.

The next part of this document covers the postincident information. Compensation is an important one. Who will pay how much for what and to whom? How is insurance involved in that compensation? Who assumes liability for certain activities on which property? Finally, the document is signed by authorized representatives from each property.

This sounds complicated and is too much information for a couple of paragraphs. That is because you will not write an MOU based on this book. Your legal folks have boilerplate agreements ready to go and you can probably fill in the blanks at their advice. If you are not using a lawyer, there are plenty of sample forms on the Internet.

Sharing of Resources

I always thought it was ridiculous that two hotels sitting right next door to each other have two separate shuttle buses, separate lawn mowers and snow blowers, and even 50-foot freeway signs. These have nothing to do with Security, but wouldn't it be nice if we could share some resources to save money? Those same two hotels might have perimeter cameras that look at the same area. Why not share cameras and pipe the feed into each hotel?

Consider people resources: The two security officers from each property probably pass each other doing their perimeter checks. What if Hotel A did it on the hour and Hotel B did it on the half hour? This reminds me of those old World War II movies where the German guards are on one side of the border with a gate and the Russians are on the opposite side (a foot away) with the same setup. Okay, they were enemies! Our two hotels are not enemies— they should be allies working toward the common goal of protecting everyone's assets.

The same applies for training—and this is where you can save some real money. It makes no sense to have one hotel train three officers for 40 hours and have another hotel do the same thing the following week. If you combine these resources, you not only save the money of training, but also you make your security programs more consistent. You read in Chapter 1 that your security will be compared to other properties in the event you are sued. What better defense than having the same training as your neighbors.

REGIONAL DISASTER PLANNING

In Chapter 10, we talked about emergency planning. Above, I mentioned the close relationship you should have with your regional emergency manager. This is where that comes together. When I first assumed my position, I started asking around about emergency planning. You have a fire, a broken water main, a gas leak—no problem. You evacuate, call the authorities, and they take care of the rest. They are the experts and that is their job.

> Besides the horrific images of death and destruction coming from the ruins of the earthquake in Japan in March 2011, we saw business continuity break down as well. Those who had mutual aid agreements, contingency plans, and backups of backups never imagined a disaster of that magnitude followed by a tsunami of even greater devastation. One example was airports. Imagine the hundreds of flights on approach to one of the island nation's many international airports. As one Delta pilot reported, they were on their final approach with little fuel, and their airport was under water. The backup airport was also devastated. The backup to that airport was already filling fast with diverted flights. The pilots had to do some fast thinking to find landing places before their fuel ran out.

Consider your plans in the event of a regional disaster. If you have agreements with other hotels, what will you do if they are also out of commission? You may not be flying an airplane, but you are responsible for hundreds of people that need a place to eat and sleep.

Then I started asking around about regional disasters. What if there is an earthquake, tornado, or citywide flood? Aren't those authorities going to be overwhelmed? So I started asking the other hotel directors and that is when I got scared. Almost all of them told me not to worry, just take care of the hotel and the rest is up to the fire department. The next day I called the County Emergency Manager and asked him the same question. He told me that is what keeps him up at night. "Frankly," he said, "in a regional emergency like that we do not have the community resources to take care of everyone. Those that we do have are going to be tending to hospitals and schools." We have seen examples of this in Hurricane Katrina and the Japan earthquake. Many people who were not prepared were left out. In Katrina, the companies that had planned for such emergencies like Wal-Mart and Toyota took care of their own employees and guests.

On that day at lunch, I made a verbal agreement with that emergency manager. I told him if he let me sit on his emergency committee and be on the list of those notified, I would make sure his important announcements got out to all other hotels in the area. I also told him my hotel would be the first to volunteer hotel rooms and convention space for evacuees when necessary. In return, I get to know before anyone else when trouble is coming and I will get first attention for my guests and employees from the authorities when it is needed.

The moral of this story is that you need to talk with these people before a crisis hits and not during. Since we set up the initial agreement, I have now been involved in many contingency planning groups, participated in regional exercises, and created a public/private group that plans and trains for disasters. Our community is more ready than it ever was.

SUMMARY

Security Directors in the hospitality business are a rare and unique type of leader. We can ensure our own success as well as those who employ us if we take advantage of the experience and style of other leaders in our industry. We just need to remember that in our business, protection of assets is our objective and our professionalism, experience, and knowledge will be the road we take to meet that objective. I wish you a long and prosperous journey, but most of all, I hope you have fun. Because as my father once said, you have to enjoy your work or you won't be any good at it.

INDEX

Printed by Publishers' Graphics Kentucky